My Swan Song for Joy

MY SWAN SONG FOR JOY

∽∾

a Sister Memoir

J9 Vaughn

Meander Publications
Hillside

Copyright © 2024 by J9 Vaughn.

All rights reserved.

Published in the United States by **Meander Publications**, Hillside, IL.

For more information visit: **meanderpublications.org**

Vaughn, J9, author

My Swan Song for Joy: a Sister Memoir

First Edition. | November 2024

Print ISBN 979-8-9906551-1-9 | Ebook ISBN 979-8-9906551-0-2 | Subjects: Memoir-Nonfiction – Accident | Best friend | Coming-of-Age | Family | Friendship| Grief | LGBTQ+ | Sister | Siblings | Tragedy | Trauma

Our books are available for purchase in bulk for promotional, educational, or business use. Please contact your local bookseller or Meander Publications by email at editor@meanderpublications.org

PRINTED IN THE UNITED STATES OF AMERICA

Disclaimer: While the author has made every effort to provide accurate information, neither the author nor Meander Publications are held responsible for errors. The stories, places, and people in this memoir are a collaboration of the author's memory, the memories of the friends and family that were consulted, and the records the author has included on their website: theincomprablej9.com. Some of the dialog has been rearranged (occurring in different scenarios) or reimagined, some of the names have been changed. Truth is not fact, memories are faulty, and all is perception, but the author tried to stay as true as true can be.

Contents

Dedications
xi

Acknowledgements
xii

Prologue
xv

Part I.
Main Body

Chapter 1.
Fools of April
1

Chapter 2.
My First Best Friend
10

Chapter 3.
Texas Fire Ants
17

Chapter 4.
Panther
27

Chapter 5.
Swim Team
33

Chapter 6.
The Sanctity of Trees
39

Chapter 7.
Sun Kissed
46

Chapter 8.
Bike Rack Bullies
53

Chapter 9.
German Shepherd Mama
58

Chapter 10.
A Corpse of Trees
71

Chapter 11.
The Kittens
83

Chapter 12.
Firecracker
93

Chapter 13.
Terrimotita y Tía Marlena
98

Chapter 14.
The Incident
106

Chapter 15.
The Falls
115

Chapter 16.
Tortoises
122

Chapter 17.
Authentic Italian Spaghetti
133

Chapter 18.
Our New House
141

Chapter 19.
My First Car Crash
147

Chapter 20.
Glass Cisne
159

Chapter 21.
Visiting the States
169

Chapter 22.
Birthday Beater
178

Chapter 23.
The Problem with Favorites
186

Chapter 24.
Dinner Interrupted
193

Chapter 25.
Grandma Vaughn's Funeral
201

Chapter 26.
When We were Clowns
208

Chapter 27.
Hansel and Gretel
217

Chapter 28.
Flight Attendant
226

Chapter 29.
Bedroom Window
230

Chapter 30.
Playing Pool
240

Chapter 31.
Phantom of the Opera
253

Chapter 32.
<u>Joy to the World</u>
259

Chapter 33.
<u>Stephen F. Austin State University</u>
266

Chapter 34.
<u>What are the Chances?</u>
274

Chapter 35.
<u>What the Water Wrought</u>
281

Chapter 36.
<u>A Pregnant Pause</u>
285

Chapter 37.
<u>The Day My Sister Became a Swan</u>
293

Chapter 38.
<u>Basement Flood</u>
299

Chapter 39.
<u>Caretaking</u>
305

Chapter 40.
<u>The Swan at Graduation</u>
317

Chapter 41.
<u>Bioluminescent</u>
324

Chapter 42.
<u>A Mother's Broken Heart</u>
333

Chapter 43.
<u>The Loss of Memory</u>
339

Chapter 44.
Pancakes
346

Chapter 45.
The Swan and the Ram
353

Chapter 46.
Journey Adjourned
358

Chapter 47.
House Spirit
374

Chapter 48.
Joy's Ashes
379

EPILOGUE
The Trial
387

Dedications

To Joy

Even though you never got a swan song

And we didn't get to say goodbye

I hope this keeps your song alive

To my Kith and Kin

You know who you are,
Ya weirdos!

Acknowledgements

There are so many people without whom this memoir would still be at the bottom of my brain, unfinished. Many thanks to Bek Huston, my dearest friend, my mate, my person. She is my home and I would be lost without her. I am grateful to my Mom who always encouraged me to write, and to my Dad, I love you both and wish Mom was alive to see this. For my living sisters, JacQueline and Kess, I am so grateful for all of your love and unwavering support. To my brother-in-law Jeff and my three niblings Katie, Sydney, and Caleb, I am grateful for your love and caring of Joy. I have so many friends who gave me amazing feedback, advice, and support along the way: Amy Hofmockle, CSE Cooney, Tina Jens, Claire Liptrot, Karin Thorgerson, Sheila Johnson, Ann Joachiam, Geoff Johnson, Ashley Sullivan, Joy Tobin, Katie Tyrrell Weimann, Lynn Cordin, Michelle Springer, Katie Redding, Carlos Hernandez, Brian and Stephanie Shaw, John O'Neill, Dave Michalak, Sally Tibbetts, Tina Jens, Meg Edwards, and many others. I am ever so grateful to the few therapist who helped and the one who is still helping me process my grief and my life.

I'm grateful to Joy's friends, especially Jennifer Harrison (Jef Majewski), who reached out to me during everything that was going on with Joy. I am honored to have been part of several writing groups – Kate the Great's Book Emporium's writers group, Writers Word Feast, The Journey Writers, The Wheaton Public Library Writers Group, Glen Ellyn's Write On!, and others who have helped me hone my craft. I am also grateful to open mics for always providing a platform to share my stories on, especially The No Shush Salon and Gumbo Fiction Salon. To the Columbia College Fiction Writing department for helping me become a better writer and to the University of Illinois's school of Information Sciences for being so understanding while I was going through such a horrible portion of my life. To my editor – Tiffany Trent and my reviewers – Tom Fate, Josh O'shea, Beth Clower, Tess Kunik, Karen Schreck, Philicia Deckerd, Amy Hofmockle, and Michelle Springer. I know I'm missing someone. Just know, I feel honored to have had your help.

Last of all, thank you to my sister, Joy. For being my sister, my tormentor, and my first best friend.

"Heartfelt, honest, raw, and wise, this genre-defying memoir tells a profoundly moving tale of sibling love and devotion. Employing personal anecdote and compelling, lyrical prose, Vaughn describes the bond they shared, and share, with their beloved sister, Joy, charting the deepening of their relationship throughout the course of childhood, adolescence, and into adulthood. This is a love that survives continental crossings, familial upheaval and conflict, great personal challenge and transformation, and, ultimately, devastating loss and grief. *My Swan Song for Joy* is that rare kind of book that centers on an incredibly unique story that somehow also manages to be entirely relatable."

Karen H. Schreck, author of *Broken Ground*

"This book is devastating in its beauty. it is honest in depicting tragedy as well as hope; difficulties alongside empowering pride. Not only a memoir, this is a collection of treasures. We can feel Vaughn's love by seeing their depiction of life through young eyes and the cataloged research material. Any two sisters, any sibling, anyone who has loved another person deeply will be able feel connected to this relationship. Joy lives on in the author's life and, because of this book, can live in ours as well."

Joshua ES O'Shea, Librarian

"While reflecting on their childhood, and their sister's tragic injury and death, J9 Vaughn artfully explores their own struggles to find acceptance in her family as a queer person. Disarmingly honest, there are spirals of both joy and sorrow in their journey toward understanding."

Tom Montgomery Fate author of *The Long Way Home*

Prologue

Everything is blue.

The color blue saturates my memory of the O'Hare International airport on the night of November 24, 2018. I am almost certain the seats were covered in a black fabric and I know there were other colors throughout the terminal. But in my mind's eye, a swath of blue covers everything.

At almost midnight, the overhead speakers announce my flight as my phone buzzes. I answer, gathering my bags. All around me, passengers are getting up and talking as they collect their belongings. A child, who had been whimpering due to the late hour, starts crying. I lean into my phone, covering my other ear.

"Hello? Can you speak up? I'm at the airport and..."

"There's been an accident..." It's the voice of my youngest sister, Kess.

My entire body becomes stone. The world stops.

Accident. How I hate that word.

"What happened?"

"There was a truck and, and Joy..." Her voice falters.

No. No no no no no no no no NO! Not Joy!

Joy, my older sister, the oldest of us four, already has a brain injury from an accident twenty-three years earlier.

Clearing my thoughts, swallowing my heart, quelling the shiver in my veins... I breathe, then ask, "What happened?"

Kess explains that a truck had crashed into the house. I gather that it was by the room where Joy was sleeping. She has already called Dad and our other sister JacQueline and the police are there and, I think, they're trying to get someone out of a truck. The driver, maybe? I'm having trouble following what she's saying as other voices on her end are trying to get her attention and on my end the announcements throughout the airport have become more and more insistent. I hear my group number being called to join the line and board the plane. I explain that I'm at the O'Hare International airport and about to get on a plane to Guadalajara, Jalisco, México...

"Yes, yes, I know." She says, taking a deep breath. "I'm sorry..."

"No!" I shake my head at the phone, fighting back frustration teeming with guilt. "You have nothing to be sorry for. I'm glad you called. But... but I don't know what to do. Do I miss my flight or..."

"I don't know. I'm sorry. I have to get off the phone. I'll call when I know more."

MY SWAN SONG FOR JOY XVII

"My phone will be in airplane mode, but as soon as I land, I'll call you. I love you!"

"I love you too."

The phone at my ear falls to silence.

I stand and get in line for the plane while calling my beloved best friend and life-mate, Bek. I explain as much as I can about what happened and ask her to call Kess. I am so confused and worried. Should I stay? What if I do and Joy is fine? Well, not fine, or Kess wouldn't have called. She's possibly, probably hurt. But she will be fine... Right? When the truck hit the house, maybe she fell out of bed and twisted her ankle or hit her head or something. I'm still worried, but how silly would it be for me to not go? I mean, my family is in Huntsville, Alabama. I'm in Chicago, Illinois embarking on a trip, THE trip connected to the class that was one of the reasons I chose the University of Illinois as my graduate school. I even received a budget from the Oak Park Public Library where I work to purchase books. It's a soon-to-be Librarian's dream, my dream, to get to go to the Feria Internacional del Libro, the international book fair, in Guadalajara. Besides, there's nothing I can do. Everything will be fine. Joy will be fine. My going or not going will not impact that. I'm not being selfish, I'm being practical.

After a brief discussion with Bek, I make the hard decision to continue my trip. Bek will check in with Kess and I will find out what happened when I land. Everything will be fine.

But the whole time, in the back of my mind, the word accident plays over and over like a mantra of misery...

Accident...

            accident...

                        accident.

I've been here before.

            Nothing is ever fine.

                        Everything is blue.

1

Fools of April

My sister's accident on April 1, 1995, completely changed my family.

On that fateful night, 22-year-old me stood on the porch of my parents' house where I was living in Naperville, Illinois fumbling for my keys. The air was sharp and cold but had the promise of spring kissing at the edges. I could smell wood burning from backyard barbeques and bonfire gatherings in that suburb of Chicago. It was night, but street lights were blazing, so not dark, not really, a gloaming sense of time. I laughed at something my companion said. He was just behind me, in the shadows off to my left. I heard his voice, but cannot recall his words; I can barely remember his face.

Before my keys hit the lock, the door sprang open. The light from inside the house silhouetted my father's frame.

He stood there silent for a second or two. I had not expected him home having gotten my dates and times confused, as I often do. Behind me, a muttering of an excuse as my date melted into the darkness.

"It's Joy." Dad's dark brown eyes were blinking back tears; a sight so rare, it left me speechless. Sorrow was clawing inside his throat. He rasped out, "there's been an accident."

Dad's shaven jaw was tight, leaving no room for speculation on the significance of the day. If it had been anyone but him, I would be thinking about it being the first of April and all the folly that entails. But my Dad was never one for practical jokes and the word hung thick in the air.

"Accident."

My head was swimming, trying to remember. Joy... she had gone out of town on... a school trip? Dad was still talking. His voice sounded so far away, as if he was on a different planet; a different plane of existence. A dog barked in the distance. I was having trouble focusing. I think he was in shock. I know I was. He repeated himself a few times and the words slowly permeated the thick cloud that had gathered in my mind. He told me that Joy was in Costa Rica where she had been chaperoning the International Club with one other teacher. They went whitewater rafting on their last day. She drowned, but she was not dead. She was revived, but in critical condition. He could not fully explain since he was having trouble understanding. Mom was in the kitchen on the phone.

They were going to fly to Costa Rica. I was going to have to...

He paused to look at me, really look at me. He and I had, over the last few years, been in a constant struggle; an ongoing argument over what he called my choices in life and what I called me discovering myself. I had turned my back on so much of what he valued. My developing agnostic, hedonistic, lascivious, androgynous, and queering lifestyle fit less and less with his conservative Southern Baptist born-again Christian household, that he had come to not trust me. After being told over and over that I was going to hell, that my choices were breaking his and Mom's hearts, that what felt natural to me made me an abomination, that if I continued down the path I was on, I would be forever lost. I had come to not trust him.

I stared back. I said nothing. I could barely breathe. I clasped my keys so tight I could feel the metal cutting into my palm. A hurricane of questions whirled in my mind, but I could say nothing.

Behind my father, I could hear my mother's gentle voice. I could not distinguish words, but I could feel the tight stretch between them. She was patient and thoughtful. But she wanted off the phone, that much I could tell. To cry? To scream? Both? To release something that had coiled so tight around her heart it would eventually tear it apart?

My dad was suddenly aware that we were still standing on the porch. That he had not let me inside. That I was shivering.

"Let's go inside," he said, stepping back, his words sliding into a whisper.

The light in the house was harsh as I stepped down into the family room and sat on the plush couch. Even though I lived there, it had never felt like home. My parents and younger sisters had moved while I was in my first year of college. I had not grown up there. Beyond the usual discomfort, I felt awkward as I tried to look relaxed and lean on the armrest. Dad didn't sit. He paced, listening to Mom who was still on the phone in the kitchen. Her words had been reduced to, "hmmms," and "uh-huhs" and "well, yes..."

"Dad?" My voice is shaking. I'm still not sure if I should speak. The air felt like I was in trouble, a familiar feeling, but also held a sad and angry tinge that made my eyes water.

Dad nodded, "Let's wait for your Mother."

I noticed for the first time a few grays in his short crow-black hair and the beginnings of wrinkles by his eyes. I saw a tightness to his lips and chin, as if he was holding a flood of emotions he could not, would not allow himself to feel.

"Yes, of course," my mother's voice was suddenly louder. "God bless you too. Thank you."

I heard a click as Mom finally got off the phone. I could not see into the kitchen from where I sat, but I heard her heave a sigh that deflated her. I knew she was sitting at the wooden breakfast table facing the window that looked out onto the tiny backyard. At that time of night, the glass would be opaque, showing her reflection as she held her face in her hands. Dad stopped pacing, waiting for her. After almost a minute of silence, I heard the wooden chair creak. But instead of coming into the family room, we heard the refrigerator door open. She was pouring herself some iced sweet tea. A very Southern thing to do. Another sigh as she stepped from the breakfast nook into the sunken family room. She nodded to Dad and was about to speak, but Dad spoke first.

"Jeani, I mean, Jeanine is here."

"Oh," she breathed, turning to look at me. She sounded neither relieved nor disappointed, just a sound of acknowledgement that something else must happen. She sat on the other side of the couch, the almost clear plastic golden cup of tea in her right hand hovering in the air as she turned her body to face me. Her green eyes were rimmed red and swimming with unshed tears. Her pale, freckled face was blotchy, like it gets when she cries, a trait I inherited. She looked at Dad.

"What have you told her, John?"

He looked alarmed, trying to figure out what he had said. The phone rang.

"I've got it," he said, a little too quick, a little too eager to escape. His hurried steps from the living room to the kitchen got him there as quickly as possible without running.

Mom shook her head as she made a kah sound of inhalation. We heard the murmur of Dad's words rise and fall as he paced from the kitchen to the dining room and back again. Mom reached between the cushions and pulled down the middle section of the couch that had a secret table with cup holders in it. She took a sip of her tea and set the cup in the holder. Weaving her fingers together, she licked her lips and took a deep breath.

"I guess I'll just start at the beginning...." Never even considering that she could just ask me what Dad said. Still, her shock was understandable.

She told me that when they arrived home, there was a message on the answering machine. While Joy was in Costa Rica chaperoning the Batavia High School International Club, she had been in a rafting accident. Everyone on the trip was in the accident and ended up in the water. But the students and the other teacher made it to shore. Joy drowned, but in the raft behind, there were two nurses.

"God sent them to save her," Mom said, her eyes shining as tears cascaded down her cheeks. "Praise God," she said, tilting her head and looking skyward.

I clenched my teeth against the tears and anger rising in me. I swallowed, attempting to banish the question that would cause us to fight. But in my head it was on repeat. If your God is so great, why did your God not stop Joy from drowning? But I breathed deep and kept my peace.

"She's in a hospital in Costa Rica," Mom continued. "She's in a coma and can't be moved. Dad and I are going to fly out tonight. We need you to stay and help your sisters. Will you?"

Of course I will! Of course! Of course...

My parents were gone for a week. I don't remember that week. As sharp as the memory of that fateful night stayed in my mind, the week was a blur—a haze of phone calls and visits and lots of food given and even more prayers said. My two younger sisters and I lived in silence, giving and receiving hugs, crying but not knowing what to say or how to act.

Our parents called with updates. They told us how Joy was doing, what the doctors were recommending, that they had found a church to pray with. They explained that Joy still wasn't stable but they would bring her home as soon as she was.

They also told us there was a man who drowned. The theory, and it's only a theory since no one saw for certain, was that Joy got to shore, saw the man drowning, and dove back in to save him. It's a good theory. Joy might've done that. Following that theory, he, a much bigger person than my tiny 5 foot nothing sister, in his last moments, might've grabbed hold of Joy's life preserver and pulled her under. It's one of the only things that makes sense because Joy, my sister who won swim meets when we were kids, was a really good swimmer. But she drowned. She died. She would have stayed dead if not for that other raft carrying those nurses who used CPR to bring her back to life.

Mom explained over the phone that Joy was in the water too long. They—that nebulous medical they—explained to my parents that the jostling from the board Joy was bound to bounced her head as she was brought up from the side of the river to the ambulance. Once inside the vehicle, she was jostled even more as they drove over rough terrain to get to the hospital. Either or both might have caused further damage to her brain. Her brain that was already suffering from oxygen deprivation from being in the water too long. But they could not leave her in the jungle beside the rapids. No. It was the only way.

As soon as Joy was finally stable–still in a coma, but stable–she was airlifted back to Illinois and my parents came with her. Her return was met with a flurry of phone calls and visits and another onslaught of casseroles. Our family, her friends, her students, all rallied. There was even a spaghetti dinner, Joy's favorite food, that her students held in her honor and collected money to help my parents with the mounting medical bills.

I didn't go. I stayed away as much as I could. I buried myself in college classes and work. I drank, I smoked, I stayed out all hours and hung out with friends, not telling them anything, or if I did, very little. The one person I did confide in, the man-boy I was dating at the time, broke things off with me. I stopped speaking about anything of consequence. I felt my life falling apart, and yet felt selfish for even considering my life when Joy was struggling to survive. I avoided thinking about what was happening with my sister as my family was struggling to cope. I did not cope. I told myself I could not. I couldn't even help myself; how could I possibly help anyone else?

I didn't visit Joy in the hospital enough. My parents and sisters went every day; her friends and even her students visited as often as they could. I went a handful of times.

I was awash with shame. I did not wish her dead, but I did wish over and over for all of it to end. When I did visit the hospital, it felt wrong. Standing by her bed with my mother or sisters or Dad or others, I felt her absence.

Joy wasn't there.

As I listened to her breathing and the machines beeping and inhaled the disinfectant so ripe and pungent in the air, I wished and willed her eyes to open. But I could not feel her.

When we were young, when she was my first best friend, I could sense her without seeing her. She could never sneak up on me. But staring at her there in that bed, I could not feel her presence. My soul reached out to her, but her soul either did not or could not, reach back. Or maybe, it just wasn't there.

Then, right before they-they of the amalgamation of medical professionals-started asking the hard question, the deep question, the fatal Hamlet-esque question of should we or shouldn't we pull the plug, Joy woke from her coma.

She woke, but she was not the same. In her eyes, I tried to find my first best friend. But she wasn't there.

2

My First Best Friend

~~~

Jersey Village, Texas

The first clear memory I have of Joy was when I was almost three years old and Joy was almost five. It was a Sunday morning in the early 70s and we were in the tiny shower of our parents' bathroom. Even at that young age, my blonde hair was short. I had a propensity of getting all sorts of things stuck in it and Mom kept having to cut it shorter and shorter. Joy's hair was long and luxurious and starting the transition from blonde to a soft brown like Mom's was. All my sisters would have hair that eventually did that. As we were finishing up in the shower, Joy slicked her hair back with water, making it almost look black like Dad's hair.

The shower was so small it only had room for one adult, maybe two, squeezed tight together, or two kids. Its frosted glass door had a metal rim around it. It wasn't the bathroom Joy and I normally used, but since Dad was out of town, Mom decided it would be easier to keep an eye on us if we took a shower down there while she got ready. She didn't want us dawdling and playing in the bath upstairs.

There was a large wall-length mirror next to the shower that was fogged over from the hot water. We should have been out and getting dressed, but Mom had left the room for a few minutes to talk to Dad on the phone. While she was gone, Joy made up a game. She told me to stand outside of the shower and knock on the door.

In a high sing-songy voice, she said, "who is it?"

"Me!" I shouted. Then I threw open the door and squealed with laughter.

"How dare you burst in on me!" She exclaimed, in that pretend adult voice as she tried to hide her naked body behind her skinny arms and hands. (I think we must've seen a scenario like that on a sitcom.) Then she slammed the door shut. She ran out huffing, "I never!"

I jumped into the shower and slammed the door.

I didn't quite understand the game, but she was laughing so I laughed too. The water was cold, but I couldn't reach the knob to turn it off. I pushed the door, but Joy held it shut.

"No," she said. "This time, you stay in and we'll do it again. Okay?"

"Okay!" I shouted.

Only I didn't realize that we were switching roles. So, as soon as she knocked on the door, I pushed it open shouting, "Me!" But because I was supposed to say, "Who is it?"

She was standing too close and got hit. She howled. Horrified that I had hurt her, I slammed the door, catching my finger in it. Panicking, I yanked my hand, causing my skin to rip as I slipped on the wet floor and hit the metal door handle with my eyebrow ridge as I went down.

Mom came running into the room to find Joy sitting on the floor wailing. "Oh, what in the world," she exclaimed, dipping down to be on Joy's level. Not hearing me over the running water or Joy's cries, she asked, "Did you slip on the bathmat as you got out?" Joy stopped screaming, whimpered a couple of times, and started to tell her what happened. That's when Mom heard my cries. Standing back up, she opened the shower door to find me writhing on the floor, my right hand covered in blood and my left eye swollen shut. She gasped.

"Oh no, Jeani! What happened?"

I couldn't answer, I was too freaked out by my eye not being able to open and all the blood. I don't remember pain, I just remember wondering if all the skin on my finger was going to come off and the thought freaked me out.

"Joy!" Mom shouted as she turned off the shower and knelt to look at my finger. It was still gushing blood. "We're gonna have to go to the emergency room instead of church today. Go get the emergency kit from the pantry in the kitchen; it's on the third shelf."

She wrapped a washcloth around my finger, instructing Joy to put on her dress and run to get what she needed.

"But Mommie, I hit my head," Joy cried.

Mom nodded, glancing over at Joy and assessing if the injury needed any immediate attention. "Yes, I know. But you're not bleeding and your sister is. We'll have the doctors check your head when we get to the hospital."

I could hear Joy still whimpering as she left the room. When she got back and handed Mom the kit, Mom quickly cleaned the wound and started wrapping my finger. Without looking at Joy, she said, "Thank you. Now run upstairs to get me some play clothes for Jeani. I don't want her getting blood all over her dress."

I don't remember anything about the trip to the hospital. I do recall watching them stitch me up and thinking it was the coolest thing to watch. Mom told me later that I said it didn't hurt while they were stitching me. But on the way home, I complained about my finger and my eye aching.

That night as I was laying in my converted crib (not a big kid bed like Joy had, but the bars were down) I remember feeling happy. It might've been the pain killers. In the dark,

I heard Joy making loud sighing sounds and wondered why she was sad.

"Joy?"

"Yeah?"

"Are you sad about my booboo?"

She snorted. "No."

"Oh. But, you're sad?"

"No, just annoyed. Nobody looked at my head."

"Oh. Does it hurt?"

She thought about it for a moment. "Not any more. But it did and Mommie promised th-that they would." I could hear her crying.

I wasn't sure what to say, so I decided to comfort her. I crawled out of my bed and climbed onto her bed. I gave her a hug with my left arm, being sure to keep my right one dangling off the side of the bed.

"Get off me!" She whisper-shouted, pushing me. I gripped the shoulder of her nightgown, not letting her get away from me. "What are you doing?"

"You're sad! I'm hugging you."

"Well, stop it!"

From downstairs, we heard the booming baritone of our

father who had gotten home that night. "Girls, you're supposed to be sleeping. Do I need to come up there?"

"No, sir!" We sang in unison.

Joy pried my fingers loose. "You can stay in my bed," she whispered through gritted teeth, then pressed her hand against my shoulder. "But stay over there."

She scooted over towards the wall as I was still half off the bed. I wiggled around until I was all the way on the bed and lying on my back. I stared into the dark, running my fingers over the bandage that was wrapped around my right pointer finger and the skin just past it. The two different textures were interesting.

"Is skin like clothes?" I asked.

Joy, whose whole body had been stiff with irritation, relaxed as she turned to me. "What?"

"Mom said they stitcheded me up like she stitches my clothes when I rip them."

Joy laughed, but kept it quiet. "You're so weird!"

Now it was my turn to be frustrated. I wasn't trying to be weird or funny. I gave an exasperated huff, then asked, "But is it?"

Joy, realizing that I really wanted to know and wasn't just being silly, thought about it. I could feel her shrug. "I don't think so? I mean, if Mom sews your clothes, you have a sewn part. But the doctor said that after a bit you'll come back and they'll take the stitches out. He said your skin will be like new."

I smiled in the dark. "New skin!? I get new skin!" I said loudly.

"Girls!" Dad's voice boomed.

"Sorry, Daddy!" I shouted.

With her teeth clenched, Joy whispered hard in my ear, "You're gonna get me in trouble again!" Then rolled away from me and faced the wall. I barely heard her mumble into the sheets, "Go back to your bed."

Sad that I had annoyed her, I slowly climbed off the bed and crawled into mine. I wondered why she thought I got her in trouble when she was the one who came up with the game and I'm the one who got hurt. Actually, nobody really got in trouble. Then I started thinking about new skin and grinned as I drifted off to sleep whispering, "New skin."

3

Texas Fire Ants

Jersey Village, TX

About half a year later on a scorching May day in 1976, Mom was sitting on her bed folding laundry. From my perspective, as a three and a half year old, it was a massive bed. It had a dark wooden headboard that had an intricate diamond pattern carved into its face and majestic rounded tops over each side of the bed, making it look a little like the back of two thrones that had been fused together. Joy and I had run in shouting at each other, only quieting when Mom shushed us. Joy asked if she would solve an argument, but Mom was fed up with our bickering and fighting. She told us to go play outside.

"But Mooooooom," Joy whined, "it's too hooooot!"

Mom's normally bright green eyes were somber and her face was even more pale than its normal white and freckled pallor. She just looked so tired. Years later, I would understand that she had chronic migraines and our high-pitched voices would pierce through her head like ice picks. She took off her glasses and closed her eyes. She pinched the bridge of her nose and sighed, "Dear Lord, give me strength." When she looked at us again, I saw that her eyes were shining with tears. She took a deep breath, blinked fast, and put her glasses back on.

She spoke in a soft voice. "Tell you what, I'm going to let you put on your bathing suits,"–something we were always begging to do– "and play in the sprinkler. Or, if Daddy hooked it up, you can turn on the slip-n-slide. Mommy is going to finish folding this laundry and take a nap. Unless, of course, you would rather help fold laundry and take a nap?" She left the question hanging in the air as both Joy and I, with eyes wide and heads shaking, dashed out of the room, squealing.

"And no hitchy-pitchy screaming until you're out of the house or you will HAVE TO take a nap!" She called after us.

We fell silent as we raced up the stairs to our bedroom to change into our bathing suits. I imagined Mom smiling as she pulled her bedroom's thick curtains closed, moved the laundry aside, and climbed into bed.

Once outside, we saw that even though the hose was attached to the spigot, it hadn't been hooked up to the sprinkler or the slip-n-slide. Dad also hadn't left the slip-n-slide out. It was stored on a high shelf in the garage where neither of us could reach. After a few tries of Joy boosting me up onto the shelves, them shaking, and me falling back on top of her, we decided the shelves were a little too unsteady to climb. We tried to get the step-ladder down, just in case we had gotten tall enough that it would help, but it was hanging on the wall just out of reach. So we grabbed the sprinkler from its spot under the shelves and dragged it out to the grass. But, after several attempts and both of us getting sprayed in the face, we realized our fingers weren't strong enough to screw the hose on.

"Jeani, why don't you go ask Mommy to come out? Tell her we can't get the sprinkler to work."

Always eager to please my big sister, I ran into the house. But when I got to my parents' room, the door was closed. This puzzled me.

The only time my parents' closed their bedroom door was at night, when they were sleeping, and on Saturday mornings, when we were allowed to watch Saturday morning cartoons but not allowed to come into their bedroom. On Saturday mornings, the door would be locked and knocking on the door was only allowed if (a) someone was bleeding so much that a bandaid couldn't help, or (b) there was a bone poking out of the skin, which meant (a) was also happening. In the unlikely event of (c) the house was on fire, we were instructed to yell FIRE at the top of our lungs before running outside and going to the neighbor's house to call 911. They told us that on Saturdays, they were sleeping in and that it was what every parent did on Saturday mornings. Why else would there be Saturday morning cartoons? But sometimes, we heard noises. Dad told us to just turn up the cartoons because they were "talking." It didn't sound like talking, at least not just talking. But I never questioned it since Saturday mornings were the only time we were allowed to watch whatever we wanted. At any other time, a show had to be pre-approved by our parents, like Sesame Street, or they had to watch it with us, like Happy Days. My favorite was always The Pink Panther Show, a show I now look back on and am pretty sure wouldn't have received the parental stamp of approval.

Once we were in jr. high, Joy and I realized that they had been having sex every Saturday morning when we were kids. We were both grossed out and delighted by the idea. As an adult, I now know that while they might have been having sex some Saturday mornings, they were probably actually sleeping in most of the time. It's so interesting how understanding shifts and changes and sometimes comes back to the thing I had learned as a kid, but from a different angle.

But this time, the door wasn't locked, Dad wasn't home, and it wasn't Saturday morning. So I slowly turned the knob and crept inside. The room smelled like fabric softener and unscented lotion, the only kind Mom ever used, due to her allergies. There was almost a sacred feel to the darkness. As quietly as I could, I tiptoed on the thick cream shag carpeting over to my mom's side of the bed. She had the covers pulled over her head and the unfolded laundry was either on Dad's side or on the floor.

"Mommy?" I whispered very quietly. She groaned. Getting a little closer, but not close enough that she could smack me, I repeated, "Mommy?"

"What?" Her voice sounded muffled as her face was pressed into the pillow.

"We can't get the sprinkler to work." I whispered, ready to dash back through the door.

"Then don't use it," her muffled voice said.

Unable to dispute this logic, I tiptoed backwards and silently closed the door behind me before dashing out to the yard.

The sun was bright and I had to squint to see Joy, who was standing in the grass with the hose in her hand. She had turned it on and a thick stream of water was glugging its way through the snakelike shell, making a puddle in the yard.

I shouted as I ran to her, "Mommy said..." But before I could get out what Mom had said, Joy had shoved her thumb into the nozzle, causing the water to shoot out like a torrent, and aimed it at me. It would have been funny if it didn't hurt. I screamed and ran from her as she chased me, laughing.

A little something about our backyard in Texas. It was vast. It was a third of an acre and had only a few trees. So it was a lot of grass that I would have the displeasure of mowing when I was in junior high after we moved back from Venezuela. Even though the land we lived on was flat, our yard was not. It had random little slopes and hills and there were multiple divots where critters had created holes and there were ant hills...so many ant hills. And not just regular ant hills. No, these were Texas fire ants. If you have never been bitten by a Texas fire ant, consider yourself lucky. While they're not the worst bites ever, the sting of their bites linger way longer than it should.

I was running and screaming but sort of having fun as I started seeing this as a game, when I tripped. I fell face first into the biggest ant hill in the entire yard. Joy, seeing me in my vulnerable state, laughed and ran over, still spraying me the entire time. She made sure I was soaked from my head to my feet. The water was pushing so hard against the back of my head that my face was smashed into the ant hill.

About then, Joy realized that I wasn't moving. She threw the hose to the side and crouched down next to me.

"Jeani, are you okay?"

I turned my head, spitting out dirt and ants. Joy's brown eyes widened. "Oooooooh...." Her mouth hung open as I cried and scrambled to get myself away from the ant hill.

Joy jumped up and screamed, "Moooooooooooooom!" while running back into the house.

Crying and brushing at my face and my body, I couldn't get them off. The water and dirt had become glue and the ants were sticking. The ants were not happy either, so they kept biting me until they died. By the time Mom got outside with Joy trailing her, I had crawled over and was laying on the hot cement patio sobbing and scratching.

"What in the world..." Mom trailed off as she shook her head and knelt next to me. She pulled me to a seated position and helped me brush as many ants off as she could.

That's when I noticed that Joy was crying and shaking. "I was just playing! I didn't mean for her to get bit like that!"

She wailed. "Y-you said we could..." Her words dissolved into tears.

Mom nodded as she helped me stand, smacking ants off my shirt and shorts and arms and legs. I felt like I was getting a paddling even though I hadn't done anything wrong. "Let's get you upstairs and into a bath. Joy, get the vinegar out of the laundry room and bring it upstairs to the bathroom, okay?"

Biting her lip, Joy nodded then rushed into the house ahead of us.

Once we were upstairs, Mom ran water into the tub as hot as I could stand it and had me take off my clothes. Joy came up the stairs slowly, almost dragging a heavy jug of vinegar that weighed almost as much as she did. Mom poured all of it into the tub. The water was so hot and the sharp smell it hurt my nose, but it soothed my burning, itching skin right away.

"Joy," Mom said, her voice calm. "I want you to go downstairs into my bathroom and get the calamine lotion. It's in the cabinet under the sink, to the left, I think."

Joy nodded and hurried out of the room. About then, the doorbell rang.

Mom turned her attention back to me. "Jeani, I want you to dunk your head several times. If you can lay back, that would be best since the ants are all tangled in your hair. But be sure to close your eyes tight, that vinegar is going to sting. I'm going to go see who's at the door, but I'll be right back."

I nodded, pinched my nose, and lay back in the water, with my eyes squeezed tight. When I came up for air, she was gone. So I did it again and again. When I came up the third time, Joy was standing there with the bottle of calamine lotion. She had an odd look on her face.

"You smell funny."

I stared at her, my eyes wide. "I think an ant is," I pointed at the water between my legs, "down there."

She set the calamine lotion on the counter behind her and knelt by the tub. She was fascinated. "Is it biting you?"

I shook my head. "No, I think it's dead. But it feels funny."

She nodded, chewing on her lower lip. "You probably have to get it out."

I made a face, but got it out. Joy and I looked at the surface of the water around me. There were so many fire ants, it looked like someone had sprinkled red pepper into my bath.

"That's a lot of ants," Joy said.

In unison, we sang the Pink Panther theme song. "DEADANT... DEADANT... DEADANT DEADANT DEADANT DEADANT DEADAAAAAAANT! D-D-D-DDANT!" And busted out laughing.

"I figured it out! You smell like pickles! Also, you look like you have the chickenpox," Joy said.

Mom, who had just come into the room, nodded. "Sorry

Jeani, you really do and it's not going to get better right away."

She had me get out of the tub and dry off. She then rubbed calamine lotion on all of my bites.

"Now you smell like medicinal pickles and look like a splotchy pink panther!" Joy snorted.

Mom, who was crouched down by me, looked up at Joy. "Don't you have anything better to do? Maybe in your room, you know, since you're grounded?"

"I'm grounded?" Joy said with disbelief. "Why am I grounded?"

Mom stood up, her hands on her hips, and stared down at Joy. "Because if you weren't chasing her, she wouldn't have fallen into the ant hill. But if that was all that had happened, it wouldn't be so bad. But you didn't check to make sure she was okay. Whenever anyone falls, you check. You know that! but you kept spraying her and that's what made the ants stick. So this is very much your fault. Now," she said, extending her arm and pointing beyond the bathroom door, "go to your room."

Since my skin has always been overly sensitive, it took a week for the ant bites to calm down. During that time, I looked like a splotchy pink panther, and smelled like a medicinal pickle. Joy thought it was the funniest thing and called me her favorite pickled panther.

"That's okay. I like panthers!" I announced.

"You don't even know what a real panther looks like," Joy retorted.

I thought about the Pink Panther show. "Where do real panthers live?"

Joy shrugged. "The zoo?"

I nodded thoughtfully, scratching at my ant bites.

Just over a year later, I would see a real live panther. But it wouldn't be in a zoo. It would be in the wild and in Venezuela.

4

Panther

Guri Dam, Venezuela

In 1977, my family moved to Venezuela for the first time. Joy was six and I was four. Dad's engineering company, Chicago Bridge and Iron, had made him Construction Manager for part of a project that was building the Guri Dam. It was a massive undertaking which would eventually provide electricity for towns and cities throughout Venezuela and, years later, become part of the political stronghold the United States had over Venezuela.

Before April, Dad had been back and forth between countries, but his company decided they needed him to move there. I never knew how long we were supposed to have stayed because Mom discovered she was pregnant with Jacqueline and we moved home before she gave birth in February of 1978. We ended up staying in Guri for about seven months, from April to just before Thanksgiving. Dad stayed a bit longer, moving back to the US just before Christmas.

It was a weird place to be living since, at that time, there wasn't even a town. Basically, the company had scooped out part of the jungle, tossed in a bunch of trailers, cleared the middle of the circle for a garden and a flag pole which had the Venezuelan flag, the US flag, and a flag that had the CBI company logo.

Years later, I would try to understand the environmental impact of what my father's company was doing. I would even write a report on renewable energy looking at how, while better than fossil fuels, hydroelectric energy impacts wildlife habitats and migratory patterns when I was in junior high.

But as a four year old, it was just life.

Everyone that lived in the trailers were connected to the Guri Dam and worked with or for my father. Joy, being older and in school already, had classes with the other kids. No one was allowed to leave the circle of trailers without an adult and there were no kids my age, only a couple of babies and kids older than Joy. So, I ended up trailing after Mom who spent her time arranging shopping trips, setting up Bible studies, and praying with the other women whose husbands worked on the dam with my Dad.

It would have been really boring, but throughout that makeshift community, we could hear the sounds of the jungle and that thrilled me. The monkeys and other primates were the loudest during the day. Just behind them, volume-wise, was the array of bird songs. But unlike the other jungle sounds, the songs of birds would permeate the night; the voices of night birds seamlessly replacing the daytime ones. Joy was scared when we first got there, but I loved all the noises from the start. I was just frustrated that I couldn't go into the jungle and see the wild animals. I wanted to play with them and, no matter what my parents or anyone else said, I knew that all the animals wanted to play with me.

The adults were always warning the kids to stay within the circle. Joy didn't need the warnings, but I did. A few of the bigger kids, I think there were three of them, would joke about going into the jungle, but none of them really wanted to go beyond the trailers unless they were in a car.

One day, when I was supposed to be taking a nap, I somehow got out of my bed and the trailer without anyone noticing. It was a beautiful day. Most days were, but that one shines in my memory. The sun was bright and hot but there was a cool breeze too. I remember sand blowing in my face as I found a path past the circle of protection. I remember hearing the delightful sounds of the jungle growing as I got closer. I remember running. I fell a few times, but got right back up and finished covering the distance to the jungle's edge.

As I approached the jungle, a huge panther stepped out from between two trees. Her enormous front paws made deep prints in the dirt that had been cleared of all vegetation for future construction while her back ones rested in the grass of the jungle. I froze. I don't remember feeling scared, just awe. I was entranced by her magnificence. She was regal and had the most brilliant golden-green eyes I'd ever seen. She radiated majesty as she lowered herself, showing me she meant no harm. A slight sigh escaped her as her chin rested on her now crossed front paws. I don't remember deciding to sit, but there was a thump as my butt hit the ground. Every molecule of my body was vibrating. I wanted to bury my hands and face in that thick black coat so bad! But even at my impulsive age, I knew that if I did, the magic would be broken and I would probably be eaten. So I sat on my hands to keep them in check. I don't know how long we sat like that, just staring at each other. It was probably only a few moments. But in my memory, those moments were an eternity.

I remember hearing, or rather feeling, the panther's thoughts. It wasn't words exactly, at least not human ones, more like emotions coming in waves off of her to me. My mind made words of what I felt.

The deep and melodic feel translated to something like, "Why are you here, little human?" The feeling was kind and had a maternal edge to it.

The question startled me. Not the fact that I was sitting across from a wild panther more than five times my size, nor the fact that I could sense what she was feeling and possibly thinking, but that she was concerned about me.

After a long pause, I whispered, "To meet you, I guess."

She laughed. I had never heard a cat, or any animal, laugh before. Her laughter was as warm as the day and as strong as the wind.

"If you have to guess, you are not ready."

"Ready for what?" I asked.

"For your journey to begin."

She uncrossed her paws and stretched, with her hindquarters in the air and her front half almost flat to the ground. But, instead of leaving, she stood up tall and studied me. From my seated position, I craned my neck to keep looking into her eyes. I noticed that her whiskers twitched in ways that had nothing to do with the strong breeze whipping my short blonde hair.

She gave a mighty roar that sent me scurrying backwards like a crab. Closing her large and toothy maw, she turned and, with regal steps, strode back into the jungle. As I stood and brushed the sand off my butt, I saw Joy stepping out from the circle of trailers, scanning the area. I ran to her and pounced. She managed to remain standing, but just barely.

"Did you see her? Did you see my panther?"

She pushed me off and gave me a quizzical look. "What are you talking about? You know what, nevermind. We have to get back home. You're in so much trouble!"

She turned to go, but I stood where I was.

"No." I said. "Not until you tell me you believe me."

She turned sideways and cocked her head. "Believe you about what?"

"That I saw a panther!" I shouted stomping my foot.

She sighed then turned fully to face me. "Jeani, if you saw a panther, it would eat you."

I shook my head. "No. Not this one, she talked to me. She was my friend."

Joy laughed. "You say that about all animals!"

"Yeah, that's 'cause I'm friends with all animals."

She shook her head again, her long darker, but still blonde hair dancing in the wind. "I hate to say it, but someday that's going to get you in trouble." She was repeating something our mom often said. She flipped around, spinning like a dancer, and started back. She shouted over her shoulder. "Get your butt in gear or I'll tell Mom where you were!"

I ran after her, leaving the jungle behind.

It would be a few more years before her prediction about my trust of unknown animals would come true. We would also be living in a different province in Venezuela. But when it did, my actions would have potentially dire consequences.

5

Swim Team

Jersey Village, TX

After Mom gave birth to JacQueline, we wouldn't move back to Venezuela until 1980. So the summer of 1979, Joy and I were on the Jersey Village swim team. Joy, at eight, had been on the team since she was five. At six, this was my second year and my first year participating in swim meets. Joy, unlike me, loved the swim meets. She was a good sport about losing, though she didn't lose too often.

One meet that I'll never forget was at the pool in Jersey Village the summer before I started first grade. It was a sunny day and there was a strong breeze. I stood with the rest of the swim team as Joy's age group, the eight and nine year olds, took their positions on the starting blocks. It was the freestyle and Joy had been practicing all month. As soon as the starter pistol went off, she was in the water and ahead of everyone.

"Go Joy!" I shouted, jumping up and down and clapping with my teammates as water splashed and parents screamed from the bleachers. Her moves were strong and sure. Even though she was the shortest swimmer out there, she was at least half a body length ahead of the next swimmer. She hit the wall and bounced up to look around.

"And the winner is, Joy Vaughn, from Jersey Village, Texas!" The announcer shouted as everyone cheered. Even the swimmers from the other team were whooping it up. One of our coaches helped her out of the water and wrapped a towel around her. She was glowing with delight as they walked around the pool towards where we were standing. I heard the coach say that Joy had beat her own record and was leagues ahead of all the other swimmers. I caught Mom's eye as she was waving and clapping in the stands. Jackie, not quite one and a half years old, was in a stroller next to Mom smiling and clapping along.

Another group went, a different age group doing the backstroke, as Joy reached where our team was standing. She was shivering a little, but still grinning. I ran over and hugged her. She usually pushed me away when I did that in front of people and barely tolerated it when we were alone, but this time she hugged me back.

"You won!" I shouted.

She laughed. "I know!"

Then it was my turn. I joined the swimmers in the six and

seven age group on the starting blocks. We were doing the breaststroke. We took our stances. I waved to Joy, then looked at my competition. The boy closest to me looked stern, almost angry. The girl next to him was giggling. She shook her head, blonde curls bouncing, and took a deep breath as she straightened her back. I couldn't see the other swimmers without leaning too far forward, so I focused back on the water.

"Jeani!" Joy laughed from the sidelines. "Go Jeani, go!"

The announcer was saying something about how the meet was going, then shouted, "on your marks, get set..." The starter gun went off and all the swimmers dove into the water. Well, everyone except me. I was frozen in that swimmer's crouch with my butt in the air, my fingers gripping the front of the diving block, and my feet planted. I could see the other swimmers reaching the middle of the pool.

"Jeani!" I could hear Joy shouting as she ran over to me. "What's wrong with you?"

A hand touched my arm. It wasn't Joy. I turned to look at my swim coach. She gave me a tight-lipped smile.

"Come on, get down."

I relaxed and got off the starting block. Joy ran up to me.

"Are you okay? What happened?"

I shook my head. She gripped both my arms above my elbows. "Jeani, I've seen you swim this more times than I can count. You can do it. I don't know what happened to you just now, but you can do this." She gave me a hug. She looked over at the swim coach. "Can she go with the next group?"

The ten and eleven year olds were already lining up on the blocks. After a moment of thinking about it, the swim coach nodded.

"Well, it's freestyle and they're much older, but there's an open lane at the end. Jeani, you'll have to swim freestyle not breaststroke and no matter what place you come in, it won't count."

I shrugged. "Really, I just want to swim."

"Okay," she said. "Scoot!"

I nodded and ran to the open lane. When I got there, a few of the kids closest to me were snickering.

"What do you think you're doing, tiny?" The whisper came from the kid closest to me. "You can't race us. We're fifth graders! You're what, a kindergartener? You can't swim with us!"

I ignored her.

The kid next to her laughed. "Don't worry about her," he said. "Even if she doesn't freeze up again she won't be able to keep up with us."

When the gun went off, I dove in with the other kids and swam. The water was cool and refreshing. I swam the fastest and best I had ever swum. I beat all of those snooty fifth graders. When I got out, there was a lot of cheering. My coach picked me up and swung me around.

"Jeani, that was amazing! It didn't count, but you were way ahead of the other kids. Next time, do it with your group, okay?"

I nodded and laughed, "okay. I promise."

For the rest of the swim meet, I sat with Mom and Jackie and we watched Joy. She swam like she was made for water; as if she was a swan in a former life. She didn't win every race, but placed each time. Her form was widely admired and talked about by those watching. She even competed in diving and got fourth place.

That night, after we went for pizza and while we were in the bathroom getting ready for bed, Joy asked me what happened.

I took my toothbrush out of my mouth and thought about it. "I don't know. I was just there waiting for the gun to go off and I looked down the line and was thinking about all the other swimmers. I thought about how coming this early meant that they left their town even earlier and must have had breakfast even earlier and they were probably hungry for lunch. Then I was wondering what they would have for lunch, probably pizza? Then I was thinking about pizza and how much I like pizza and I was wondering if we were going to go for pizza and... and then I realized that the gun had already gone off and the other swimmers were already in the water. I didn't know if I should dive in or get off the block or what. So I just stayed there."

"You're stupid," Joy laughed. "But at least you weren't scared."

I laughed. Then, realizing she was serious, I brushed my teeth some more. Watching her in the mirror as she washed her face, I held the brush between my teeth and my cheek. "Wait. Do you get scared?"

She nodded and whispered, "Every single time I swim."

I was surprised. I always thought Joy was the bravest person in the world. "Why did you do it if you were scared?"

She shrugged. "I don't like being scared, but I am, lots of times. Instead of just letting my scarediness win, I do the thing I'm scared of anyway and it's almost always not as scary as I thought it was." She grinned. "Besides, I'm a really good swimmer!"

I nodded. "Yeah you are!"

6

The Sanctity of Trees

~

Union Point, GA

I was a high energy wild child, the opposite of my calm and composed older sister, and had trouble figuring out how to calm down. But high in a tree's branches, with nothing to distract me and needing to stay balanced, I could breathe and just be. Mom said that as soon as I could walk, I was trying to climb trees. Joy called my ability to find a good climbing tree my special skill. I fell out of a lot of trees trying to find the perfect one. But I never broke a bone and whenever I did find that tree, it was worth every time I fell.

One year, during the 1978 family reunion on my dad's side, I couldn't find any place to hide. There were benches and picnic tables under the pavilion where the family set up, but there were so many people, so many relatives around that anywhere I turned, they were asking me questions. I couldn't just go sit at another pavilion since the entire area we were in was filled with other families getting together for the Fourth of July weekend. I had played all the games and eaten all the food and felt like my brain was short circuiting. When one of my cousins suggested we play hide-n-seek, I was all in. But instead of hiding in and around the pavilion like all my cousins did, I ran as far as I could while still in earshot of whoever was counting. I quickly found a tall tree to climb. I made sure it had lots of foliage to hide in. The sun was bright and sweat was sliding down my back. It pooled in my hair as I climbed. I could hear the, "ready or not..." and climbed faster. I didn't stop until I reached the highest sturdy branch of the tree. Climbing out onto it, I sat with my back against the trunk, panting. After my heart stopped racing, I stared through the leaves at the world. I could just make out our pavilion and see all my relatives milling around. They looked so small. I let my legs hang off the opposite sides of the branch and swung them. The wind picked up, causing the tree to sway. I closed my eyes, enjoyed the cooler air.

"Maybe I'll live here forever," I thought sleepily as I leaned my back firmer against the tree.

I don't remember falling asleep, but suddenly I was facedown on the branch and jerking awake. I almost screamed as I wrapped my arms and legs tight against the branch, gasping.

"I could have fallen!" I thought, suddenly very aware of how high up I was. I stared down through the tree leaves and branches and began to cry. I had never been afraid of heights, but I was suddenly very aware that I could fall.

"Jeani?"

I opened my eyes and saw Joy standing at the base of the tree looking up. I tried to call out to her, but found that I had lost my voice. Could she see me? I wasn't sure. I tried to wave, but my arms refused to move. They were glued to the tree.

One of the cousins, who was beyond the small bit of ground I could see from where I was, shouted at Joy, "Are you sure she's up there?"

Joy stopped looking up and shook her head. "No, but I think I'm going to climb up and see if I can see her from a higher vantage point."

"Van tach what?" The cousin asked. It was one of the younger boy cousins. He stepped a little closer and I could just see the top of his crewcut head.

Joy laughed. "So I can see her from up high."

The cousin shook his head. "You might fall."

She laughed again. "I doubt it. I'm really good at climbing trees." To demonstrate, she pulled herself up onto the closest branch and started shimmying up the tree and to the next big branch.

"Your funeral!" The cousin shouted after her then ran off to see what everyone else was doing.

Paralyzed and unable to say anything, I watched Joy climb. She wasn't climbing my tree, she was climbing the tree right next to mine. Even though it was shorter, it was an easier climbing tree. When she was about halfway up, she stopped and sat on the widest branch. She looked over at my tree and, with only a few leaves between us, I could see that she was looking right at me.

"Everyone is worried," she said in a calm, conversational voice. "We're all looking for you."

I said nothing.

She sighed. "Look, I know we were playing hide-n-seek, but the game's over. I don't know why you decided you needed to hide in a tree and I don't care. But Mom and Dad are upset and," she pointed at the sky that had gotten dark, "it's almost night. You should come down right now so they know you're alright."

"I can't," I whispered.

Leaning forward, Joy held her hand at her ear, "I can't hear you! What did you say?" She looked like she might laugh and, for some unknown reason to me, it made me mad.

"I can't!" I shouted.

"Can't what?" She shouted back.

"I can't climb down!"

"Oh," she said, leaning back. "Are you like one of those stupid cats that gets stuck in a tree but forgets how to get down and then the family has to call the fire department to bring their ladder and..." She shook her head and started laughing. "You're not a cat. But you are a weirdo!"

I sat up on my branch and put my small hands on my hips. "I am not! I'm just scared to..."

"No," Joy cut me off, her voice stern but calm like Mom's would get when she was dealing with my, what she called, backwards logic. "You can't be scared 'cause you got up there, okay? You can get down. You always do. Just do what you did before, but backwards."

The wind was getting even harder and I realized it wasn't getting dark because it was night, it was getting dark because there was a storm.

"I can't," I cried.

"Of course you can." Disdain dripped from Joy's lips as she climbed down from her branch. "Watch me, it's easy!" She wrapped herself around the tree trunk and slowly lowered herself down to the next branch. "Now you!" She shouted at me.

I gathered my courage and copied her. I was a bit shaky, but I got to the next branch.

"Great!" She shouted at me. "Now do it again."

Slowly we made our way down our trees, branch by branch, with her talking me through every step. Joy, not having climbed as high, got to the ground first. But she didn't leave me. Even when it started raining, she stood there shouting encouragement until I made it all the way to the ground. As soon as my feet hit the ground, her hands were on my shoulders and she was staring into my eyes. The rain was coming faster, but she stood there staring at me. After a few seconds, she spoke.

"Jeani, I get it. Sometimes I have to get away and be alone too. But it's important to pay attention to what's going on 'cause if Dad had found you..." She shook her head. "Next time, just tell me where you're going, okay?"

"Okay," I nodded.

"Okay," she repeated, then grabbed my hand and we ran to the pavilion as the rain pelted us.

When we got there, everyone else had packed up and were heading to their cars. Mom was bouncing a crying baby Jackie on her hip as Dad put the last of the stuff away.

"Finally!" Mom said, waving for us to join them as we raced to the car. Once we were all inside, Mom gave Joy and I a towel to share as Dad drove.

Years later, in 1986, when I was fourteen, I was over my fear climbing the upper branches of tall trees and climbed an even taller one at a cousin's house. Once again, I was doing it to get away from my family. It wasn't an official family reunion, but there was a large gathering at one of our cousin's houses.

I forgot my deal with Joy and that time, she didn't find me. Dad did. When I finally came down, I got a whoopin' in front of my cousins. While the spanking didn't hurt too much, the humiliation stayed with me and the look of reproach from Joy made me wish I'd stayed up in that tree and never come down. I wish I had told Joy before I climbed that tree.

7

Sun Kissed

Jersey Village, Texas

Despite the Texas heat, summer was my favorite season during my childhood. The public pool wasn't far from our house in Jersey Village and swimming was my favorite activity other than climbing trees. The pool was further than the high school but closer than the elementary school. In 1979, Joy and I rode our bikes there all summer even when we didn't have swim team practice. On any given day, except Sunday, if the weather was good, we would be at the pool from open until close.

At 7 years old, I was still struggling to make sense of letters and words. Mom had started reading Freckle Juice with me. I loved it. Joy, of course, had already read all of Judy Blume's books and didn't like her as much as I did. She said they were baby books. I told Joy that she said that because she was a Beezus. (I was, of course, a Ramona.) She wasn't amused.

Back to freckles. Whenever we went to the pool, Mom, Jackie, and I would get more and more freckles. Joy took after Dad and didn't freckle. Despite all the sunscreen, my skin would burn and be splattered with freckles while Joy got a lovely even tan. People would compliment her, telling her how lovely her skin was.

On one bright and sunny day in early August, Joy and I had gotten out of the pool and were reapplying sunblock to each other. I had to move her long hair out of the way to get to her already tanned back. Joy's hair had gone brown over the winter, but she used lemon juice and Sun In to bleach it a golden blonde. Some other moms from around the neighborhood were talking to our mom over by the gate where she had just shown up with Jackie. I watched her bounce Jackie on her hip and laugh at something one of the other mothers said. She looked so happy. When she looked over, I waved to her, forgetting I had the sunblock in my hand and squirted a big blob in Joy's hair.

"Hey!" she shouted, touching her head and holding up a hand covered in white greasy goo. "You got it in my hair!"

I held the offending container aloft. "Sorry!"

"Whatever," she grumbled, wiping her hand on her towel.

I held the sunblock out to her since she was supposed to do my back after I did hers.

She shook her head, trying to rub the goop from her hair.

"I don't think so." She glanced over at Mom who was coming our way, then leaned so close I could feel her breath on my ear and snarled, "And don't tell on me 'cause I'll tell Mom you squirted the sunblock into my hair on purpose." She waved to Mom, then jumped into the pool and washed the rest of the sunblock out.

Mom sat down on the lounging chair Joy had vacated and started slathering sunblock on her arms. "Jeani, could you do my back?"

"Only if you do mine!" I grinned.

"Sure," she said. Glancing over at the diving board, she asked, "Did Joy not do your back? I saw you doing hers."

I shrugged. "I forgot to ask." It wasn't technically a lie.

"Okay," Mom said. After I finished, she looked over at the diving board. Joy had just reached the front of the line and was climbing the tall ladder. Mom shaded her eyes with her hand as Joy walked down the vibrating board and dove. We applauded and whooped for Joy. Mom turned to me and rubbed my back with the sunblock.

"Hey Mom," I said, chewing on my lower lip as I thought. "Do you like your freckles?"

She made a sound that fell somewhere between a laugh and a scoff, then sighed. "You know what, when I was young like you, I didn't like them. I knew several boys and a few girls who would make fun of my freckles." I gasped. The idea of anyone making fun of my beautiful mother upset me. Joy was walking over to us, still dripping. "But then," Mom continued, "I decided that each freckle was a kiss from the sun."

I looked down at my arms and smiled at all the kisses. "Well, the sun must love you and Jackie 'cause y'all have all the kisses."

Mom laughed as Joy sat on the edge of Mom's chair and I went to go swim.

Later that day, after Mom had left with Jackie, Joy and I were walking over to our bikes. I noticed that Joy had a weird look on her face. As a few of her friends walked past us, her face broke into a smile. They shouted at each other.

"Later gator!"

"After while, crocodile!"

"See ya soon, baboon!"

They laughed. But once her friends were gone, Joy's face fell and she had that weird look again.

"Whatcha thinkin'?" I asked as I skipped along beside her.

She tilted her head and looked at me sideways. "Nothin'."

By then, we had reached the bikes and we were too busy fiddling with the combinations to talk. I noticed that we had stayed longer than anyone else, besides the lifeguards. I started to say something to Joy about how cool it was that we had been the first to the pool and we were the last leaving, but she had already gotten onto her bike and was peddling away. I quickly threw my leg over my bike and hurried after her.

"Joy!" I shouted. "Mom says you're supposed to wait for me!"

She glanced back at me, annoyance etched in her face. "Sorry."

I could tell she wasn't sorry. She was trying to speed away from me, but I was pretty fast. There weren't any cars on the road so we rode side by side. After a few minutes of silence, I couldn't take it anymore.

"Joy, I'm sorry if I did something to make you mad. I didn't mean to. But could you tell me what it was? Was it getting the sunblock in your hair? If so, I already said sorry."

Joy huffed, but said nothing. I was getting more and more frustrated. I pushed my bike harder. I passed her then made a sharp turn in front of her, setting my food down hard on the pavement, causing my back tire to flip out like a shark fin. I almost fell off my bike as she squealed to a stop.

"What the bananas, Jeani!" She shouted, her face red with fury. "You could've gotten both of us killed!"

I doubled over with laughter. "What the bananas?" I howled, then chittered like a monkey.

"Stop it!" She shouted, trying really hard to be mad at me, but I could see a grin pulling at the corner of her mouth. Before she could say anything else, she saw a car coming around the corner ahead of us. She waved me over and we both bumped our bikes up on the curb and over to the sidewalk.

After a few cars passed us, she gave a big dramatic sigh.

"Look. The reason I'm upset is 'cause I don't have freckles."

I grinned wide. "Oh we can make freckle juice, like in the book That'll be so..." I stopped before I said 'fun' because Joy was crying. "Oh no. I..."

She shook her head and I fell silent. "It's just... I mean... Mom said freckles are kisses from the sun!" She cried harder.

"Oh," I said, realizing why she was upset. I thought about it for a few seconds, then an idea came to me. "But you tan and you know what a tan is, don't you?"

She sniffled. "What?"

"It's a bunch of freckles that got all smooshed together! You get the most kisses! I think the sun licks you! I think the sun is in looooooooove with you!"

"Ew!" she laughed as I made kissy, slurpy sounds. She wiped her nose on the towel slung over her shoulder. "Well, I guess that's better than the sun just hating me."

I snorted, crossing my arms and tilting my head at her. "Everybody likes you. You know that, right?"

She shrugged. "I mean, I guess. But sometimes, I'm not

sure. I mean, what if everybody's just pretending?" She shook her head and laughed a little. "I mean, not you. You like me best, don't you?"

I nodded. "Of course!"

The wind had picked up a little and the sun was starting to set. The street lights had started buzzing like they always did before coming on. "Come on," Joy said, mounting her bike and looking up at the street light next to us as it flickered on. "You know how much trouble we'll get in if we don't get home before dark."

I got on my bike and pedaled after her. I was glad she was no longer upset and that something I said helped.

8

Bike Rack Bullies

Jersey Village, TX

In September of 1979, when I started first grade, I got to ride my bike to Post Elementary School with Joy and her two friends. They were sisters who lived just around the corner from us and were closer in age to Joy. The three of them had been riding together since Joy was in first grade. That year, Joy was in third, and I think one of the sisters was in third with her and the oldest was in fourth grade. They were both very shy and quiet. Of the four of us, I was the most outgoing.

When she was told to take me with her, Joy complained. She said my tagging along was annoying, and her friends didn't like it and she doubted I could keep up, which was a total lie because I could bike faster than Joy. Mom listened to her for a while, but she finally reached her limit.

"Enough. I'm sorry you have to put up with your sister. But that's the way life is," and she would listen to no more complaining. "If you keep it up," she said as she tossed some sheets into the dryer, eyeing Joy who had opened her mouth to continue, "you will have to do everyone's laundry for a week."

Joy huffed and marched out of the room. She stopped complaining around Mom, but she would complain at me every chance she got. The sisters we road with didn't seem to mind me too much. They even seemed to like my never ending observations of the world. But Joy couldn't stand it.

Only a few weeks after the start of the new school year, we began having trouble with a few fifth grade boys. They were mostly bigger kids and would hang around the bike racks after school. It wasn't just us; they would block anyone from getting to their bikes. But they would scatter as soon as a teacher showed up. It went on for a couple of weeks whenever we were leaving school, but their harassment eventually petered out. A few of them ended up in detention and the rest were finding other ways to occupy their time.

About mid-October, even though this was Texas and it didn't get all that cold, it got rainy, so most kids were either taking the bus or getting rides. One day, there were only our four bikes left at the rack. It was raining so the playground was empty. As we approached our bikes, four of the boys, including the kid who lived across the street from Joy and I, were standing in front of our bikes. They didn't say anything, they just stood there with their arms crossed over their chests, looking intimidating. They all had slicked back hair, either due to the rain or a poor attempt to copy the Jets from Westside Story, and one even had the beginnings of a mustache. Our neighbor was the smallest of them, but he acted the toughest and at lunch would often brag about how his dad had been in prison and that his brother got hauled off to jail for drunk and disorderly or something like that. He spent a lot of time in detention.

"I'm going to tell my mom," Joy said to our neighbor with a slight tremor in her voice, "and she's going to tell your mom and you're totally going to get in trouble." She was shaking with her fists clenched at her side.

He laughed. "My mom won't care."

The sisters exchanged a knowing glance, as if to say, he's right. We all knew his parents had split up and his mom was constantly working. She often didn't get home until the wee hours of the morning, or sometimes sunrise, and slept until noon or later during the week. I knew, from a previous encounter, that he was telling the truth. His mom wouldn't care. What could we do?

"We should just walk home," The oldest sister whispered.

"Come on," said the biggest of the four boys. "There are four of you and four of us. It's even. Let's fight!"

Another boy laughed. "We can't fight 'em, they're girls."

The boy from across the street, who was the shortest but still taller than Joy and I, cracked his knuckles and said, "Isn't it sexist of us not to fight them? After all," he shrugged, "feminism."

Suddenly, I had a bright idea. Joy was still taller than me at that point, so I stood on my toes and whispered in her ear. "I've got an idea. We can't fight 'em and tattling won't work, but maybe we could trick 'em?"

"Trick 'em?" she asked.

I nodded, shielding my mouth and told her my plan.

"What're you saying?" One of the boys shouted, looking a little nervous.

Joy grinned at me. "I mean, you could get infected. But if you're willing to chance it..." She shrugged.

"I am." I said.

She took my arm and, using her body to shield what she was doing from the boys, she whispered while she drew with her finger. "Circle, circle, dot, dot. Now you've got your cootie shot."

I rubbed it into my arm for good measure, then marched over to the biggest boy. He laughed.

"What're you gonna do, squirt?"

I made a 'come here' motion with my finger. He leaned down until his face was inches from mine. He snarled. I grabbed the collar of his jacket, tilted up onto my tippy-toes, and planted a big wet kiss on his mouth. Jumping away from him I shouted, "Cooties!"

He stumbled backwards wiping at his face. "Ewwww!" He howled as he ran away.

With my hands on my hips, I looked at the other boys and puckeed my lips. "Who's next?"

They all screamed and ran away. Even the boy from across the street!

Joy and our friends laughed. Clapping her hands, Joy hollered, "Look at 'em run! Scared off with a kiss!" She shook her head and ruffled my hair. "Guess you're not so bad after all, squirt."

I was elated. She never complained about me riding with them again. Bonus, those bullies left us alone the rest of the year.

9

German Shepherd Mama

Punto Fijo, Venezuela

Towards the end of the summer of 1980, my family moved back to Venezuela. That move took us to Judibana, a small parish in the town of Punto Fijo, the capital city of the municipality of Carirubana in northern Falcón State. While this put us on the southwestern coast of the Paraguaná Peninsula, I don't remember going to the beach during that stint of living in Venezuela. But we could always smell the ocean. Punto Fijo was nicknamed "La Ciudad del Viento", the city of wind, because of the constant breeze coming off the ocean from almost every direction.

Dad's company put us in a one story stucco house with a front lawn that was so small Mom would send Joy and I out with scissors to trim the tiny patch of grass. I think we were getting punished for something since I remember seeing Dad push around one of those non-motorized lawn mowers on another occasion, or she might've just sent us out there because we were hot and bored and whining. Since there was constant wind, there was no air conditioning so the windows of the house were always open. Mom was miserable with allergies and she was pregnant again. Despite the wind, the heat and her migraines often overwhelmed her.

One weekend in September–I know it was a weekend because Dad was home–we were having breakfast when Dad announced that we were going to a party. Someone from his work who lived nearby was having a barbecue and there would be kids our age and a piñata and games and possibly even fireworks. The party was starting later in the afternoon and would be going into the night. Mom took her napkin off her lap, wiped her mouth, and placed it on the table.

"John, I need to speak with you in the other room." With a bit of difficulty, she got to her feet and walked into their bedroom. Even though she was only four or five months pregnant, her pregnancy was causing her back pain, especially when getting out of chairs. From where I was seated at the table, I could see her sitting down on the bed. Because their room was dark, I couldn't see her face. Still, we could all feel the wave of disapproval coming from her.

Dad sighed, got up, and started walking to the room. He paused and looked at Joy. "Make sure the baby finishes eating before she gets down." He closed the door behind him. Joy and I exchanged a look. A fan had been placed between the tiny living room and the even smaller kitchen to circulate the air. But the fan in the bedroom had been turned off to conserve electricity. For them to close the door and not turn on the fan meant business. Jackie was happily singing and eating her bacon, oblivious. Joy put her finger to her lips, clutching her napkin in her hand, as she leaned down to switch off the fan. Still in our seats, we leaned towards the door, listening.

I kept eating the rest of my eggs, glancing at Joy as Mom and Dad's voices got louder and softer, then loud again. But we didn't really need to lean far to hear them. It didn't matter how quiet they got, the walls in that house were thin that with the fan off, we could hear every word.

"John, you didn't say it was a party. You said it was a work get-together. Are we supposed to bring a gift?"

"I don't think it's that kind of party." Even though we were in the other room, I was pretty sure Dad was rubbing the back of his neck. He did that whenever Mom was upset with him. "I think if we just bring your potato salad like you planned, that will be fine."

"John! There is a difference between a work barbecue and a party at someone's house! You had said families with kids, but a piñata? That sounds like a birthday party."

"Honey, they do things different here. Maybe they have piñatas at all their parties. I don't know!"

"Will there even be anyone who speaks English? My

Spanish isn't that good and, honestly, yours is a bit shaky when it doesn't have to do with construction. The girls barely know any Spanish."

"Joy seems to be picking it up quite quickly."

Joy preened. I stuck my tongue out at her.

"That is not the point and you know it!"

"Jo, I don't know what to tell you. You said you wanted to meet more people and for the girls to make some friends. You know we're having trouble finding an English speaking church, so I thought this might be a good solution."

"John, you didn't invite us to somebody else's party, did you?"

There was a long pause. Jackie burped really loud and looked like she might cry, so Joy and I distracted her with funny faces until she giggled. We could hear that Mom and Dad had started talking again, but the baby's laughter got too loud to understand what they were saying.

"Girls!" Dad shouted from the bedroom. His voice had that no-nonsense-you- better-do-what-I-say-or-else tone to it. "Clear the table, do the dishes, and clean up your sister; then go play outside!"

"Yes, sir!" Joy and I said in unison. Joy switched the fan back on, then did what he said.

Later that afternoon, we had to put on our Sunday clothes, wrap an almost new doll (it was one of mine because I never played with it) in some wrapping paper, and tied it up with one of Joy's hair ribbons. That way, we were both contributing to the gift. Dad had called the family throwing the party and found out that yes, the party was a birthday party for the daughter of one of his workers. While Mom was helping us get ready, he assured Mom that they actually wanted us there.

After he left the room, Mom sighed. She was sitting on the bed Joy and I shared and helping me with my hair. She shook her head. "They're not going to tell you that we're not welcome," she muttered around the hair elastic in her mouth, yanking the brush through my tangled hair. "You're their boss." I didn't dare say anything, but squeaked as she yanked on my head again. "Jeani, you have to brush your hair at least once a day if you want to keep it long like Joy's." I glared at Joy who was sitting in front of the vanity running a brush easily through her glossy brown hair. She caught my look in the mirror and gave me a smirk.

The people hosting the party lived only two blocks away from us, so we walked there. Joy carried the present, I carried the potato salad, and Mom pushed Jackie in the stroller. Dad took the lead.

"Your Dad's gonna take off without us!" Mom huffed through gritted teeth. "If we lose him, we'll just turn around and go back home."

"Mooooom!" I whined, "I wanna meet some kids!"

"Me too," Joy whispered.

Mom sighed. "I was only joking."

But we knew she wasn't.

By the time we turned the corner, Mom was panting. There were barriers at both ends of the street, blocking off any cars. Dad, who had been standing in the street with another man, rushed over and presented us. "This is my lovely wife Jo, our three kids, Joy, Jeani, and Jackie. And as you can see, we have another one on the way!" He was so proud as he patted Mom's belly.

Mom, still catching her breath, brushed his hand away and held it out the dish she was holding. "I brought potato salad."

A Venezuelan woman, almost as short as Joy and I, appeared from behind her husband.

"This is mi esposa," he started in clear and precise English, but she ignored him and spoke over him in Spanish as she took the bowl and Mom's hand, leading her to the house.

"She says you need to sit down, Señora Vaughn." her husband announced after them. "She will get you some water too. Don't worry about tus niñas. They will play with the other kids!"

"We brought a present," said Joy, holding it out in front of her, a slight tremor to her hands.

A young girl, about my age, with a long black braid flipped over her shoulder, appeared in front of us. "Gracias... I mean, eh, t'ank you! I put with others." She grabbed Joy's hand and led her into the yard of the house Mom had disappeared into. There was a table piled high with presents.

I had spotted a group of kids in the yard and tugged Dad's sleeve. "Dad! They're all wearing shorts and t-shirts!"

He nodded. "Well, I might've misunderstood. But go ahead and play. As your mom says, you're gonna get dirty no matter what you wear."

I had been mad about wearing a dress, but was thrilled about the permission to get dirty. I ran over to the kids. There were five boys and two other girls, not including the girl with the long braid who walked over with Joy trailing behind.

I waved wildly to them as I came closer and said, "¡Hola! ¡Mi nombre es Jeani! Y esta es mi hermana Joy." They welcomed us and we were soon running and playing with them. They explained the game they were playing with that Venezuelan speed so I missed quite a bit of it But Joy got it and explained that it was similar to tag; a game with pretty universal rules.

As the sun was getting low on the horizon, a few of the kids had gone into the yard across the street. Curious, I followed. In a large basket next to a dog house, a mama German Shepherd was nursing seven puppies. The mama was eyeing us nervously, but the kids were doing a good job keeping their distance. I sat down, cross legged and rested my chin in my palms with my elbows pressed into my knees. The kids around me were very animated as they spoke. While I could understand most of what they were saying, I couldn't follow the conversation.

Without turning to look, I felt Joy behind me. "Isn't it amazing?" I said, my eyes fixed on the puppies. "I just want to pet all the puppies and hug the mama."

Joy, who had been able to follow the conversation, squatted next to me. "The kid whose dad owns the dog says she's really protective and will bite you if you touch them."

I looked at her, my eyes wide. "But don't you want to pet them more than anything in the world?"

"Not if it means I get bit!" Joy shook her head, standing up. "But hey, if the mama goes away, I double dog dare ya to pet the puppies." She laughed. "Look, everybody's gonna play another game, it's kinda like kick-the-can except they throw a shoe instead of kicking a can."

"Maybe it's called throw-the-shoe?" I asked, my eyes still on the puppies.

She laughed. "Yeah, maybe. Wanna play?"

I shook my head. "I'll stay here."

"Okay," Joy shrugged, then ran off.

I watched as the puppies finished nursing and curled up to sleep. The sun was setting and the sky was a vibrant pinkish orange. The mama dog ambled off to find some table scraps by the barbecue. I watched her until she was out of sight, then crawled over to the puppies. They were so tiny! I looked all around, but nobody was paying attention. Slowly, I reached into the basket and petted each puppy. They were so soft and made little happy sounds as I petted them. I picked one up and held it to my chest, humming with my eyes closed.

I heard a growl behind me. My heart pounded as I put the puppy back and crawled away from the basket. The growl got deeper and closer. I turned to see the mama less than a foot away, meat juice dripping from her snarling snout. Her front feet were splayed and her ears back. I continued scooting backwards, away from her puppies, too scared to scream or get up. She barked deep and charged me, knocking me over. All I saw was fur as she pounced, her mouth biting and ripping my dress and my chest, my arms pinned at my side by her large paws. But just as suddenly, she was gone. I opened my eyes and saw her dangling in the air, whimpering as her owner held her by the collar.

Tears streaming down my face and blood covering my chest as I cried in my poor Spanish, "¡Por favor, no la dolor! ¡Es mi culpa! ¡Es mi culpa!" over and over as others rushed over. "Please!" I cried. "She didn't do anything wrong! It's my fault!"

The man, who had lowered the dog so her back feet were touching the ground, stared at me. He shook his head then hooked her collar to a chain. She was still growling, my blood mixing with the meat juices as it dripped from her snout. He was speaking with sharp but soft words. I couldn't tear my eyes from her as unknown arms wrapped around me and I was carried inside, still crying.

Several of the mothers gathered and attended to my wounds. Mom held my hand. She was shaking as she petted my head. The other ladies removed my tattered dress and washed the blood off to find a single bite wound in the middle of my chest. Mom whispered, "Oh, thank God! The wound isn't even that deep." Then she prayed.

All of the kids had gathered around me. One of the boys said something and they laughed.

"Joy, what did he say?" Mom asked.

Blushing, Joy said, "He...um...he said that she's lucky she's still a kid and doesn't have..." Her entire face went red as she searched for the appropriate word. Then in the quietest voice she said, "...breasts?"

Mom nodded, her own freckled face going pink.

"Is, is, is she go-gonna be o-okay?" I sobbed.

Creasing her brow, Mom asked, "Is who gonna be okay?"

"Th-the dog!" I wailing. "The-they're not gonna shoot her, are they? I heard that if a dog bites somebody, th-they..."

"Oh honey, no!" Mom hugged me. "That's not going to happen." Even with my head hugged to her chest, I could tell she wasn't certain. "But I'll check and..."

A loud bang made everyone jump and I screamed. I hopped off the table, about to run out of the house with only my underwear, socks, and shoes, but Mom grabbed my shoulder.

"Shut up, Jeani!" Joy shouted, clutching her ears against the noise of other explosions. "They didn't shoot the dog, that was fireworks! You're so..." I could tell she was going to call me stupid, but she stopped and glanced at Mom.

The women were talking in broken English with Mom on how best to care for my wound as they bandaged me up. The girl with the long braid came over with a shirt and shorts. I hopped off the table, thanked her in Spanish, and put them on. She hugged me.

"You best gringa friend. You make party so exciting!"

Joy rolled her eyes.

The girl grabbed my hand and Joy's hand. "Come see!"

"What's fireworks in Spanish?" Joy asked, ever eager to learn. The girl stopped in the doorway, looking confused. Joy pointed to the sky. "¿Cómo dices las luces?"

"Petardos," the girl said, pulling us out through the front door.

As we stood on the lawn in awe of the beautiful display of colors, Joy leaned over and asked, "Does it hurt?"

I shrugged. "A little. I was more sad than hurt. I thought we would be friends."

"Who?"

I looked at Joy, surprised she had to ask. "Me and the mama dog, of course. I always get along with animals!"

Joy shook her head. "You're so weird! And no, you don't.

You just think you do." She took a deep breath. "Jeani, I'm so sorry."

Distracted, I tapped on the braided girl's shoulder. "Do you know what they did with the puppies' mama?"

She looked helplessly at Joy who translated. She made an "ah" sound then launched into an explanation.

I couldn't hear her because of the explosions and could only understand a few words like dog and fireworks. "What did she say?" I asked.

"They put the mama and the puppies inside the house because of the fireworks. They didn't want them getting scared and run off or bite anyone else. They're not gonna hurt the dog 'cause you definitely caused her to bite you."

I nodded, feeling foolish but relieved that the dog was going to be okay.

After a few minutes of watching the fireworks, Joy leaned her head on my shoulder and whispered, "I have to know! Do you forgive me?"

"For what?"

"For daring you!"

"Oh, of course," I said, hugging her.

Pulling away, she looked down at her previously pristine dress and saw my blood on. "Ew!" She pointed at the shirt I was wearing. "You're bleeding through your shirt and got blood on me. Thanks a lot!"

"Of course!" I said, smiling wide and putting one arm over her shoulder, "That's what sisters are for!"

"To bleed on each other?" She asked. I nodded and we both laughed as we went back to watching the fireworks.

10

A Corpse of Trees

Jersey Village, TX

My mom was worried about me. In 1979, I was almost seven years old and still unable to read. When I wrote my A-B-Cs, they'd sometimes come out backwards or upside down. Even when I wrote my name, the first thing I was taught to write after the alphabet, it was a mess. My 'J' was backwards, the 'e' was upside down, my 'a' was backwards, the 'n' was sometimes backwards, sometimes an 'm' and sometimes it turned into a 'u'. Then my 'i'... Well, I usually got my 'i' right.

A year later in 1980, when we were living in Punto Fijo, Venezuela, Mom would find someone to evaluate me with

Dyslexia and help me develop coping skills. For now, let's return to Jersey Village, Texas in the spring of 1979.

"Jeani! Hey, wait up!"

I could hear Joy pedaling after me, but I didn't want her to catch up and see me crying. So I pushed my bike faster, the hot spring air whipping my tears and snot across my face and into my tangled dirty blonde hair.

"Jeani!"

Joy's voice was falling farther and farther behind as I turned off Congo Lane, taking the corner onto Solomon street faster than I should. I almost toppled over, but managed to keep my balance as I swerved through cars in the intersection. This caused several cars to honk at me and tires to screech, but I didn't care. I made it to the other side and pumped my pedals even faster, popping up onto the sidewalk. I rode under the bright sunlight. The Jersey Village High School was across the street from me and had just let out. The high schoolers looked like they were playing live action frogger as they bounced and weaved through the slow moving traffic. Several horns blared as teenagers laughed. A couple were ahead of me walking slowly and holding hands.

"Get out the way!" I shouted.

Startled, they jumped apart as I flew between them.

The girl in the sundress shouted, "what the F, kid!"

The boy, who was wearing jeans and a t-shirt, shouted, "Yeah!"

I could barely hear the girl say, "Yeah? That's all you have to..." before her words were sucked away with so many other sounds.

I didn't pause when I came to the intersection of Australia street, just glancing over as a car pulled up to the stop sign. My front wheel bounced back up onto the sidewalk in front of the car and I looked right again, but this time down that sidewalk to see my friend's back as she walked home. I thought about calling after her, but knew that she wouldn't understand why I was so upset. So I kept going.

When I reached Singapore Lane, my street, I didn't turn. Upon reaching Seattle street, just past the furthest portion of the high school's parking lot, I finally stopped pedaling. I glided, easily steering my bike to bounce off the sidewalk and out into the empty street. On my right, there was no sidewalk and I was reminded of one of my favorite books, "Where the Sidewalk Ends". Even though I couldn't read it, I liked to look at the pictures. I could usually get Joy to read a poem or two. She would let me pick the first one, but the second one would always be, Sister for Sale. She would even do the pose in the book like someone auctioneering. It always made me giggle.

It didn't make me giggle thinking about it. All I could think about was the fact that I couldn't read, couldn't read, couldn't read...

I let the inertia of the bike carry me past Seattle's intersection with the tennis courts on my left. I could hear some high schoolers playing and talking. I was glad they couldn't see me through the green netting since I was still crying. To my right, was a large, round, squat metal water containment unit with a purple falcon, the high school's mascot, painted on it. I rode past it and reached the West Gulf Bank Drive where Solomon street ended in a T. In front of me was a parking lot to a large industrial building. To the right was a dead-end and to the left, the road wrapped away from me. I turned right, slowing down, and went to where the road ended. I hopped off my bike and walked it onto the grass. There were a few trees and lots of unkempt shrubs and brambles. This area was behind a row of tall fences to the backyards of Seattle Street and behind the large parking lot of the industrial complex. It wasn't really anyone's space and that's where I wanted to be, someplace that was kind of nowhere and where no one was around. A liminal space.

I leaned my bike against a tree in a way that made sure no one could see it through the shrubbery even if they were standing at the end of the street. If they came onto the grass and walked towards me, they would probably find me. But it was good enough. I chucked my backpack off and threw it on the ground. Then, after glancing around to make sure no one would hear me, I screamed. I screamed as loud and as long as I could, until I had no more screams left in me, then crumpled to the ground in tears.

I must've fallen asleep from exhaustion 'cause the next thing I remembered was being nudged in the side and someone saying my name. I groaned and willed myself to go back to sleep. But the nudging continued, so I opened my eyes and saw that it was getting dark.

"Jeani! Come on, get up!" Joy nudged me again with her foot.

I brought my head up and looked at her. "What?"

She sat in the grass beside me. "Mom's really worried."

I looked away from her, sat up and shrugged. "So?"

She pushed my shoulder, "so you need to get home so she knows you're alright!"

I raised an eyebrow and looked over at her. She was sitting primly with an expression that said, 'Me? I am innocent of everything!' and I knew Mom probably didn't even know I hadn't come home and most definitely wasn't worried. But if I didn't come home before the sun fully set and it was time for super, Mom would know and Joy would be in trouble too. I shook my head and got up.

As I brushed the dirt off my back and my butt, I asked, "What'd ya tell her?"

Joy grinned. "I just said you ran upstairs when we got home. I've been in my room reading, so I didn't see when you left again."

"Left again?" I asked.

She nodded. "Well you must have. Your bike wasn't in the garage. Mom was surprised she didn't see you since she'd been in the kitchen the whole time."

"I'm just so super fast and quiet," I said as I picked my bike up from where it was laying on the ground.

But I couldn't keep a straight face and started laughing. Joy joined in, as she picked her own bike.

"Oh yes," she giggled between gasps, "you're practically invisible and silent!" She almost folded over her bike as she howled with laughter.

Once we got our laughter under control, we rode home and made it through the door just before dinner.

After dinner, Dad was drowsing in his recliner watching sports and Mom was working on some mending. Joy had gone into the living room to read since it was my night to clear the table and do dishes. I was very much lost in thought and gasped, almost dropping the stack of plates I was carrying from the table to the kitchen, when Joy appeared in front of me.

"Don't do that," I said through gritted teeth. She had her bare left foot crossed over her right and was leaning her right shoulder casually against the harvest yellow fridge as she used a nail file to clean under her fingernails. I squeezed past her and the half island to get into the kitchen and over to the sink. "I thought you were reading." I turned on the water and started rinsing the white plates with a light blue design around the edge.

After they were done and all the dishes were in the dishwasher, I turned to look at her. She hadn't answered me, but I really hadn't asked a question. She was just standing there, looking at me.

I sighed and whispered, "why aren't you reading?"

She shrugged, then took my hand. With a finger to her lips, she led me into the laundry room and out the door that had been propped open so it wouldn't screech against the latch. Once outside, she walked me past the grill and over to the wooden picnic table Dad had set up earlier for the barbecue picnic we were going to have tomorrow. I sat on one side and she sat across from me. It was dark enough that I couldn't make out her expression, though the light from the tiny window above the sink in the kitchen and the large bay window by the breakfast area provided quite a bit of light. I leaned way back, looping my fingers under the bench, and looked up at the sky. It was too bright around me to see much of anything, but the air was crisp and I knew the universe was up there. I sat back up and looked at Joy. She had her hands folded in front of her on the table and was staring at me.

"What?" I asked.

She tilted her head. "I'm waiting for you."

"For me to... what?"

Her sigh held more exasperation than Mom's when we were dawdling before church on a Sunday. "For you to tell me why you rode off without me and why you were sleeping in the woods."

I snorted a laugh. "That's hardly the woods. It's a corpse of trees at best."

"Copse of trees. And where did you hear that?"

I shrugged, swinging my feet and tapping a random

rhythm out on the table with my fingers. She gave me a scolding look and I stopped. After a second, I remembered she wasn't my mom and definitely not the boss of me and started tapping my feet.

"Look," she said using her most earnest tone as she reached across the table and took my hands in hers. "I'm worried about you. When I found you, you were asleep on the ground."

"I like sleeping on the ground," I grumbled, trying to yank my hands back, but her grip was tight.

"Be that as it may," she said in her most adulty voice. "That was dangerous! What if I hadn't found you? You could have kept sleeping and caught hyper thermal and died."

I shook my head. "I would've awoken if it got too cold. Besides, you can only catch hyper thermal in Ant's arctica. It was in the movie I saw in my class so you know it's true."

"Be that as it may," she said again. I was beginning to wonder who had said that phrase to her. "You are my sister and I don't want you to get hurt. Maybe if you woke up after dark, a van man would come along and kidnap you!"

I shook my head. "I know stranger danger. I wouldn't get in a van. Well, I mean, except ours."

"But what if you thought it was uncle Clarence 'cause it was dark and he said he was going to take you home but he lied."

"Oh, so really he just wanted to kidnap me and steal my bike?"

"What?" Joy exclaimed, releasing my hands as she threw hers up. "Why would he want to steal your bike?"

"To sell it, of course. But then, you'd see it for sale and you'd tell mom and dad that you think the man selling the bike was my kidnapper. But they wouldn't believe you and mom would cry and dad would yell at you and you'd get grounded. But you'd sneak out and meet up in a secret place with the greatest detective of all time, Sam Nav!" I clapped my hands, thrilled with this new story idea for the mystery I had been telling her and mom for over a year.

Joy groaned. "No! Not Sam Nav!"

"Why not? Sam Nav is great!"

"Sam Nav is you!"

"Um, I'm not a detective. Besides, Sam Nav can't be me because I'm kidnapped and my bike's stolen by the van man with the handy mustache... I mean... you know those ones that make a twirly? Those types of villain mustaches?"

Joy shook her head. "Look, stop being silly. Krista saw you crying in the hall today and then you rode off without us, which you're not supposed to do. Then you almost caused an accident when you were weaving through the traffic, which is really bad. But then after that, you didn't even come home! Jeani, what's going on?"

I wanted to tell her she was wrong. I wanted to say that Krista was mistaken. I wanted to do anything but what I started doing, which was cry, like a baby.

"Oh Jeani!" Her voice got soft and melodic as she took my left hand in both of hers. "What happened?"

Before I could answer, we heard the backdoor open and mom saying, "Girls? Are you out here?"

"Yes ma'am," Joy said, as I sobbed. "We're over at the picnic table."

"You know you're not supposed to be," Mom's scolding faltered as she came nearer and her eyes adjusted. "What happened?" She asked Joy. She pulled me into a hug as she sat down.

"I don't know," Joy said. "She's just... crying."

Mom nodded, rocking me. Once my crying had subsided into hiccups, she tilted my face to look up at her with a finger under my chin. "Think you can tell us what's going on?"

I looked at Joy and took a deep breath. "Th-they were being mean at school and called me s-stupid and a dummy and m-my teacher said you shouldn't pick on her 'cause sh-she's retarded a-and you can't..."

"She said what?" Mom's voice had a hard edge to it and Joy's eyes were as wide as dinner plates.

I flinched a little at Mom's tone since it was the same one that she used when I got in trouble. I shrunk down a bit and whimpered, "R-retarded?"

"Which class was that in, which teacher? That is ridiculous. Even if you were retarded, which you are not, she had no right to say such a thing to any child and definitely not my child!"

"I-I'm not?" I whispered.

Even in the dark, I could see Mom's face soften. "You most definitely are not. You are one of the smartest, most creative seven year olds I have ever known."

"Yeah!" Joy practically shouted. "You were just making up another Sam Nav story while I was trying to figure out why you had been crying. I mean, you make up stories all the time. And you just said a corpse of trees! It wasn't quite right, but it was close. Copse of trees was one of my vocabulary phrases and I'm in third grade."

"B-but I can't write," I said, looking down at the table.

"Yet," Mom whispered into my ear.

"Joy could write sentences when she was my age. I can't even write letters right."

Joy laughed. My head snapped up and I glared at her.

"Joy," Mom's voice had a warning to it.

"I'm laughing because that is ridiculous. Jeani, you never want to do things the same as me. You always have to do it your own way. Why would this be any different?"

I just stared at her. I hadn't known until that moment that she thought I was deliberately doing things different from her. If she only knew how much I tried to be like her, but couldn't.

"She's got a point, Jeani." Mom said. "Look, on Monday, I'll go to school with you and have a talk with your teacher. Then we will get someone who understands how to help you. A tutor, or something. But right now, I want you two to head inside and get ready for bed. You don't want to miss your Saturday morning cartoons!"

Both Joy and I said no, then raced each other into the house and up the stairs. Joy won, of course. She was always ahead of me.

11

The Kittens

Puerto Ordaz, Venezuela

After getting pulled out of school and finishing the year with homeschooling lessons from the US that Mom ordered through the mail, Joy and I hadn't had a chance to make any friends. So that summer, we spent most of our time together. Our favorite thing to do together was ride our bikes that Dad had shipped from the US.

The house we lived in was a single story with a tiny walled in patio. When it rained, the patio was on just enough of a slant that the rain would create a pool. Joy and I loved that little patio! As long as it was only raining and not storming, Mom would let us put on our bathing suits and play in the water. We would pretend that we were out in the ocean. We made up stories about saving each other from terrible sea monsters or that we were the sea monsters. It was lots of fun.

One day, Joy and I were outside scanning the sky for clouds. It had rained a bit earlier but not enough, and we were tossing around the idea of going for a bike ride, but feared getting caught in a storm. The weather was like that, very lovely most of the time, but when we hit the rainy season, it was totally unpredictable. As we realized there was not a cloud in the sky, we heard something that sounded a little like screaming and a lot like a squeaky toy.

"What's that?" Joy asked.

I shrugged, squinting at the sun, willing clouds to cover it. Then we heard the sound again.

"Mew, mew!"

Jackie, who had been singing to herself, or perhaps the flowers, over by the teeny-tiny garden in the highest corner of the patio, had stopped singing and ran over to us. "I heard it! What was it? Was it a cat?"

Joy and I shushed her to listen. The mewling got louder and sounded like there was more than one.

"I think it's coming from next door," I whispered, worried that the cats would hear me and run away. "I wonder if the kitty is hurt and needs help?"

The house next door was under construction, but the construction workers had gone home for the day. The house they were building was much bigger than our house and it towered over us. All around the house was dirt where a lawn, or maybe a large garden, would be added. Backing up to our wall was a drain for the water. Maybe the construction workers had seen the way the water got trapped on our patio and wanted to prevent such a thing happening there. I felt bad for whoever ended up living there 'cause they wouldn't get a free pool like us. It wasn't like the water stayed forever, it drained away after a few hours.

Joy grinned, then quickly took on a look of concern. "Oh, you are so right! It would be wrong not to check."

I nodded and ran over to the spot where there was a gap in the barrier that had been put up at the other house behind our wall. I was just about to climb the wall to go through the gap when Joy yelled, "My turn!"

Joy and I had snuck over a few times after the construction had stopped when Mom was away from the house. Neither of us stayed very long–we were too scared of getting caught–but we took turns investigating and being the lookout. Being the lookout was so boring! But she was right. I begrudgingly stepped back and let Joy go. I sighed as she disappeared from view.

"Where is she going?" Jackie whispered, thrilled and appalled.

Startled, I looked at Jackie. I had forgotten she was there. Seeing this as an opportunity to not have to be the lookout, I knelt down to look into Jackie's freckled face. I placed my hands on her shoulders and took on a somber expression. Her brown eyes were wide. I studied her face for a moment, knowing if I didn't explain it just right, we would be in serious trouble... Or, at least, I would.

"What would Jesus do?" I asked finally, flooding my face with as much spiritual compassion as I could.

She crinkled her three-year-old face, trying to figure out what I meant.

"If Jesus heard someone in trouble," I explained, "what would he do?"

"He would help them, of course," she stated with righteous conviction.

"Exactly. And that's what Joy and I are doing. Now what I need you to do is stay right here. That way, if there's someone or some animal in trouble and we think we can save it, you can help us."

"How?"

I took a moment to think, since I really just wanted her to stay where she was so she wouldn't tattle. "Well, if it's a cat, carrying a cat from there to here would be difficult, but you could help us. Do you think you can handle that?"

She nodded so hard I thought her head might pop off.

"Okay," I said, bouncing up. "We're counting on you, so don't move."

I climbed onto the wall, through the gap, and hopped down to the muddy ground. I walked around for a bit, but I didn't see Joy or hear the meowing. I was just about to go inside the house, something neither Joy nor I had been brave enough to do yet, when I spotted her crouched in the far corner of the yard by the drain. I ran over to her.

"What are you..." she started to ask, then shook her head. "Never mind. It doesn't matter. I'm glad you're here. You can help me get this grate off."

"This great what off?"

She stared at me quizzically for a moment, then understanding hit her. "Not great, grate. As in the grate over the drain." She pointed to the red grate that lined the yard.

I was still confused, but then I heard, "Mew, mew!" I looked down through the bars and saw a pile of fur with tiny eyeballs.

"Kittens?" I asked, vibrating with excitement and anticipation.

She nodded. "Yeah, but it's wet down there. I don't know where the momma cat is, but they might drown if it rains again. We HAVE to get them out!"

With that, we worked together to get the heavy grate off. Around us, the slight breeze that had been with us all day was picking up. I looked up at the sky and saw some ominous clouds starting to form.

"Not now!" I shouted at the sky. But the sky didn't listen and two large drops hit me on the forehead.

Once we got the grate off, it was sprinkling. Joy climbed

into the drain and handed me a kitten. I took it, ran over to our gap, climbed through, and held the kitten out to a startled Jackie.

"Kitten!" She squealed.

"Yes," I grunted, straddling the space between the gap and our wall while holding the kitten aloft. "Take it!"

She did and I ran back to Joy.

When I was handing Jackie the third kitten, we heard thunder rumbling in the distance and I saw Mom step outside of the house. "Girls, you need to come insi..." The word died on her lips as she saw the two kittens at Jackie's feet and watched me pass her a third one.

But before she could regain her composure and yell at me, I ran back to Joy.

"Mom's outside and saw Jackie with the kittens!"

Joy handed me a kitten then held her hand out to me. I gently set the kitten down and helped my sister out of the drain.

"It's okay," she panted, "that was the last one." She looked back at the drain. "We should put the grate back."

I nodded. Still keeping an eye on the last kitten that was wiggling around like it didn't know how to use its feet very well, we managed to slide the grate back into place. I scooped up the kitten as we ran back to our break in the wall. When we got there, Jackie and the three kittens were gone. Mom was standing there with Jessica, the baby, on her hip. She was shaking her head as she stared at us.

"I don't know what to do with the two of you!" She made a sound that was somewhere between a growl, a laugh, and a sigh. "Come on, the rain's about to get really hard. Let's get this kitten and the two of you inside before it does." She turned and headed for the house.

Joy and I stared at each other, stunned. We hadn't known exactly what to expect, but we thought for sure she was going to be mad. But she wasn't... was she? As we got into the house, she led us to the laundry room where Jackie was sitting in the middle of the floor with three kittens crawling all over her.

"There are four. We can name them our middle names," she whispered.

"Why are you whispering?" I asked.

She shrugged and laughed. "Who gets which kitten?"

"I should get first pick 'cause I'm the oldest and I was the first to hear them." Joy had her arms crossed, like she was ready to fight. I shrugged, gently petting each of the kittens, not caring.

Jackie was also petting each one, imitating my gentle touch. She sighed, "Good. I couldn't pick a favorite 'cause they're all so beautiful and fluffy and I love them all."

Joy picked the short haired orange tabby and named her Clarisse, her middle name. I got the black one and named her Marie. Jackie and Jessica both got brown tabbies named Leanne and Dennise.

Mom called a friend she'd made at the new church we had started attending. The woman had cats and was a retired veterinarian or vet tech or something to do with animal care. She came over after it stopped raining with a bag of cat food and a couple of litter boxes. She checked them out and, according to her, Dennise was Dennis and Clarisse was a Clarence since they were both boys. But that was okay since our uncle Clarence was where Joy's middle name came from and Dennise came from our Mom's uncle Dennis.

We also borrowed a cat bed and a baby gate to keep them in the laundry room. The lady and a few other people at church told their friends about the free kittens spread. Mom's allergies were too severe for us to keep them.

We'd only had them a couple of days when tragedy struck. One morning, when we got up to take care of the kittens, we found Joy's orange tabby Clarence and Jessica's brown tabby Leanne had died in the night. We had a little funeral for them, but I think Dad ended up disposing of their bodies elsewhere since Mom was not okay with burying them in the tiny garden.

We were all upset, but Joy was mad.

"It's not fair that your stupid black kitten got to live and my beautiful orange kitty died!" She stormed off to her room and slammed the door. When I tried to enter our shared room, I found that I couldn't. The bedroom door didn't lock, but Joy had blocked it with the dresser. I could hear her crying through the door. I decided not to tell on her and went to play with the kittens. After a bit, I got bored since all they seemed to want to do was eat and sleep and Mom told me to not bother them when they were sleeping.

"Why don't you play with Joy?" Mom said when she saw me pouting.

I shook my head, bouncing my body against the wall I was leaning on. "She's sad."

Mom nodded as she dusted the shelves. "Well, why don't you go play outside?"

"Can I bike by myself?" I asked hopefully.

"No," Mom said without turning. "If you want to stay inside, you can help me clean."

"That's okay," I said. "I have a very important something outside."

Mom laughed. "Okay. You go take care of your very important something."

I hurried outside before Mom remembered that Dad had told me I was supposed to help her whenever she asked.

It was the first and last time we had kittens. Once I became an adult, I would have many pets, work for a few years at an animal shelter as a Feline Care Supervisor, have a job after that as a dog walker / pet sitter, and foster kittens for several years.

Joy told me that after losing that one kitten, she would never have cats again. "It's too sad." She said. "Plus, why would I have a cat instead of a dog? Cats are dumb."

12

Firecracker

Puerto Ordaz, Venezuela

In February of 1981, we moved back to the United States so my youngest sister Jessica was born in Houston. She had green eyes like Mom while Joy, Jackie, and I had brown eyes like Dad.

Once the baby was old enough to travel, we moved back to Venezuela. This third move landed us in Puerto Ordaz and Dad's company helped enroll Joy and I in a public school with a bilingual curriculum. The school had an open floor plan with outside halls. It was lovely! Each building was a standalone classroom. But we were there less than a month when things started going wrong.

The first indication of trouble were the whoops and

hollers out in the hallways. Our teachers told us to ignore the noise. They were just some ignorant teenagers who had dropped out of school.

Another day, my teacher paused during roll call and sniffed the air. "Does anyone else smell..." She sniffed again, then ran out the door.

Each student stayed in their seats as we heard raised voices. The teacher ran back into the room.

"¡Vamanos!" She shouted, waving and clapping to get us in line. We could smell smoke from a small fire in a trash can in the courtyard. The students had to stand with their grades in separate parts of the field behind the school. I waved at Joy over with the fifth graders, but I wasn't allowed to go to her. A sweep was made. It felt like forever, but probably took only half an hour.

A few days later, the teenagers were back, running through the halls, laughing. Class stopped, but we didn't leave. That night, at home over dinner, Joy told our parents about the fire and the teenagers.

"Do you feel unsafe?" Dad asked.

I shook my head no, Joy nodded.

"Maybe tomorrow, instead of having them bike, I can drive them in and talk to whoever's in charge." Mom said. We only had Dad's company car.

"Not tomorrow," Dad said. "I have a big meeting. You can call and next week, I'll arrange a ride into work with someone from my team."

Mom agreed.

The following school days were peaceful. But on Friday, the teenagers were back. The teachers closed their doors and kept teaching. Rocks flew through open windows, hitting desks and concrete floors. The teacher ran over to the window crank, but stopped, as we heard glass shatter. Then bang! A gunshot? Students screamed; more bangs.

"¡Métete debajo de tus escritorios! Get under your desks!" My teacher shouted. She peeked out then slammed and locked the door. I crouched under my desk with hands over my ears. Something flew in and hit the teacher's desk. It exploded and shot off bright lights. Students cried and screamed. The teenagers were laughing and banging walls and trash cans. I wrapped my arms tight around the metal legs of the desk too scared to think, pray, or cry.

Once the fireworks stopped, we rose and sat at our desks, trembling. Our teacher unlocked and peeked out the door, then closed it gently.

"I'm going to check on things. You will be safe here. Do not leave."

She locked the door behind her. A few minutes later she came back and told me to come with her.

"Get your things," she said, pointing a shaking hand at my bag.

I followed her. When we got to the office, she had me sit on a hard orange plastic chair and spoke with the receptionist, then left.

Maybe they thought I had something to do with all the craziness. I didn't see how, but since I constantly got in trouble at home, I thought it could be true. Plus, I was new.

It felt like years had passed when my mom walked through the door with Jessica swaddled to her chest and Jackie held by a hand. She looked pale and worried, so I kept quiet. She signed me out and we got a cab.

Staring straight ahead, Mom explained. "Someone threw a firecracker into Joy's classroom and it landed beside her desk. It exploded inches from her. The nurse said Joy couldn't hear. She was taken to the hospital." She turned. Her eyes were shining with tears. I hugged her. Jackie started crying, so I hugged her too.

At the hospital, Mom asked me to sit with Jackie. The smell of sweat overpowered the disinfectant. They had no air conditioner or it wasn't working. The fans only blew the stifling, sweaty air. Mom came out with the doctor, I stood and shook his hand, which surprised him. In Spanish, he explained that Joy couldn't hear out of her left ear, but Mom couldn't understand. My Spanish was never as good as Joy's, but I was able to interpret.

"He said that if her hearing doesn't come back in three days, we should see another doctor. But he's pretty sure it will."

Mom cried from relief. "Jeani, ask him if Joy can come home."

I nodded. "¿Puede mi hermana va a la casa hoy?"

It wasn't a perfect translation, but the doctor understood and nodded. "Si. Cuando terminemos, puedes llevarla a casa."

I nodded to Mom. "He said yes."

Mom sat and nursed Jessica next to Jackie who had fallen asleep. I stood as we waited.

I wondered what it would be like to have a deaf sister. I decided to learn sign language. I would be the best sister and Joy would be so pleased to have a sister like me looking out for her. She would thank me and call me her best friend. When I realized that Joy could still hear with her other ear and then she could hear fine in less than three days, I was almost, though not quite, disappointed.

13

Terrimotita y Tía Marlena

Puerto Ordaz, Venezuela

Marlena was one of the most beautiful women I have ever known. Her eyes were dark pools of the cosmos and she had lovely dark brown skin. She would kiss my forehead with her soft full lips and she always smelled like lemons and almonds. I loved whenever she visited. She called me her Terrimotita, saying I was like a small earthquake as I bounded through a room. She would laugh at my jokes, no matter how silly they were, and she talked to me like an equal, not a goofy kid. I could listen to her talk with her Guyanese accent for hours. At eight years old, without realizing it until years later, Marlena was my first crush.

She went to the church we found only a few months after

moving to Puerto Ordaz (always a priority with my parents) and soon was coming over every week to help Mom with the cleaning. She made her living as a maid, so my parents hired her. But then she started showing up twice and sometimes, three times a week. This distressed Mom because Dad had only given her enough money to pay her for once a week, but Marlena told her not to worry.

"I come to spend time with you and these sweet girls," she said in her gentle voice with its rhythmic Guyanese cadence. "Yes. This is what good Christian women do."

She explained that she was homesick for family and insisted that Joy, Jackie, and I call her Tía, the Spanish word for aunt. She had moved to Puerto Ordaz from Georgetown, Guyana without any family. I didn't know any of the details, but from what I overheard the adults saying that it was a bad situation.

In November 1981, she arrived early and in obvious distress. She was trying not to cry, but the tears kept leaking out. Mom had just put Jessica down for her morning nap while Joy and I were clearing the table and washing up after breakfast. When Mom saw her, she led Marlena away from the cleaning supplies and into the kitchen and asked her what she wanted to drink. Marlena kept protesting that Mom shouldn't be waiting on her. Mom shook her head.

"That's silly. When a friend's upset, this is what we do. We take care of them." Marlena burst into tears, cupping her hands over her face as she leaned over the table. Mom gently lifted her thick black hair and rubbed her neck. She leaned close to Marlena, whispering. "Marlena, you have been such a comfort to me. You are a friend who helped take care of us. Please let us do the same for you. We can talk about whatever it is that is bothering you or, if you don't want to talk about it, we can pray. We can even just sit in silence. Let me be here for you." She stood back up and smiled. "Now, what would you like to drink?"

Getting her tears under control, Marlena sniffed and said, "I would very much enjoy a glass of cold water." Mom leaned over and wrapped her arms around her. Marlena slumped into Mom's embrace and started crying again. Over her shoulder, Mom waved for Joy and I to take Jackie into the other room and play. Marlena turned her head slightly to see us slowly backing out of the room. She motioned for us to come back.

"Oh Jo, could your girls stay? I need family I love around me now."

Mom smiled, nodding. "Of course! I just didn't want them getting in the way." Marlena motioned us over and we all hugged. Mom untangled herself to get iced water for our guest and iced tea for herself.

"Can I get some milk?" I asked, thinking this might be the perfect time to get an extra cup of milk. I loved milk.

Smiling, Mom agreed. "But only if you pour some for Joy and Jackie."

I clenched my teeth against my protest that Joy was perfectly capable of getting her own milk and just nodded.

I knew if I gave her lip, Mom would most likely say no milk.

Once we were all seated around the table, Joy and I with our cups of milk, Mom with her iced tea, Marlena with her iced water, and Jackie sitting on her lap with a sippy cup, Marlena smiled. Only her smile was broken. Usually her smile was the widest and brightest thing on the planet. The little crinkles of skin next to her mouth made it even brighter. But that day, it was the smallest and saddest smile I'd ever seen.

I felt tears pricking the edges of my eyes. I leaned forward, touched her hand, and whispered, "I'm so sad you're sad!"

She started crying again, then leaned over and hugged my head into her chest. "¡Mi preciosa Terrimotita!" she said. "You are so sweet! I am very sad. My family, almost all, have died."

"Oh no!" exclaimed my mother. I was still buried in Marlena's bosom, but I could feel Mom put her hand on her arm. Marlena let me go and leaned into Mom, sobbing.

I stared in wonder at her. Her whole family? How could that happen? I sipped my milk as Marlena took a long drink of water. Joy had grabbed the tissues from the living room. Grateful, Marlena hugged her then wiped her eyes and nose.

"Just before I left Guyana, many of my family were going to a new church called the People's Temple. They kept telling me I should go too. So I did. But there is something wrong with that church. The man in charge, he is named

Jones and is from your California. I do not like how he speaks. Not that he's American, you understand, " her worried eyes were on Mom who nodded. Marlena shook her head. "No, I just did not feel the holy spirit was with him. So when the service is over, I tell my family I do not wish to go back. They are mad at me and tell me I am wrong. They threaten me, saying I must go to their church because something bad is coming. I am scared and cannot bear their anger. So I flee to Venezuela with my friend and find work. We also find a good church and praise Jesus the right way. I hear about how my family had moved to the Temple and given much of what they own to it. But today, my uncle who is not my uncle but a friend of my family, arrived. He also would not join the church and received threats, but had stayed nearby when his sister and her daughter joined. He told me he had been looking for me for two years. I had hidden myself because of the threats. He told me that everyone in the church was dead." She sobbed, clutching Mom's hand tighter. "They drink poison because the Jones man tells them to, saying it was what Jesus wants." She gasped a sob, then exclaimed, "My Jesus would never do that!"

Crying softly, she cuddled Jackie who was still happily sucking on her sippy cup, oblivious to the sorrow around her, but loving the attention. Mom, with her hand over her mouth, had removed her glasses and was wiping her eyes. Joy and I were also crying, sad that Marlena's family had died and that she was sad.

Joy, who had been sitting on my other side, got up and

took Jackie, who had fallen asleep, from Marlena and put her to bed. When she came back, she told me to move so she could sit next to Marlena. I looked at Mom, but she just motioned with her head for me to move. Once Joy had my seat, she took both of Marlena's hands in hers.

"Tía," she said with a very serious voice. "You are our family. Whatever we can do, we will. Right, Mom?"

"Of course!" Mom said. "You let us know what you need and we will do whatever we can for you."

"Yes!" I chimed in, not wanting to be left out. I hopped up and stood behind her, massaging her shoulders. "We love you, Tía!"

Marlena hugged Joy and Mom and kissed my hand. "This," she said. "You being here for me, this is what I need."

Just before Christmas, Marlena moved back to Guyana to take care of the affairs of her family. Our church had raised funds to help her go and she promised to write. I was sad because, even at eight, I knew I would never see her again.

"I miss Tía," I told Joy one evening. We were both flopped on our beds after a bike ride.

"Then you should write her a letter like I did."

"Did you already send it?" I asked, flipping over.

"Not yet," Joy said. "Mom said I could put it in with hers so we only have to pay for one postage."

"Could you tell her that her Terrimotita misses her in your letter?"

Joy sat up and faced me. She put her hands on her hips and cocked an eyebrow at me. "Why can't you?"

Without making eye contact, I shook my head, dragging my hands along the shag carpeting. "My writing's terrible. She won't be able to read it." Then I rolled up onto my bed and burst into tears. Joy left the room.

A few minutes later, I was still curled up on the bed sobbing, thinking Joy was mad at me. Joy came back holding an envelope. Instead of saying anything, she sat at the roll top desk, grabbed a pen, and pulled the letter out of the envelope. As she wrote, she said the words out loud. "P.S. Jeani, your Terrimotita, wanted me to tell you that she misses you very much. She loves you almost as much as I do, but she is bad at writing letters so she asked me to do it instead. Sincerely again, Joy." She put the letter back in the envelope, sealed it with her tongue and wrote, "and Jeani" under where it said, "To Tía from Joy." Then she grinned and wrote, "your Terrimotita" under my name. She held it up for me to see.

"Thank you," I said, sitting up and wiping my eyes.

"You know, you should really write letters. I write to my friends in Texas all the time. When we move back, I'm gonna have friends who remember me."

"I have friends," I said, my voice sounding sullen even to my ears. "I just hate writing letters 'cause my writing's so bad."

Joy stood up and waved the letter at me. "You know how you get better? You practice." She skipped down the hall give Mom our letter to add to the bigger envelope.

I knew she was right, but it was so hard. Years later, I would regret not following Joy's letter writing example. Instead, I laid back on my bed and fell asleep dreaming of a world in which Marlena came back and was my age.

14

The Incident

Puerto Ordaz, Venezuela

During that summer, we were pretty isolated. Most of the houses around us were new and unoccupied and we'd only made a handful of friends through the church. None of them were within walking or biking distance and we only had the one car Dad needed for work. During the week, Mom was stuck at home with the baby and a three year old while Joy and I got to go out and bike around. Reflecting on that time, I don't think Mom was doing all that well, but I was too young and selfish to understand that. Joy and I were having a great time.

At least, we were, until The Incident happened.

The first time The Incident happened, it was storming outside. Mom was laying down in the bedroom with a migraine and we could hear Jackie singing to herself in her room where she was supposed to be taking a nap. Our baby sister Jessica had just woken up from her nap and Mom had asked us to watch her for a bit. Joy and I were in the living room playing a game of cards on the floor while the baby wiggled on her blanket. That's when we heard Jessica shout, "Dummy!"

We stared at each other, eyes wide.

Joy asked, "Did she just say..." but couldn't finish since dummy was one of the many forbidden words in our house. What we watched, what we read, where we went, and most importantly, what we said, was strictly monitored. If we put each other down, if we gave sass, if we said a bad word (and that included words like dummy and stupid), we got our mouths washed out with soap and would be spanked and/or grounded. We decided we must've heard the baby wrong.

The next day, when Joy and I were out playing on the porch, Mom heard her say it. She also thought she'd heard wrong. But then Jessica bounced up and down while opening and closing her hands with an outstretched arm, singing, "dummy, dummy, dummy!" in a very demanding tone.

"Joy Clarece and Jeanine Marie Vaughn, you get in here right now!" Mom shouted out the kitchen window that faced the porch. Upon hearing our full names, we knew we were in trouble and ran inside.

"What's wrong?" We asked simultaneously, hoping against hope that there WAS something wrong, like maybe one of our sisters was on fire or something, and not that we were in trouble.

"This!" Mom exclaimed, pointing to Jessica who was sitting on the floor sucking her fingers.

We stared at our baby sister, wondering what, 'this', could mean. Hearing a whimper behind me, I looked over at the table to where Jackie was seated. She was crying. I looked back at Joy. Neither of us knew what Mom meant. I mean sure, I often felt that babies were wrong for lots of different reasons. They're just so sticky and stinky and screamy. But I also knew that my mom didn't share my sentiment.

I jerked my thumb at Jackie. "What's wrong with her?" At that, Jackie cried louder.

Mom dismissed her with a wave of her hand and a head shake. "Don't worry about her." (I swear Jackie's crying got even louder.) "You two need to tell me who has been teaching the baby to say certain words."

I looked at Joy again, but she still looked as baffled as I felt. Then, the baby spoke.

"Dummy," Jessica said, holding out a wet hand.

"That!" My usually soft-spoken Mom was shouting for the third time in only a few minutes. "She just said dummy! Now, where would she learn that kind of language?" Her hands were placed firmly on her hips. "Maybe from her two oldest sisters who are always picking on each other?"

Jackie, who had stood up from the table to stand beside and just slightly behind Mom, sniffled and nodded. "Sh-

sh-she called me dummy!" Then she started howling again.

I wanted to roll my eyes and tell her to stop being so sensitive. But Mom's stance wasn't one to mess with. You don't push buttons when Mom's hands are on her hips.

"Go to your room," she said through clenched teeth. "Both of you!" She took a deep breath and breathed out, then growled. "I want you to think about what you've done. You are both grounded for two weeks."

Joy and I protested, but it did no good. Once we were in our shared bedroom, Joy punched me in the shoulder.

"Ow!" I said, rubbing my arm. "What'd you do that for?"

"For getting me in trouble. Duh." She sat on her bed that was about a table's length away from mine, and glared at me.

"I did not! You're the one who taught Jackie to call me an ugly ole hag and chase me around the house when Mom was out. But I got in trouble for yelling at Jackie when she did that. Ha, this time you got in trouble too!" I cringed, certain that Joy would whap me again.

But she just laughed. "I'd forgotten about that! That was hilarious. She was just a little older than Jessica is now. Good times. But hey, I taught Jackie to never say it when Mom and Dad are around."

"Yeah, well, you shouldn't have taught her that at all. It's not very Christian."

She fell over onto her side, rolling on her bed, giggling maniacally. No matter what I said, she just laughed harder, though not louder, so Mom wouldn't hear her.

Finally, super annoyed at her, I hissed, "I know you did it. I'm a good Christian girl and I only get in trouble when you make me get in trouble."

She stopped laughing, sat up, and wiped her eyes. "Are you saying I'm not a good Christian?"

In our house, that was almost the equivalent of calling someone a bastard.

Jutting out my chin, I nodded. "I totally am."

She jumped on me with a loud, "Aaaaaaaah!" pulling my hair and shoving me. I hit her and she screamed.

"You two better stop making all that noise!" Mom shouted from the living room. "Otherwise, you'll be grounded for four weeks!"

We quickly separated and faced the opposite walls.

That night, when Dad got home, Jessica said it two more times at the dinner table. "Dummy, dummy!"

"This is what I was talking about, John." Mom's voice was weary. She'd had to deal with her two oldest daughters bickering and claiming that the other one must've taught the baby the rude word and with Jackie crying over and over as Jessica continued to say, "Dummy," all day.

Dad looked at us, then after dinner marched us into the bathroom where he washed our mouths out with soap. As we each held a bar of soap in our mouths, trying not to let our tongues touch it, he lectured us.

"I am very disappointed in the two of you. It is your duty as older sisters to set a good example for your younger sisters. You are not acting like good Christian young ladies today and I will not have that in my house. Do you understand me?"

We both nodded, our eyes fixed on his dark brown ones.

"Now, one of the things you're both going to do while you're grounded is read your Bibles and find verses that talk about how what you say reflects the inner person or about how setting a good Christian example is so important or even just about how sisters should treat each other 'cause your Mom tells me you've been fighting too. That's not very ladylike." He raised his eyebrows.

I hated the word lady, but I almost laughed since he had the funniest way of wiggling his eyebrows when he was being silly and him raising his eyebrows reminded me of that. But I managed to just cough as we nodded. Hearing my cough, Dad decided we'd held the soap in our mouths long enough.

After he left the bathroom, we washed our saliva off of the soap and made sure to put those bars far away from the bathtub. Nobody wanted to use soap that had been in someone else's mouth to wash their body. Then we washed the soap off of our tongues.

"At least it was Dove soap," I said, brushing my tongue. "Irish Spring always makes my tongue feel all tingly, in a bad way."

Joy, who had been scrubbing her tongue with a wet washcloth, stared at me. "You're so weird. I can't believe your mouth's been washed out so many times you have a preferred soap."

I shrugged and got ready for bed.

The next week was the worst. We couldn't go outside and ride our bikes when it was sunny or play in the water on the patio when it rained. Joy, who loved to read, wasn't as bothered by the grounding as I was. I loved reading too, but because of my dyslexia, I was very slow and it frustrated me quickly. I tried to convince Joy to read out loud to me, but she refused since she was still mad at me. So I found other ways to entertain myself like dancing through the house and singing until Mom told me to stop because I was being too hitchy-pitchy and her head hurt. She probably had one of her migraines. So I would then bring out all the LEGOs and all my stuffed animals and create stories with them. This was fun for a bit, until Jackie wanted to help and Jessica got a LEGO under her knee when she was crawling. Such a wailing! Mom looked like her eyes might pop out of her head as she told me to pick up everything and stop making the baby cry. She wished out loud for summer to be over so we would be in school and out of her hair.

Six days after Joy and I had been grounded, Marlena, who

helped Mom with the cleaning and insisted we call her Tía, came over. After she finished cleaning, she sat on the floor playing with the baby while Mom got dinner ready.

"Oh did you hear that?" She asked in her beautiful Guyanese lilt.

Joy and I, who had been sitting at the table drawing, looked at each other. Jessica had said, "Dummy," again. But Marlena didn't sound upset. She sounded delighted.

"¡Que bueno, niñita!" She cooed in Spanish.

"What did she say?" Mom asked, wiping her hands on her apron as she came out of the kitchen, smiling.

Both Joy and I shrank in our seats and stared at the table.

"Dame." Marlena said, giving the baby the toy she had been holding, and grinned.

Mom froze. Since I was still staring at the table, I felt rather than saw her give us a sidelong glance of disapproval. "The girls taught her that ugly word thinking it was funny and..."

"What ugly word?" Marlena asked in a perplexed tone. "She is just saying 'give me' in Spanish."

Both Joy and I looked at each other and mouthed, "Dame." It all made sense! Every time Jessica said "Dame" she had been making monkey begging motions by grasping and ungrasping her hand towards something she wanted.

That night Mom discussed what Marlena revealed to us with Dad and our grounding was lifted.

Joy asked, "Will the week that we were wrongly grounded and the mouth washing go towards our next punishment?"

Dad laughed. "No. It'll be a good reminder, a lesson, that sometimes, Life is not fair."

I stared at him thinking how it wasn't Life that had grounded us, Mom had. But I didn't dare say that out loud.

Years later, the portent of Dad's offhand comment would hit our family so hard, we would almost shatter. If my family had a coat of arms, our heraldic description would be, "Life is not Fair". It's not that Life was terrible, there were many bright moments, but completely unexpected and unavoidable things kept happening, especially to Joy. Joy's life should have had that phrase as an epitaph.

15

The Falls

Canaima National Park, Venezuela

In 1982, we were still living in Puerto Ordaz. Mom's brother, our Uncle Doug, his wife, Aunt Celia, and their two kids, Heather and Colin, came to visit. Our parents were such good friends that years later, when Dad retired, he, Mom, and Joy moved to Huntsville, Alabama to be near them. Other than my dad's brother Uncle Clarence who worked with Dad and who Joy got her middle name Clarece from, they were the only family that visited us in Venezuela. I was impressed that anyone did. Since they had come all that way, we took a vacation to the Canaima National Park. Our parents booked a stay in a cabin near the water. The younger kids–Jacqueline, Jessica, and Colin–stayed with friends in Puerto Ordaz.

To get there, we took a small plane from the port of Puerto

Ordaz and got to fly past Salto Ángel (Angel Falls), the tallest uninterrupted waterfall in the world. It was breathtaking. I was about nine when we took that trip and it is still a visceral memory. The air had a fresh, soft, earthy smell to it. I remember leaning my face against the window, thrilled at this incredible sight. There was so much growing on this wall of a cliff. We saw moss, vines, flowers, and even trees growing out of the edifice. We saw parrots, macaws, and toucans. These birds had colors that would rival any rainbow. They flew in and out of the foamy blue water that sparkled in the sunlight. I wanted to jump into the water; to be part of the flow; bask in the light that made the rocks shine. After that flight, I was obsessed with waterfalls.

Canaima National Park is in the southeastern region of Venezuela, along the borders of Brazil and Guyana. While we were there, we saw amazing landscapes. The habitat is home to wildlife such as the jaguar and mountain lion as well as a variety of native flora and fauna species. Along with all of that and the Angel Falls, the park protects several astounding tepui, or table-top mountains, that are found in South America, especially Venezuela and Guyana. Tepui means "house of the gods" in the language of the people of that area, the Pemón, who are the fourth largest indigenous community in Venezuela.

As we traveled from the airport to the camp, our tour guide, a jovial man who spoke in halting English, stopped the car and had us get out. He pointed out a Capuchin bird with its bright orangey yellow plumage and almost skull-like face. Then we got to hear its weird, fog horn-like, call. He pointed out how the bird inflated its throat to make that sound. We also got some amazing fruit from a street vendor. I have not been able to find the delicious fruit that had skin thicker than a lime, with fruit that was almost orange in color and textured similar to a nectarine, but tasted nothing like either. The fruit was definitely a stone fruit, but I've not found anything in my reasearch about it in the years since we were there. It was the most delicious fruit I've ever eaten.

When we arrived at the camp, we discovered that our cabin was only a few yards away from the beach. The adults shared one room while Joy, Heather, and I shared another. We were sad when it rained for our first day there. But the second day was sunny and, as soon as we finished breakfast, we were ready to go swimming. We had to wait half an hour to digest our food, so we took our time getting ready. As soon as our moms said it was okay, we were in the water. Aunt Celia and Mom were sunbathing while Dad and Uncle Doug were off doing something. After we had been swimming for a few hours, Aunt Celia called Heather over to her, and asked her to get something from her room. While Heather was gone, I noticed a smaller waterfall not too far away. It splashed into the body of water we were in. Joy had been swimming with me and saw me swimming over to it. When I got out of the water, she yelled at me.

"Where ya goin', Jeani?"

We both knew we weren't supposed to go away from the beach. But the waterfall looked like it was so close and it was technically part of the beach. I didn't tell her where I was going, I just went. I'm not sure why, but she followed instead of telling Mom.

There was a little path leading from the beach to the top of the small waterfall. I guess small is relative. It was small compared to seeing the tallest falls in the world, but so are all other falls. It hadn't seemed that big or quite so far away when I was looking at it from the water. but it took a bit to get to the top and looked a lot bigger once I was standing on the bank of the river that fed it. There were a bunch of rocks that stuck out just above the water. They made a path that went from one side of the river to the other.

"What are you doing?" Joy shouted, as she scrambled up after me. But then she looked around and gasped. "It's really pretty up here."

I nodded, smiling. "I want to cross it."

Joy stared at me, her face crinkling. "That's stupid."

"Nuh-uh!" I crossed my arms.

Joy laughed. "Well go."

I dropped my arms as I looked at the rapidly flowing water and the distance between where I was standing and the first rock. The water was swirling so fast around it. A few of the rocks further away had water flowing over them. Both Joy and I were barefoot. I hesitated.

"Dare ya," Joy whispered in my ear. "Double dog dare ya."

I should have known better with the whole dog bite a few years back. I still had the scar on my chest. But I couldn't resist the challenge. I stepped onto the first rock. It was a little slick with water, but steady. I put both feet on it, wavered a bit, then balanced. The next rock was bigger than the first one, but further away. I held out my arms for balance. I could feel my heart pounding as I jumped to it. I landed well. Joy laughed behind me as she stepped on the first rock. The next few rocks were closer, so I stepped easily to them.

"Joy Clarece and Jeanine Marie Vaughn! You get back here right now!" We turned to see Dad standing on the bank. His face was red and he looked really mad. Joy immediately started back.

I refocused on the rock before me. There was only one, then I would reach the opposite bank. I was closer to the other side. I thought it made sense to keep going. The idea of turning around on that slippery rock made me more nervous than disobeying my father. From the tone of his voice, I knew I was already in trouble. What would it hurt to take two extra steps and accomplish something Joy didn't? I took one step to the next rock and my foot slipped. I screamed as my arms windmilled. There was nothing to grab onto! My movements seemed to slow as I felt my food slide in the muddy earth beneath the water. My toes hit a rock wedged in the mud. It stopped my descent, but only just. Then the rock started sliding. I screamed even louder, grasping at the air as I tried to fall backwards instead of into the flowing water. Just as the rock gave way completely, a hand grabbed mine and pulled. I looked up to see Joy standing in the water, her feet wedged under the rock my back foot was sliding away from. Dad was running up behind her and grabbed my arm just as Joy lost her grip on my other hand.

That night, I got a lecture from both Dad and Mom. I told them it was all my fault, that Joy had just followed me to make sure I was okay. Mom cried and hugged me. "You could have died!" she choked out. "Do you realize that? What you did was very, very dangerous!"

I nodded, crying too. Even though I understood my mistake and promised never to do it again. I still got punished. Dad spanked me and sent me to bed without supper.

As I crawled into bed with a sore behind, I felt sorry for myself. I laid on my stomach, my face buried in my pillow. Joy was the first one to come back after supper. She sat on the lower bunk across from mine and stared at me. I rolled onto my side. She hadn't been spanked or sent to bed without supper, but she hadn't been allowed to stay up late since she followed me instead of getting an adult.

"I told you it was stupid."

I fell back on my pillow, sighed, and stared at the underside of the bunk. "Yeah, you're right."

Joy made a 'huh' sound. "You're not going to argue with me? That's weird!"

I laughed. "No, I guess not. You kinda saved me. If you hadn't grabbed my hand, I would've..." My words stopped in my throat as my eyes filled with tears. "I mean," I choked out. "I could've fallen down the waterfall and I could've died!"

Joy came over and shoved me over, laying down next to

me. Then she hugged me. "But you didn't." She sighed, rolling to lay flat on her back and stare up at the ceiling. "I'm so sorry I double dog dared you. I shouldn't have done that... again. Why didn't you tell Mom and Dad?"

I shrugged. "It's not like you made me do it. It was my choice."

She pulled back, took my face in her hands, and stared into my eyes. She stared tearing up, "you really scared me." She pushed me away and we lay side by side, staring up at the underside of the top bunk.

"Look," she said after a minute of silence, "don't do that again, okay?"

"I won't," I whispered, rubbing at my eyes.

"Oh, come here," she said, hugging me.

She saved my life. I just wish I could've done the same for her.

16

Tortoises

Caracas, Venezuela

Just before Thanksgiving of 1982, we packed up our house in Puerto Ordaz. Joy and I were excited to go home for the holidays, but we were sad to leave our little house. Back in Texas, the Mardis family, our cousins, had been caretaking our home while we were overseas. With their family of four and our family of six, it was a crowded Christmas on Singapore Lane, but one filled with love and laughter.

In January, we were supposed to move to Caracas, but we couldn't get into the house we would be living in. Dad's company, Chicago Bridge & Iron, was renting a house for us from a rich Venezuelan family. They were in the process of building an even bigger house directly behind the one we would be moving into and they had run into some construction delays. So Mom and Dad had to scramble for accommodations. Since Mom wanted Joy and I to start school at the start of the semester, she didn't want to delay our moving. Even though Jackie wouldn't be starting kindergarten until the fall, Mom said that the school we were going to go to, Escuela Campo Alegre, had a pre-kinder class. Jackie was over the moon to get to start school early. So arrangements were made for Joy, Jackie, and I to stay with the Romano family for a week.

There were some delays, but Mom kept saying, "thank goodness we're still in the same time zone."

In the taxi ride to where we would be staying, Mom sat in the front seat with Jessica on her lap while Joy, Jackie and I were in the back. Mom kept swiveling around to tell us something else she had forgotten to say. She had to shout about the traffic sounds, which included lots of honking as the Caracas traffic loved to honk their varied musical horns, and kept having to push her hair away from her face since the driver kept all the windows down. He didn't know much English, but he did know, "no AC."

"Now don't forget to be gracious. Thank your host for every meal and... Pay attention, Jeani and Jackie!"

"Yes ma'am," we answered in unison, pausing our pushing. I slid closer to the door so Jackie wasn't right up against me. Satisfied, she spread out her dress on the seat around her. Jessica started crying. As soon as Mom turned her attention to her almost 3 year old, Joy rolled her eyes and I giggled.

"Now," Mom said, turning again, as Jessica slurped her

bottle. "You will all be respectful and kind and do what you're told. Got it?"

A cascade of, "yes, ma'ams," rang through the car.

After Mom turned back around, Joy leaned over Jackie's head to whisper to me. "I'm nervous."

I thought about it for a minute and realized I wasn't at all. "I'm excited," I smiled at her.

She shook her head, letting me know that was the wrong thing to say, then turned to look out her window. I sighed, but before I could turn to look out mine, Jackie said, "me too! I'm nervous and excited!"

I laughed, Joy rolled her eyes, and Mom smiled, "of course you are."

The Romanos were an Italian family that had a very neat one story stucco white house with a black roof. Their front lawn was gated with a wrought iron fence and there was quite an array of plant life keeping their house shaded and invisible from the street. The foliage was so thick, when the car we were in pulled up, we couldn't see it until the gate opened and we were driving up the driveway. When we got out of the car, Joy, Jackie, and I each had the one book bag we were allowed to bring on the plane and a single suitcase stuffed with everything, including two sets of brand new uniforms for school. (The Venezuelan Ministry of Education, required uniforms for all school students in all grades as a sign of respect and a show of decency.) Joy and I had white shirts since we were both in elementary school while Jackie had red shirts as she would be entering kindergarten.

The Romanos had three kids around the same ages as Joy and I. The two boys, Luca and Angelo, had black hair and tawny eyes. Anna, the girl, had almost black eyes, and dark brown hair.

They were all delighted when we arrived. The boys each gave a quick hello, then grabbed our suitcases and ran them into the house while we stood there. Anna, still standing where they had been lined up to greet us, giggled. Mrs. Romano stepped out of the house on slingback wedge sandals as her boys rushed past. She was shorter than five feet tall and had her long dyed blonde hair swirled up on the top of her head. Her '60s beehive protruded from a sun hat with a hole cut out of the middle. Her skin was very pale and she was wearing large sunglasses that covered most of her face.

She smiled, throwing her arms wide and spoke with a thick Italian accent. "Welcome to my home! Or, as we say in Italian, Benvenuto in casa mia!" She hugged each of us and kissed our cheeks.

Jackie hugged and kissed her back, announcing, "I love your garden!"

Mrs. Romano laughed with delight. "Oh, I like this one!" She took Jackie's hand and told her all about her plants as she led us into the house.

For as small as the house looked on the outside, it was

pretty big on the inside. The living room was sunken with thick brown shag carpeting and the kitchen was massive with the most up to date appliances you could possibly buy from the late '70s. There was a breakfast room between the kitchen and the living room and a dining room off to the side through an archway. While the kitchen was very bright with windows and all white appliances, the other rooms were dark brown from ceiling to floor.

Anna was a big reader, so she and Joy clicked immediately. They wandered off to Anna's room, discussing books. Mom stayed talking to Mrs. Romano in the kitchen as the boys led Jackie and I through a door off the kitchen. Unlike the front yard, there were no trees and the only bushes were against the tall wooden fence in the backyard. There was a gray stone patio and a grassy area that sloped up onto a hill at the back. It wasn't a large yard, especially not compared to our quarter acre in Texas, but for a city yard, it was pretty decent. The grass almost reached up to my thigh, it was so tall. But I noticed that there were zig-zags of bald areas all over the yard.

"Do you see them?" One of the boys asked.

"See what?" Jackie squinted to see what they were talking about.

I stepped out into the yard, and started following one of the zig-zags. It ended in a large mound of dirt. The mound moved. I looked back at everyone still standing on the patio, my eyes wide. It wasn't a mound of dirt, it was the largest tortoise I had ever seen. I squatted down beside the slow moving creature and put my hand on its rough shell. I could feel the heat from it.

I squealed, "it's so big! I bet Jessica could ride it!"

"What is it?" Jackie asked, running out to me.

"No!" Anna shouted as she and Joy stepped outside. I yanked my hand back from the shell as if it had been burnt and looked over at her. "They're very sensitive. The shell is part of their bones and they can feel through it. They're not meant to be ridden! But you can pet them. They like that."

Jackie squatted down next to me. We both ran our hands along the shell very slowly and with great care. Jackie and I looked at each other and giggled.

"It feels so rough," I said. She nodded.

Joy and Anna came over to us and Joy leaned down to touch the tortoise. The boys were running around us, whooping and hollering. One of them was doing flips. Anna ignored them and told us all about giant tortoises.

"They're herbivores and they thrive in warmer weather. We have three and this one was really old. Our dad got her when he was a kid. The two others are younger males. They can potentially outlive our whole family!"

"Did your dad get two boys and a girl on purpose?" Joy asked.

Anna gave her a quizzical look. "What do you mean?"

"I mean, since he has a daughter and two sons."

Anna smiled. "No, he had them all before us."

Mrs. Romano stepped outside and called us all in for lunch.

After lunch, we were set up in the rooms we'd be staying in. When we were done unpacking, Mrs. Romano said we had a few hours before dinner. I followed the boys back outside and ran around with them, doing flips and playing tag.

After a couple of hours, Mom and Mrs. Romano came out to the patio and sat at the little picnic table. They kept talking, then Mrs. Romano said she was going to go start dinner.

"Could I help?" Mom asked.

"No, you are a guest," Mrs. Romano patted Mom's arm as she walked past her.

Mom nodded, then turned to look out at the yard. That's when she realized I was out there with the boys instead of in the house with my sisters.

"Jeani, could you come here?"

I ran over to her. She looked me up and down and shook her head. I had grass stains and dirt caked on my play clothes and I was sweaty.

"Jeani, I know you want to run around and play and get dirty especially with a couple of boys who can keep up with your energy. But we only have so many clothes for the week you're here and you've already ruined this shirt and shorts. Mrs. Romano has enough to do with her three kids, she doesn't need to be doing laundry for our family. Please keep your clothes clean."

I said yes ma'am over and over.

"Also," she said, standing up and stretching her back, "I'm gonna need you to be an example of Christ's love and patience. They're Catholic, so they do things differently. You need to be polite and watch your manners. Got it?"

I nodded.

"No tantrums, talking back, or any of that nonsense. You will treat Mrs. Romano with respect and you will be on your best behavior here and at your new school. Okay?"

I nodded again, secretly betting with myself that Joy wasn't going to get 'The Lecture'.

She sat back down. "And keep an eye on your little sister. You'll all be going to a new school, but this is only the second time she'll be in a school that's not preschool. I really hate that I won't be here for your first week of school, but I'll see you off tomorrow morning. Mrs. Romano says that many people use the buses, but her kids go in with her driver. That's pretty fancy for your first week of school, isn't it?"

I nodded. Mom wasn't prone to rambling unless she was

nervous and I realized she was really nervous about leaving us here. I leaned over and hugged her. She seemed startled at first, but then hugged me back. I squeezed a bit harder then let her go and sat in the chair next to her.

She gave a little laugh. "What was that for?"

I shrugged, still stroking her arm. "I think we both needed it."

"Good thinking!" She said, smiling wide.

"Where's Jackie and Jessica?" I asked, thinking I could probably play with them until dinner.

"They're both taking a nap since they were so exhausted from the flight."

"Oh," I said, looking out to the yard. "Did you see that they have giant turtles?"

"No, I haven't seen, though I've been told."

"Oh, you have to," I said, jumping up and grabbing her arm. "They're so cool!" I followed a different zigzag with Mom in tow and found one of the younger and smaller male tortoises. His shell was practically black. I showed Mom how to pet him and told her all I remembered of what Anna said about the tortoises.

We were all so exhausted from traveling that we went right to bed after supper. The next morning came way too early and we were off to Escuela Campo Alegre, the international school that taught in English and Spanish and accepted students from all over the world. I barely remember anything from the first few days, since I was getting so little sleep. As soon as I fell asleep, Joy would wake me up and say I was kicking her. By Wednesday night, she was done.

"Either stop kicking me, or sleep on the floor!"

"I don't mean to kick you," I whined. "I'm not even awake!"

"I don't care," she hissed into my ear. "If you don't think you can control it, take your pillow and the blanket Anna left on the laundry hamper and sleep on the floor."

I rolled over and tried to ignore her. But she literally kicked me out of the bed and threw my pillow at me.

Instead of fighting her, I remembered what Mom said and stayed on the floor. It wasn't the most comfortable, but it was better than being woken up every two hours by Joy.

Since I couldn't just run around and play and the boys were on sports teams so they didn't come home with us, when I finished my homework, I tried to hang out with Joy and Anna. But they were always just talking. I suggested a few games, but neither of them wanted to play anything.

I spent most of my time out in the little backyard. I told myself, inside the house was too crowded. Jackie would come out with me sometimes, but not often. I started thinking of it as my praying time since I would sit and pet the tortoises and pray in my head.

It's only for a week, I wrote in my journal over and over. On Thursday after school, Mrs. Romano told us that Dad had called. He, Mom, and Jessica would be joining us on Friday. We were outside, so I did several flips as Jackie clapped her hands and Joy hugged Anna. We would have a home soon!

17

Authentic Italian Spaghetti

Caracas, Venezuela

Mom and Dad and Jessica flew in Friday evening and let everyone know that the house was finally ready. We would be, as Dad put it, out of their hair, on Sunday. Mr. Romano, who we hadn't yet met, came home Saturday morning when we were all sitting down for breakfast. He was a large man, in height and stature. His hair was as black as Dad's, but wavy and he had a matching mustache. When he came in, he set down his briefcase, tossed his hat to the coat rack, and made a beeline to the kitchen where his wife was pulling some biscuits out of the oven. He waited until she had put the pan down before swooping her into a big bear hug and kiss. She giggled and kissed him all over his face.

Setting her down, he walked into the dining room where Mom and Dad were eating. Since there had barely been enough room for all the kids around the breakfast table, the adults were eating at the dinner table. He introduced himself to Dad, shaking his hand roughly. Dad gave a laugh, saying that he had quite the grip.

Mr. Romano looked at him for a moment, then said in a thick Italian accent, "Yes, I have manly grip!" His deep voice rumbled as he sat down, joining them for breakfast.

Saturday night, we all gathered in the kitchen. Both families stood in a circle around the island, holding hands and heads lowered. Mr. Romano looked like he was getting ready to pray, when Dad asked if he could pray. Mr. Romano gruffly said yes. I peeked at him and he looked a little annoyed.

"Dear God. Thank you for allowing us to find wonderful friends with the Romano family. We know it was your wise hand that led us to such a family whose house is overflowing with love and kindness and who opened their doors to us. We thank you for this bounty of food we are about to receive. In Jesus name..."

Before Dad was able to say Amen, Mr. Romano spoke in his loud, heavily accented, voice, "As it says in your word, 'Use hospitality one to another without grudging. As every man hath received the gift, even so minister the same one to another, as good stewards of the manifold grace of God.' Amen."

Mr. Romano barely let go of his wife's hand before turning his dark eyes on Dad. His entire body seemed to vibrate with challenge as he said, "That was from first Peter, chapter 4, verse 9 of the King James Bible."

Dad gave a chuckle and clapped the larger man on his shoulder twice, then dropped his hand. "I don't doubt it. You have a great grasp of the Bible! I wish I could quote scripture and verse as well as you."

The other man relaxed a bit and smiled. He grabbed Dad's shoulder and shook it. "It has been good having you and your family in my home."

His wife clapped her hands together. "We line up here and take plates then get the food... Jo, what is...?"

Mom smiled, "buffet style."

She clapped again, her gold bracelets jingling against each other. "Yes! We have spaghetti, bruschette, prosciutto, gnocchi, risotto..."

Dad chuckled again. "Other than spaghetti, I don't know what any of that is, but it all smells amazing!"

The two boys pushed ahead of us, so Joy and I hung back with Jackie. Mom had taken Jessica through the line with her, which I thought was totally unfair, but I kept my lips shut tight.

I noticed Joy was smiling. "You're so happy!" I whispered in her ear.

"Am I?" She whispered back. "I guess I'm just really excited 'cause real spaghetti from real Italians. I mean we've had amazing lasagna and other really tasty Italian dishes, but I thought we weren't going to get to have spaghetti since we're leaving tomorrow."

Joy's wide smile held until she was standing on the step stool Mrs. Romano used to be able to see into the big pot of spaghetti. She looked at the other pots on the burner, then back at that one. Her face took on a concerned look as I helped Jackie get some food onto her plate. Catching my eye, she said, "can you get mom?"

I stared at her. "Why?"

She stuck her fork in the pot and scooped out some spaghetti. It was glistening with what looked like butter and bits of meat clung to it, but looked plain otherwise.

"I can't find the sauce. Please get Mom?"

She so rarely said please, I nodded. Looking at Jackie I asked, "hold my place and watch my plate, okay?"

"Okay!" She sang out and did a little twirl.

As I headed out of the kitchen, I palmed a breaded mushroom from one of the many platters on the island. I knew Dad said it was impolite to start eating before we sat down, but I was hungry. I shoved it into my mouth and chewed really fast as I walked past the kids table in the breakfast room where the three siblings were tossing a single tiny potato to each other and giggling. I stopped just outside of the dining room and chewed, chewed, chewed, then swallowed. It was too dry and didn't go down. I coughed, spraying breadcrumbs as I stumbled into the room.

"Jeani, you okay?" Mom said, getting up.

I was leaning over, my hands on my knees, still coughing. She grabbed her glass of water and hurried over to me. I took it and drank as she patted me on the back. The water was so cool and lovely. I held the fancy glass goblet with both hands and peered over the top of it. Everyone at the table had stopped eating and talking and were looking at me.

Mom patted me on the back. "Okay now?"

I nodded, slowly lowering the goblet, wishing I could keep it. I liked drinking out of real glass, but knew that Mom would never let me with my tendency to drop things. She took it gently from my hands.

"Glad you're okay. Why don't you go back..."

"Joy needs you," I cut in, sounding way more urgent than I meant to.

"Oh no," Mrs Romano gasped, getting up and dropping her cloth napkin on her chair. She rushed past us into the kitchen muttering in Italian.

Mom and I exchanged a glance then hurried after her. As we got there, Mrs. Romano had her hands on her hips as she stared up at Joy still standing on the step-stool.

The only big change was that Joy's look had gone from concerned to panicked. She looked over the small woman's head to Mom.

"What's wrong, Joy?" Mom asked, her voice held a note of caution as she saw Mrs. Romano's upset expression.

Mrs. Romano threw up her arms. "She not like my spaghetti and she not even taste it!"

"No, I... Mom, I just said that I like red sauce on my spaghetti and..."

"Red sauce," Mrs. Romano practically spat. "That is not..." She stormed out of the room towards the back bedrooms muttering in Italian.

Joy was crying as she stepped down from the step stool. "Mom! I didn't mean to..."

I watched in bafflement as Mom went over to Joy and comforted her instead of scolding her. But then I remembered that Mom hadn't said anything about me eating, and almost choking to death, on the mushroom before I sat down to eat at the table. I took a deep breath and listened as Joy explained what happened.

"I – I didn't mean to be rude. I was confused by the spaghetti because there was no sauce and meatballs to put on it. When she came in here, I asked, where's the sauce? An – and she said, the sauce is in the pot with the noodles. Then I said oh! Does it not have any, and I couldn't remember the name of the red sauce... Marinara! That's it! But that was what I meant and I didn't mean to be rude or disrespectful or..." She broke down crying and Mom hugged her.

Noticing me standing there, Mom handed me Joy's plate and motioned for me to put it on the small table next to the door that led into the breakfast room.

"Jeani, why don't you and Jackie finish fixing your plates and go sit down to eat?"

Slightly startled, I looked at Jackie who was sitting on the floor eating the garlic bread, breaded mushrooms, and salad she had gotten, with her hands. I nodded to Mom, got Jackie up off the ground, and put some of the spaghetti on her plate. I realized it wasn't just butter, but a very light creamy white sauce. I sent Jackie to the table and went back to finish filling my plate. Mrs. Romano came back into the room and went over to Joy. She was now talking softly. Joy gave a little laugh at something that was said, then nodded and hugged Mrs. Romano. I dawdled over the last few things to put on my plate so I could see what happened. Mrs. Romano swirled a fork in the spaghetti and brought it over to Joy

As Joy chewed, her eyes lit up. "Wow! That was great! I think that might be my new favorite spaghetti!" Mrs. Romano laughed and hugged her. I hurried out of the room.

The next day, I woke up when Joy got out of bed. She was trying to be really quiet, but she had to step over me and she ended up stepping lightly on my finger. I crawled up onto the bed and rolled onto my stomach to watch her as she sat at the little desk writing.

"Whatcha doin'?" I asked, yawning.

"Shhh, go back to sleep," Joy said, not even turning to me.

I looked around the room and saw that Jackie was sound asleep.

I whispered, "maybe I'll go back to sleep later, but if I don't know what you're doing, I won't be able to get to sleep with all the wondering."

Joy sighed, "I'm writing a card to give to Mrs. Romano to apologize for being rude and thank her for her hospitality."

"Oh," I said, stretching. "Where did you find a card?"

"It's just some paper." She held the folded paper out to me with an illustration of a big pot of spaghetti with steam rising out of it. There was a fork hovering just over the edge of a pot and a noodle was being sucked into a face that looked a little like Joy's. Above the face was the word DELICIOUS in all caps.

"That's cool," I laughed, then gave a big yawn. "You're like super nice and stuff."

Joy turned back to her writing. "Yeah, I know."

18

Our New House

Caracas, Venezuela

That weekend, we went to our new home. It was on a busy street and had a red brick wall around the property. As Dad pulled up to it, he pushed a button on what I thought was a garage door opener. But instead of lifting, a large white gate rolled aside and we drove into a spacious car park area. I looked up at the house. Then tilted my head to look up even more. It was a skyscraper!

I watched the gate roll back into place as I got out of the car and heard the loud sounds of the city traffic become muffled. Joy elbowed me in my ribs. I turned to say something to her, but realized Dad was talking.

"...lots of stairs up to the house proper, but once we get up there, it'll make sense. So grab anything you can carry 'cause we want to make as few trips back and forth as possible."

Mom gave an audible sigh as she picked up her suitcase. Jessica, who had been running around in circles with Jackie, fell down and started crying. Mom knelt down to check and see if she was okay. Joy and I put our backpacks on and grabbed our suitcases then lugged them over to the stairs.

"You weren't kiddin'!" Joy shouted as she bumped her bag up the concrete steps. I was still at the bottom staring up. There was a white railing along the right hand side of the stairs and a stone wall on the left. The stairs themselves wound around and I couldn't see where they ended from the bottom. There had to have been hundreds and hundreds of steps! I started trudging up, dragging my suitcase behind me.

I paused after about 20 steps and looked up. There were about 30 more to go, but not hundreds like I had thought and I could see that Joy had reached the top. She disappeared from view. I kept going. Her head reappeared and I thought she was going to fall over the side. But she was just leaning over the side, shouting.

"Dad! The door's locked!"

Dad, who had been unloading everything else from the car, looked perplexed. "What?"

"The door is locked!" Joy shouted again.

"Oh!" Dad shouted back. "Just a sec."

I reached the landing and saw that it was a pretty wide area. I put my suitcase over by Joy's stuff, then stood next to her.

"They look so small," I said, " like ants."

Joy giggled. "They're not that far away."

"John," Mom's sharp voice cut the air. "Don't you dare!"

I looked over the railing to see that Dad had been winding up to throw the keys up to Joy and Mom's voice stopped him before he released.

"You know they only gave us so many keys and if you lose those on our first day..." She shook her head.

Dad nodded, "you're right. Jackie, go run these up to your sisters and don't drop them."

"Yes sir!" Jackie sang, skipping over to him then skipping up the stairs. "Here ya go!" She dropped the keys in Joy's hand, smiling wide, like she expected a prize.

I laughed. "You didn't bring anything else up with you? You have to go back down and get your stuff."

"Aw," she said, her buoyancy deflating. "I wanted to see the inside of the house."

Joy shook her head. "Sorry. You heard what Dad said, you have to bring something with you to get into the house."

It wasn't quite what Dad said, but Jackie believed her and went back down.

Joy unlocked the door and we grabbed our stuff. My first impression was that there was a lot of yellow. The yellow was in the entryway and the living room off to the left. But the walls going up the stairs inside were creamy white. We decided to head upstairs with our luggage before investigating the rest of the house. Dad had told us that we would have to share a bedroom and Jackie and Jessica would share the other bedroom. We were determined to get first pick. The carpeted stairs wound around and around and we were both panting before we reached the second floor. We found a bathroom on the left next to one bedroom. Across the hall was another bedroom. It was slightly bigger, so Joy started dragging her suitcase in there.

"But what about that one?" I asked, pointed to the open door that revealed a much bigger room at the end of the hall.

"That's obviously Mom and Dad's," she said, rolling her eyes. "Come on!"

"Are you sure?" I asked, following her. "Dad said whoever gets in first can claim whatever room."

"He didn't mean that one," she said, tossing her backpack on the bigger bed. I put my stuff on the other one, then went across the hall to look at the little kids room.

"We picked the right one! This one has smaller beds." I ran to the master bedroom and found that there was a king sized bed and an attached bathroom. There was also a lot of floor space. "It's not fair that our room isn't as big."

"Well," Dad's voice boomed behind me, making me jump. "When you get a job and have your own house, you can have the biggest room."

"With an attached bathroom," I added.

He grinned, setting down the two suitcases he had brought up. "Yes, with an attached bathroom. Now let's head back down and bring the rest of the stuff inside. I think your Mom's going to be taking a nap after she puts Jackie and Jessica down." He headed down the hall, but before descending, he turned to look at us. "Unless, of course, you two want to take a nap?"

"No sir!" Joy and I sang out in unison, running down the stairs ahead of him.

The next day was Monday and, even though we were exhausted from unpacking, we had to go to school. At least I was finally well rested. Having my own bed to toss around on gave me a much better sleep than I'd had the entire time at the Romanos.

Joy, Jackie, and I were picked up by a yellow school bus that looked just like the ones from the United States. We discovered a few of the friends we had made during our first week of school, were on the bus. Joy, who had spent most of her time with Romano girl, sat alone. She didn't even try to make friends on the bus. On Thursday, as we were waiting for the bus, I asked Joy if she wanted to sit with me.

"Why would I want to do that?" She asked.

I blinked at her. "So you won't be lonely." She tilted her head and stared at me until I felt uncomfortable. "What?"

"It's just, you'd think that after all these years, you'd know me better. Being alone doesn't mean I'm lonely. I like sitting and reading a book on our way to school. All your jibber-jabbering with your new friends isn't what I need. I guess I'm just too mature for that."

The bus pulled up and she got on before I could say anything. As we bumped down the road, my friends and I chatted and laughed. I kept sneaking peeks back at her. I had thought she had been jealous of me with all my friends. But she was just reading. There were even a few kids her age who tried to talk to her. After politely answering their questions, she went back to her book. She looked happy.

19

My First Car Crash

❦

Caracas, Venezuela

Just like the other places we lived in Venezuela, the weather in Caracas was beautiful but with more noise and air pollution since it was a major city. Caracas was also confining. Joy and I couldn't go out on our bikes because the streets were not safe and the city didn't have much in the way of sidewalks. I missed the bike rides Joy and I took through the neighborhood when we lived in Puerto Ordaz and running around the streets with the local kids when we were in Punto Fijo. We had our bikes, but Mom and Dad only let us ride around the carpark and that got old really fast.

In February 1983, we celebrated Dad's, Jessica's, and

Jackie's birthdays in our new house. By mid-March, we were settled into our new home, new school, and new church. It was a nondenominational church that prided itself on accepting anyone who believed in Christ and was born again. While there were some significant differences, it was, as Dad put it, as close to Southern Baptist as spittin'. The building itself was a converted one story house. They had removed the wall between the living room and the dining room and put in a small riser for the choir and the pulpit. It had chairs for the heads of the church to sit in front of the choir facing the congregation. Dad, having been a Deacon in our church in Texas, was asked to be one of the heads of the church. He agreed. It was hard to hold onto a pastor since Caracas was a transient city, so Dad ended up preaching a few times. But what he and Mom loved to do was facilitate small Bible study groups.

One Saturday evening, Dad and Mom were hosting a dinner and a Bible study at the church. The woman who usually led a youth class was out of town. After dinner, Dad asked if we wanted to play outside.

"As long as you don't go into the street," Dad told the kids, "y'all can play in the front or the back. There should be enough light for some games. Otherwise, you can join us for bible study and prayer. But if you do that, you will be expected to be quiet and respectful."

There were five kids, not including Jessica because she was just two and had fallen asleep. None of us wanted to stay inside. So we agreed and went outside.

The sky was cloudy, making it impossible see any stars or the moon. While there was light on the front porch, it only reached as far as the patio's edge. It would be hard to see each other in the actual yard that was full of holes and divots. Joy, being the oldest, took it upon herself to be in charge.

"Let's play tag!" One boy shouted.

Joy shook her head. "If we play tag, we might as well call it falling and busting our faces. Next idea?"

"Freeze tag?" a younger girl suggested.

Joy thought about it for a moment, then shook her head again. "Same problem."

"Why don't we just play hide-n-seek?" The first boy piped up.

As Joy was about to say no, his sister jumped in. "Yeah! But with the rule that no one can run. We could make the porch the safe space."

Joy thought about it. "Can everyone promise not to run?" We all nodded. "Okay, who will be the seeker?"

The boy who suggested the game waved his arm. Joy nodded and told him to face the building with his eyes covered and count to 100. He did and we dispersed.

I started to climb my favorite tree, but realized that would be too obvious, and hurried over to the driveway where the cars were lined up. I thought I was pretty clever, but found that three other kids were already huddled on the far side of two cars. I crouched low as I heard the counter reach 50, and scurried towards the garage. As soon as I was far enough away from the other kids, I squeezed myself between two cars that were parked close together and squatted into the shadows.

"100! Ready or not, here I come!" I could hear the boy moving into the yard away from me. The three kids who had hidden on the other side of the cars quietly made their way to the porch.

"Ah-ha!" The seeker shouted. The other kids screamed and started running.

"No running!"

I looked over the hood of the car to see Joy between two cars off to the side. She'd had the same idea!

Hearing Joy's voice, the boy who had tagged two of the other kids, hurried over. I slid to the ground and crawled under the cars until I reached the end of the driveway. I glanced back and saw the boy looking where Joy had been, but she wasn't there anymore. He turned to the row of cars I was under, but went up the driveway instead of down. I crawled out into the streetlight, still on the driveway but right next to the road, and ducked down half walking, half running up the other side of the cars. I thought if I could reach the garage, I could sneak around it, go through the backyard and slip into the house without anyone being the wiser. Then sneak out the side door onto the unlit portion of the porch. I would pretend I had been there all along. Feeling very proud of myself, I started trotting, still hunched over. I heard something behind me, so I peaked back over my left shoulder, not slowing. Not seeing anyone, I turned back and smacked my head so hard, I bounced backwards. Everything went black.

"Do you think she's dead?"

The voice drifted around me in the darkness. It sounded familiar, but I couldn't place it. I was aware of other voices, but none of them made sense. There was pain, lots and lots of pain, in my head over my right eye. I moaned.

"Not dead!" Another voice shouted. "She moaned!"

I wanted to tell them to be quiet, they were hurting my head. But my thoughts weren't reaching my mouth. I told my right hand to touch my forehead. It took a minute, then I could feel my arm lifting and my cold fingers touched a small swollen spot just under my hairline and over my right eyebrow. I moaned again, not from pain, but from the relief of my icy touch. I held my fingers there, feeling the knot grow.

"Jeani," came a commanding voice, "Jeani, can you hear me?"

I knew that voice, it was Joy. I wanted to say, of course I can hear you, but my mouth still wasn't following instructions from my brain.

"Can you open your eyes?"

I managed to squint, but closed them tight as the light from a flashlight burned into my already throbbing head.

I covered both of my eyes and pushed the word, "don't," through my lips.

"Don't what?" Joy asked. I could hear what I thought was excitement in her voice. Was she enjoying this?

"Don't light," I whispered, keeping my hands over my eyes.

"Oh," she said, the light moving away. "Sorry. Can you get up?"

I thought about that for a few seconds, then slowly sat up. My entire body ached, causing me to moan some more.

"What's going on?" Dad's voice bounced all around me.

"It's Jeani! She hit a car!"

Dad, coming up beside the circle of kids, started bellowing. "What were y'all doing in the street? Didn't I tell you not to go into the street? I thought you were old enough to..."

Joy shouted over him, "She didn't!"

Dad's flow of words fell. Crickets chirped as none of the kids dared to speak.

"What?" He asked, kneeling down beside me.

Joy gave a frustrated snort. "She didn't go into the street. A car didn't hit her. She hit a car with her head!"

Dad gently moved my hand and gave a sharp inhale. Kneeling beside me, he had me follow his finger. I could just see it by the street light. "I'm sorry to do this, but I need to shine a light in your eyes to check your pupils." I almost asked him how he knew to do that, but then I remembered he had been a volunteer firefighter in Jersey Village. The light hurt, but I was able to keep my eyes open. After he was done checking me over, he hugged me.

I leaned my head against his chest and could feel his heart pounding. Tears spilled out of my eyes and my body shook with sobs.

"Hey, hey. No need for tears. You did a really good job. Let's get you inside, okay?"

"Okay," I whimpered.

The voices of the other kids got louder as they rushed into the church, calling for their parents who, in turn, were calling back to them. Above it all, I heard Mom.

"John, what happened?"

Dad reached the backroom, which had once been a family room, and lowered me onto the couch. Mom sat beside me and helped me sit up to take a sip of the cold water.

Dad said, "apparently, our girl has been in her first car accident." As Mom and several of the other adults gasped, he quickly added, "but she hit the car, not the other way around."

The light in that room wasn't too harsh as I slowly opened my eyes. Everyone was staring at me. There was concern and worry, but there were also looks of amusement and confusion.

"She what?" Mom asked.

"Oh my!" One of the women gasped. "That is quite a knot! We should put some toothpaste on it. Hang on, I think we have some left by the last pastor in the downstairs bathroom."

Mom mouthed toothpaste to Dad who just shrugged. Someone put another glass of water in my hands and I drank about half of it, then remembered I had to pee. I hopped up and rushed to the bathroom.

"Jeani?" Dad called after me. "Are you throwing up?"

"No," I called through the door. "I just really had to pee."

Some of the kids giggled.

As soon as I opened the door, one of the adults I did not know stepped in with me. Crouching to get eye level with me, she rubbed toothpaste onto the knot. "It'll help the swelling go down," she explained.

I looked back at the mirror. My right eye was swollen half shut and the knot above it was almost glowing blue from the gel toothpaste she had slathered on it. "It's glowing," I said.

She laughed, stepping out the bathroom and held the door for me. I was dizzy, but she caught me before I fell. When we got back to my couch, Mom was sitting where my head had been. I laid down, with my head on her lap. She gave the woman a quizzical look.

"It'll help the swelling go down," the woman repeated.

Dad told Mom not to let me fall asleep then went to talk with a few people. Mom stroked my hair and jostled me awake anytime I drifted off. The families were leaving, wishing me a speedy recovery as they said their goodbyes. The toothpaste woman popped her head around the corner and waved as she and her husband left.

Mom had me sit up so she could refill my cup. Dad and a couple of other men came over and laid hands on my head and shoulders, praying. I tried not to flinch away, but I really wanted to. Whenever there had been a laying on of hands with me, it was because I was in trouble. They would pray that I not continue down the evil path and that I would soon come back to Jesus.

As soon as the praying was over, Joy asked, "did anybody check the car?"

Dad looked at her. "Why?"

"Because she's got such a hard head! Maybe she caused a lot of damage."

Everyone laughed. It hurt my head, but I laughed too.

Dad, Joy and I stayed the night at the church. Dad didn't want to move me again and knew it would be hard to get me into the house with all those stairs. Dad and Joy took turns keeping me awake. Joy read to me from her book. Dad sang. Even though it was supposed to keep me awake, I found his soft baritone soothing and kept drifting off. He said it was okay for me to sleep for a little bit at a time, but he would wake me and check my pupils.

At one point I woke to hear him and Joy talking.

"Is she gonna be okay?" Joy's voice was small and worried.

"Of course she will," Dad said. "We just have to make sure she doesn't have a concussion 'cause that can lead to a brain injury."

Joy nodded. After a couple of seconds of them sitting in silence, Joy whispered, "I was mean to her. I mean, more than sisterly meanness. She was trying to be nice and helpful 'cause she's got friends already but doesn't think I do. But I do. I have friends at school, they just don't ride our bus. I was kinda insulted that she thought I needed her help and, um, kinda called her a baby."

Dad chuckled. "Thank you for telling me. I think you should apologize to her, but also ask God for forgiveness."

Joy nodded and prayed while Dad woke me up. "You okay, sweety?"

"Yeah," I said, my voice heavy.

"How's your head feeling?"

I thought about it for a minute. "Well, it still hurts, but it hurts less. I just feel really sleepy."

Joy, who had finished praying, said, "me too."

Dad looked at her. "Don't you have something to say to your sister?"

Joy nodded. "I'm sorry I was mean to you about the bus."

I reached up and hugged her. "You're forgiven. Do you wanna lay on the couch with me?"

Joy nodded and climbed under the blanket with me. "You smell like mint," she grinned, "and look like your head has a headlight." We laughed.

Dad smiled then started singing his favorite Peter, Paul, and Mary song.

```
        "Oh once I had a little dog
            His color it was brown
         I taught him for to whistle
            To sing and dance and run
     His legs they were fourteen yards long
             His ears so very wide
         Around the world in half a day
             Upon him I could ride

             Sing derry-o day
            Sing autumn to May"
```

I hugged Joy and we smiled at Dad as we joined him in the chorus,

```
            "Sing derry-o day
            Sing autumn to May

        Oh once I had a flock of sheep
          They grazed upon a feather
          I'd keep them in a music box
           From wind or rainy weather
```

> *And every day the sun would shine*
> *They'd fly all through the town*
> *To bring me back some golden rings*
> *Candy by the pound"*

We laughed at the candy. "I want candy," I said dreamily.

"You're both supposed to be falling asleep," Dad said, with mock sternness. "If this is getting you more riled up, maybe I should stop."

I fake snored and Joy giggled, then quickly turned her giggle into a yawn. "Please keep singing," she said, "this is my favorite verse."

I giggled. Of course it was.

> *"Oh once I had a downey swan*
> *She was so very frail*
> *She sat upon an oyster shell*
> *And hatched me out a snail*
> *The snail had changed into a bird*
> *The bird to butterfly*
> *And he who tells a bigger tale*
> *Would have to tell a lie"*

My eyes were closed and I could hear Joy's deep breathing.

Dad leaned over and kissed Joy's forehead and the top of my head. "Good night my lovely goofy girls." He touched my cheek and I looked up at him. "I'm glad you and your sister take care of each other. I'll wake you up soon, okay?"

I nodded and fell asleep.

20

Glass Cisne

Caracas, Venezuela

By the end of April, my family had been living in Caracas, Venezuela for about three months. A group from the small, missionary run church we went to invited Mom to join them on a visit to the glass blowing factory just outside the capital. Since there were other kids going, Mom asked Joy and I if we wanted to go. Joy said yes, but was kind of blasé about it. Since I had taken to imitating her reactions to things, wanting to be a teenager like my sister, I answered in the affirmative in the same manner she did.

But my head was buzzing. Up until that point I had never thought about how or that glass was made. Wasn't it grown like wood but in water? Wasn't there a glass equivalent of a tree? I had heard of lumber mills and thought maybe a glass factory was like that. But it was a blowing factory, so maybe glass is found in the earth and you have to blow it up with dynamite. Maybe it was like bricks that I had learned were made of earth. But glass is different from bricks or wood or coal. That night, I dreamed of glass forests underneath the ocean.

The next day, after driving to the meeting place, we wandered along the sidewalk, chatting. The air was fresh and the sun was bright. A cool ocean scent on the breeze contrasted with the spicy smells bursting into the air whenever we passed an open restaurant door or window. We had to almost shout to be heard above the city traffic.

When we reached the factory, we were taken on a tour and got to see where the sand was brought in. We learned about how glass is made from sand and heat and pressure. We were shown the vats of different types of minerals and chemicals they used to make colored glass. When we reached the area where the glass blowing took place, the tour guide had us stand near a railing to watch the artists work. We were pretty far from the fire, but the heat came at us in shimmering waves that we could see in the air. The tour guide, a Venezuelan man about Mom's age and quite handsome, spoke in Spanish while one of the ladies from the church translated. A hush had fallen as all the kids were silent, entranced.

I had so many questions like, if you took an hourglass outside when it was really, really hot, would the sand become part of the glass and if you take a glass bottle of coke to the beach and set it in the sand, are you threatening the sand and can sandcastles be made into glass castles in a lightning storm? But as he pointed to each glassmaker and explained what they were doing, I became mesmerized and all my questions flitted away.

The tour guide told us how, about 30 years ago, the owner of the factory came to Venezuela from Italy. Since he was a glassmaker back in Italy, he decided to build his own factory in Venezuela. He kept talking and the woman kept translating, but I stopped listening because I was enthralled by the magic. Each worker, all men, were taking blobs of liquid glass on long poles then shoving them into a hole to the furnace. The man would put the other end of the pole to his mouth and blow into it while he spun the pole. Heat shields covered the holes when the poles were pulled out, but no one wore goggles or any protective gear except gloves and they would randomly take them off. They all moved so fast! Each glassmaker was at a different stage of the process and it was hard to know where to look.

I grinned at Joy. "Isn't it so cool?"

She raised an eyebrow. "Don't you mean hot?" We laughed.

The tour guide motioned to the closest furnace where a blower had just pulled the glass out of the furnace and another glassmaker was using metal tongs to shape it into a vase while the other man spun the rod. I was dizzy just watching them.

I raised my hand. The tour guide stopped talking and smiled at me. His big grin showed a few missing teeth. His smile got smaller as he pulled his lips over his missing teeth. The translator adjusted her glasses. She had big hair that reminded me of Texas and always spoke louder than necessary. She wore clothes that my Mom had described as matching her big personality. She had been staring at him and stumbling a bit over the translation since, like most Venezuelans, he spoke fast. When he stopped, she turned to see what he was looking at. Upon seeing my hand up, she sighed.

"What do you want, Jeani?"

As a kid, I was often oblivious when I was irritating people. But even I could hear her annoyance. I didn't reply to her, I spoke directly to the tour guide, motioning to the railing we were next to. "¿Por qué esta bar no está caliente para tocar?"

His grin widened, forgetting to hide his teeth. I think he was pleased that I asked my question in Spanish. He explained that since the heat was airborne from the fire, we could feel it easily on our skin. But for it to heat the railing, it would take either direct contact or consistent exposure over time. He pointed to the fans they had going that drew cooler air from outside the factory to cool off the air making the metal not in direct contact with the fire stay cooler to the touch.

"Now," he said, switching to broken English. "Who want help make glass?"

My hand shot up and he picked me. He had me stand next to the closest glassmaker. I watched his actions closely, then did what he did. Within seconds I was holding the long hollow rod, dipping it in the liquid glass, then

MY SWAN SONG FOR JOY 163

hurrying it over to the furnace. As my glass-blob went in, I spun it carefully, with the glassblower's assistance. The glassblower had me hold the rod closer to the middle and spin it while he blew into the opening. We both brought it out, showing everyone it was a platter, and everyone applauded. The glassblower continued working on it as I was ushered back to the group by the tour guide. I was sweating and flush but also exploding with delight.

"Now," he said, "Want to see making small glass figure?" All the kids and a few adults exclaimed with excitement. He clapped his hands together. "Good, good! What animal?"

We all shouted at once. I wanted a monkey and heard shouts of dog, horse, cat, burro, ant, and many others. The adults were quieter, but I could tell they wanted to join in the cacophony as they said things like, "Wouldn't a little parrot be so sweet?" or "My friend from college had the cutest little glass frog" and things like that.

The translator lady wanted to get control back so she clapped her hands and shushed everyone. "The only kid who didn't shout was Joy, who just raised her hand. That is very good manners, Joy. What would you like?"

Blushing, Joy lowered her hand and whispered, "A swan."

"What was that?" The loud translator lady said.

"She said a swan!" I shouted.

I was so mad! When I raised my hand to ask a question, she acted as if I spit at her. But when Joy did, she had good manners. I glared at the woman, but she turned away, trying to describe a swan since she didn't remember the Spanish word for it.

With her head still lowered, Joy whispered, "Cisne." Since I was the only person close enough to hear her, she looked at me with pleading eyes. I sighed.

"¡Ella quiere un cisne!" I shouted.

The tour guide gave me a thumbs up and motioned Joy over to him. He asked Joy if she wanted it to be any particular color. She shook her head. He relayed it to one of the glassmakers who motioned for Joy to join him. She lowered her face and shook her head, staying where she was. The tour guide waved for him to continue. We watched as a new smaller glob of glass was chosen for the task and put into the heat. The glassmaker spun it for a bit, removed it, and laid the rod across what looked like two sawhorses with grooves cut in the middle. He used big metal pliers to pull the strands of glass and curve them. His movements were so fast, quickly setting down the pliers and picking up what looked like a flathead screwdriver to shape the feathers and face and beak.

The glass artist held the swan out for Joy's inspection when it was done. She blushed slightly, nodding her head and smiling wide. She clasped her hands to her blushing cheeks. Her eyes followed the swan as it was brought to hover over a cushion where it was knocked free of the rod.

The tour guide explained that the glass had to cool, then led us to the gift shop. Inside was a myriad of small figurines, glass bowls with glass fruit in them, vases, and fancier glass pieces of art behind a long counter. Mom and the other church ladies told the older kids that they could touch things, but had to be very careful. But the younger kids were not allowed to touch anything. We had to walk through the shop with our hands in our pockets. If we couldn't do that, we were warned, we'd have to wait outside. But if we were really good, each mother promised to purchase one small glass figurine for each kid.

My palms itched with my desire to touch, but I followed Joy and kept my hands in my pockets. Joy made a show of gently stroking the glass figurines. With each stroke, I got more and more angry. It wasn't fair that she got to touch things! She was only two years older than me. She wasn't even doing it right. She hadn't picked a single one up.

I walked over to Mom and whined to her about the injustice, pointing out that I was closer to the older kids' ages than the little kids, who were all at least five years younger than me. She squatted down to my eye level. Her green eyes were extra serious and big behind her square glasses. Her brown hair was curled and sprayed into a cloud that practically hovered around her head like a halo.

"Jeani, you know you can be clumsy. Joy has shown us that she is very responsible and careful. When you show us that you can be that responsible and careful, you can come into places like this with your hands out of your pockets. Does that make sense?" I nodded, staring at the white collar of her soft pastel blouse that had a small drop of mustard on it. She stood back up, her knees popping beneath the tan slacks she wore. "Good. If you feel you can't control yourself and must touch something, you can come and take my hand like a little girl."

I stood straight, stuffing my hands deeper in my jean pockets. "I'm not a baby, Mom."

"Then act like a big girl."

I sighed and nodded, wandering off to find Joy. When I found her, the tour guide was talking to her. I watched as he handed her the glass swan. She took it gently, then pointed to Mom. The man walked past me and, with the help of the translator, told her that they decided to gift the swan to Joy. He thanked her for having such a creative daughter. He said they had not made swans before and found it to be a lovely addition to their collection. Mom gave him a warm smile and said, "Gracias."

"Did you hear?" I almost jumped at Joy's breath on my neck. "They gave me the swan for free! How cool is that?"

I looked over my shoulder at her. I almost said something mean, but decided to swallow my jealousy. "Yeah. But isn't it really hot?"

She laughed. "Not anymore!" She held the swan out to me. "Touch it! It's so cool to the touch."

"I can't," I pouted, "I'm not allowed to take my hands out of my pockets."

Joy made a face then grabbed my arm with her free hand, pulling me towards the exit. "Mom! We'll be just outside," she called as we hurried past.

Once outside, she held the figurine out to me. "Here, you can hold it."

I was still feeling pouty. "Aren't you afraid I'll break it 'cause I'm so clumsy?"

She made an exasperated sound. "Jeani, just be careful, okay? If you break it, I'll tell Mom, so don't break it."

Still not trusting that this wouldn't somehow get me in trouble, I kept my hand in my pockets and asked, "Why are you being nice?"

She brushed strands of her long brown hair out of her face as the wind danced around us. With a serious expression, she looked me in the eyes. "Look, if you hadn't said what I wanted out loud, they probably would have made some stupid bird I don't even like. You helped me get this, okay? So you can hold it. The glass feels really cool, in both temperature and just, you know, coolness."

Slowly pulling my hands out of my pockets, I took it from her and ran my fingers along the curve of the neck and onto the swan's back. It was so smooth and delicate but so solid. I held it up to the light and saw rainbows in the glass. It was almost cold despite the heat coming from the factory next to the shop. "It's kinda heavy for how small it is, isn't it?"

Joy gently took it from my hands, weighing it with her own. "Well, duh. It's solid glass."

"Glass is so weird and amazing!"

Joy laughed. "Let's go back inside, okay?"

I nodded and stuffed my hands back in my pockets. We wandered around, but didn't find any monkey figurines.

Mom bought me a horse head that changed the light to rainbows when I looked through it, just like Joy's swan did. They wrapped both of our glass figurines in paper and we each got our own boxes. Mom got a large golden glass platter with glass fruit that she would proudly display on the dining room table for years to come. It would even survive the trip from Venezuela to the United States.

On the ride home, Joy and I each took our glass treasures out of their boxes. We weighed them with our hands and found that they were just about the same.

"Isn't it funny how these glass pieces started out as sand?" I asked, trying to see the rainbow in my glass horse head, but finding it was too dark in the car.

Joy thought about that for a minute as she carefully put her glass swan back into the box. "I don't know if it's funny," she said, "but it is interesting."

"Yeah," I nodded, stuffing my horse back into its box. "That's what I mean." I yawned and leaned against the empty baby seat between us.

Joy gasped, her face lighting up. She leaned forward. "Mom, since man was made of clay and clay is like sand, does that mean that humans are, like, related to glass?"

Mom chuckled. "I mean, I guess? After all, all of God's creations are connected on some level."

Joy settled back, petting her swan box, and nodding, satisfied. "That's what I thought."

21

Visiting the States

Georgia, Alabama, Texas, Florida, & over International Waters

In the summer of 1983, Joy and I flew back to the United States by ourselves. It was Joy's idea and she came up with a bunch of different ways to make money including babysitting, cleaning houses, being clowns for birthday parties, and selling jewelry. Our parents paid for the larger part of the trip and they carefully arranged which relatives we would stay with, our flight schedules, and who would drive us around.

I don't remember a lot about the trip. It was a whirlwind in which we didn't want to offend any of our relatives, so we went to every house we were asked to visit. Since we'd had so many requests of "speak Spanish for us" the last time we were home, Joy and I put together a silly routine. It was fun and demonstrated our prowess in Spanish. It went a little like this:

We would approach each other from opposite sides of whatever room we were in and wave as we were walking towards each other.

"¡Hola mi hermana!" [Hello my sister!] Joy would say.

"¡Hola mi amiga!" [Hello my friend!] I would respond and we would shake hands.

Joy – "Necesitamos hablar de algunas cosas muy importante." [We need to talk about a few important things.]

Me – "¿De Verdad? ¿Por qué?" [Really? Why?]

Joy – "Porque estamos aquí en la casa de nuestra familia y se requiere una actuación de sus primas / sobrinas venezolano-viviendo." [Because we are here in the house of our relatives and a performance of their Venezuelan-living cousins / nieces is required.]

Me, with my hands on my hips and my chin jutting forward, acting upset. After all, who doesn't want a bit of drama? – "Pero, ¿qué pasa si no queremos discutir nada?" [But what if we don't want to discuss anything?]

Joy, with the back of her hand to her forehead. – "¡No tenemos otra opción porque estamos monos que actuando! Bueno, al menos lo eres." [We have no other choice because we are performing monkeys! Well, at least you are.]

This is when I would bust out my superb monkey sounds and start dancing and jumping around the room, pretending like I was a monkey.

Joy with her arms thrown up in despair. – "¡Parada eso ahora mismo!" [Stop that right now!]

Me, still dancing and making monkey chittering noises. – "¡Nunca!" [Never!]

At that point Joy would turn to the audience, looking really sad, and say, "¿Ves lo que tengo que aguantar? ¿Por qué no pude haber sido hija única?" [Do you see what I have to put up with? Why couldn't I have been an only child?]

Then she would fall to her knees, pretending to cry as I pretended to groom her hair and eat bugs out of it. We would bow to lots of laughter and applause. Since we had fun with it, our family did too. Joy got a little annoyed when we had to do it more than once in a day and I got bored of the script, so we came up with a second one in which I turned into a butterfly since we both liked to say mariposa, but that one never did quite as well.

It was a strange and exhausting trip. Other than our Spanish routine, only a few brief interactions stood out. We were so busy trying to visit every relative that Dad had put on our itinerary, we didn't have much time to just have fun. I don't blame Dad. He had suggested the itinerary to get us to and from places and so everyone would know where we were when. I don't think even he had thought how exhausting it could be. The main problem was, no one thought about jet lag or being tired or overwhelmed or crabby. Years later when I asked the relatives we visited if they remembered that trip, the main thing that stood out was our Spanish demonstration. They'd comment on how brave we were for taking the trip with just each other for company. But what we did while we were visiting them? No one remembered much. At every place we visited, we barely got there before we were turning around and leaving. Each visit was too short.

When we were in Alabama visiting Aunt Shirley and Uncle Laverne. Not his real name, just what my sisters and I called him because he gave each of us boy names – Joy was George, I was Sam, Jackie was Pete, and Jessica was Mike – he was Laverne because of the Laverne and Shirley show. A bunch of our second cousins were over visiting their grandparents and we were all watching a movie. Someone decided that since their grandma, our Aunt Shirley, was busy making dinner, she wouldn't notice if the sheet of brownies she had just taken out of the oven went missing. There were so many kids strewn about the room – some on the plush carpeting, others on the loveseat and couch – that the cousin carrying the tray had to step gingerly through the bodies to set the tray of delicious smelling brownies onto the coffee table. Before anything was said, we had all fallen on the brownies, devouring their chocolatey goodness like lions on a herd of sleeping gazelles. Joy stared at us with her mouth hanging open. I looked over at her, smiled with chocolate teeth, and held out a brownie to her. She jumped out of her chair.

"Aunt Shirley!" She shouted, running to the kitchen.

I quickly shoved the brownie into my mouth and went back to the tray to see if there were any left. If I was getting in trouble, it would be with a belly full of brownies. They were the best brownies! Almost hot enough to burn the mouth but not quite, super chocolatey, and still a wee bit gooey in the center.

A few seconds later, Joy led Aunt Shirley into the room and held her arm out to us as if to say, "See?"

Aunt Shirley stood there glancing over her glasses at us. Her coiffed beehive bobbed as she leaned down to ash her cigarette in one of the ashtrays scattered throughout the house. I was sitting with my hands folded between my knees trying to look innocent, but pretty certain there was chocolate smeared across my face. The other kids, having finished off the brownies, were back to watching the movie.

Aunt Shirley held her cigarette out, her thumb under her jaw as she tapped the side of her mouth with her pinkie, looking like she was figuring out a math problem. Taking another drag, she blew out the smoke, then leaned down to Joy.

"Okay," her gravely sweet voice sounded amused, "you're gonna have to be more specific about what everyone's doing wrong. Did they not offer you a brownie?"

Joy looked perplexed. "No, they ate the brownies. Weren't they supposed to be for dessert?"

Aunt Shirley stood back up and laughed. "Oh, is that all? I guess they had their dessert first and they won't get any after dinner." She strode back towards the kitchen still laughing and saying, "Goodness!"

Joy sat down, almost pouting. I thought about trying to cheer her up, but she had told on us. Plus, there was a movie to watch and I had a belly full of brownies.

On our flight back to Venezuela, Joy and I had seats together. We fell asleep, leaning against each other. About halfway through the flight, Joy woke me up. The entire cabin was dark because they had an inflight movie on. She had the little window screen pulled up just enough so we could look out but not bring in so much light that people watching the movie would get mad. She pointed out the window. I leaned over her and looked. I saw that we were flying high above the clouds. They looked so soft and comfy.

"I wish I had a bed made out of clouds," I whispered, my voice feeling dreamy.

She laughed quietly. "Then you would be laying on water. You do know that's what clouds are made of, don't you?"

Shaking myself more awake, I looked at her. "Of course I do. I was only saying if they were as comfy as they look, they would make a good bed. Much better than your shoulder, at least."

Her eyebrow shot up. "My shoulder is at least comfy enough for you to fall asleep and drool on."

I laughed. "Did I really drool on your shoulder?"

She nodded and pointed to an obvious wet spot on her sleeve where my face had been. I touched the corner of my mouth and my fingers came away wet.

"Yep, that's mine." Then stared past her out the window.

"Wow," her voice reeked with sarcasm. "Aren't you just the sweetest?"

I smiled wide and kissed her on the cheek. "Aw, that's nice! I'm glad you think so!"

She wiped her cheek. "I do not think so. I was being sarcastic."

"Oh!" I said, leaning back and feigning surprise. "You don't think I'm the sweetest?"

"No, I..." She stopped and narrowed her eyes at me. "You KNEW I was being sarcastic!" Then grinned the biggest grin. "You know Jeani, I think you're not such a baby anymore if you're getting nuances like that."

I rolled my eyes. "Whatever. I'm not as dumb as you think I am."

"I don't think you're dumb. I just think you sometimes miss the more subtle aspects of conversation."

I thought about that and decided she might be right. How often did people get frustrated with me when they had to explain things two or three times? How many times had Joy told me someone was being sarcastic when I thought they were being truthful? Did I ever know what people really meant? Was everyone making fun of me? Did I care? I paused my questioning thoughts and looked at Joy.

"You're right," I said. "I don't always understand sarcasm or stuff like that. But I don't really care if someone's making fun of me. I mean, if someone I don't know makes fun of me, I don't care. But if it's someone I like or love, it hurts my feelings or make me mad. Does that make sense?"

Joy laughed. "Whatever! You're such a sensitive softy, you'd probably cry if anyone really made fun of you."

I crossed my arms over my chest and sat back against my seat. I blinked my eyes, telling myself not to cry. "You're mean," I whispered.

I could feel her leaning towards me, but refused to look at her. She brushed my hair away from my ear and whispered, "You can't even stand to hear someone yell at their dog."

I flipped my head and yelled at her. "That is totally different! If someone yells at their dog, they're being super mean! I don't get sad, I get angry!"

I guess I was really loud 'cause all around us, people who

were watching the movie shouted and people who had been asleep woke up and added their shouts.

"Keep it down!"

"¡Cállate!"

"Shut your pie hole!"

I sunk into my seat and whispered, "Sorry."

Joy, who had also sunk down, whispered just loud enough for me to hear, "You're such an embarrassment."

I was so glad we were heading home.

22

Birthday Beater

Caracas, Venezuela

By October of 1983, the family had been living in Caracas for nine months. Both Joy and I had our own set of friends and it didn't seem like the family would be moving for a while. One Saturday morning, a few weeks before her thirteenth birthday, Joy made a declaration at the breakfast table. She said she was too old to share her birthday party with me.

"It's not fair that just because Jackie and Jessica's birthdays are at the opposite ends of the month, they don't have to share a party like Jeani and I do. I'm practically a teenager now. I should have my own party. Or at least a sleepover."

Jackie, who was sitting next to me smiling and humming as she ate her pancakes, turned to look at Joy. "I could never share a party with Jessica. She's still a baby!" As she whipped back around, she bumped her empty orange juice glass. It fell into my lap.

"Hey," I said, putting her cup back on the table. "Be more careful!"

"Sorry," she said.

I rolled my eyes and cut a big bite of pancake off, smearing it with syrup. Leaning my chin on my left hand, I scooped it into my mouth.

Jackie grinned and with a sing-songy voice said, "Jeani, Jeani, strong and able, get your elbows off the table!"

I got my elbows off the table and stuck my tongue out at her. She stuck hers out at me.

"Girls," Dad said in a warning voice. "If you keep that up, you're going to have to leave the table."

"Yes Daddy," Jackie sang and I mumbled. Grabbing the syrup, I up-ended it and squeezed.

Joy let out a long, deep sigh. "Am I invisible? Does anyone even hear me? Can I have a sleepover for my birthday or not?"

"We hear you," Mom muttered as she glared at me. "Jeani, that is way too much syrup!"

I stopped squeezing and looked at my plate. It looked like my pancakes were an island that was sinking into a sea of sticky golden goodness.

"You're going to have to eat all those pancakes and that lake of syrup," Dad said in his overly stern voice that suggested he was trying not to laugh. "We do not waste food in this household."

I nodded and started eating the syrup with a spoon. It was really sweet.

Mom, who was directly across the table from me, squinted. Her lips were pinched tight, like she too was trying to keep a giggle in. After taking a deep breath through her nose, she said, "I don't think so, young lady. It looks like you have enough syrup for at least one more pancake and you will not be eating that with a spoon."

"So I get another pancake? Thank you!" I picked up my fork and stabbed a pancake off of the dwindling stack and added it to the soggy ones on my plate.

Joy grunted. "See, this is what I'm talking about! Nobody pays attention to me."

I paused, my fork halfway between the plate and my mouth, syrup dripping on the table.

"No matter what I'm talking about or doing," she pointed at me, "she'll interrupt me or do something so you have to pay all your attention to her or," she pointed at Jackie who had stopped humming, "her or," she pointed at the baby who was now crying, "her! It's like 'cause I'm the only good kid, you never even notice me."

I tilted my head. "But I thought you were practically a teenager."

"Shut up," she snarled.

Mom, who was now standing and bouncing the baby on her hip, looked at Dad. He stared at Joy, his fingers interlaced, his elbows pressing into the table.

Jackie, unable to stop herself, whispered, "Daddy, Daddy, strong and able..."

"Uh-uh," Mom warned. "Not now, Jackie."

Dad's focus hadn't wavered from Joy who was now standing stiff. "Young lady." His voice was calm and even, causing Joy to slowly sink down into her seat, her back still ridged. "I will not tolerate such an outburst at the breakfast table. You can go to your room right now."

With a loud screeching sound, Joy pushed her chair from the table and ran to her bedroom, crying. Jackie and I went back to eating our pancakes as Mom and Dad talked in low tones.

"Maybe we can let her have a sleepover," Mom said, putting the baby back in the highchair. "She could have a few friends from church and school for her birthday."

"I don't think we should reward this behavior," Dad said.

Mom, cut a few more pieces of pancake for Jessica and nodded. "I know. But she's right. She's rarely the one getting into trouble and I think it would be good for us to celebrate that."

I was licking the rest of the syrup off my plate while Mom

and Dad were distracted. Jackie said, "Mom, Jeani just licked her plate!"

"Jeani!" Mom snapped. "You are excused from the table. Since it's your day to do dishes, clear the table. You better wipe it really clean since you got syrup on it." She pointed at a few spots where my fork had dripped.

"Yes ma'am," I sighed. Then, when her back was turned, I glared at Jackie who stuck out her tongue and wrinkled her nose at me.

It was a few days later before my parents told Joy she could have her birthday party sleepover. She was so excited, she invited every girl she was friends with. The party was set for a couple of weeks later, just before her birthday.

The day before the party, the two of us were hanging out in the carpeted downstairs family room. I was looking out the window to the car-park area. Joy was going on and on about her party.

"And I get to make the cake!" Joy announced. She and Mom had been working on her baking and cooking skills.

I looked at her from where I was laying on the floor coloring and set down the crayon. I rolled onto my side to look at her. "What kind of cake?"

"German chocolate," she said.

In unison, we said, "My favorite!"

She glared at me. "It's only your favorite 'cause it's my favorite."

She wasn't wrong, but I wasn't going to tell her that. I shook my head. "I love chocolate so it can be my favorite too!"

"Whatever. I guess you can have some. Anyhow, Mom said if I get the batter ready before they get home, she'll help me put it in the oven. That way, it can cool overnight and we can frost it in the morning. Do you want to help me make the cake?"

I sat up. It was so rare for Joy to voluntarily let me help her, I forgot I hated baking. "YES!" I shouted. "Will I get to lick a beater?"

She nodded. I smiled wide. Cake dough was my favorite. We raced each other upstairs.

Joy was, of course, very bossy. If I hadn't had the promise of a beater, I would have stopped helping. She read the list of ingredients while I climbed onto the counters and got everything including the mixer and the mixing bowl from the cabinets. She had me line the ingredients up and pass them to her while she very carefully measured everything out. She had only ever used the mixer under Mom's supervision, but she had gotten permission to plug it in and mix it all together as long as she was very, very careful. Once she was done, she stuck her finger in the batter and ate a glob.

"Perfect!" She said, sitting on one of the chairs next to the counter. She looked at the clock on the wall by the fridge.

"Mom and Dad should be home soon." Then she just sat there.

"You said I get a beater," I told her after she hadn't moved for almost a minute.

She looked at me and grinned. "Oh yeah!"

She picked up the mixer and pulled at one of the beaters as she pushed the release button with her opposite thumb. But her finger bumped the start and the mixer burst to life. She screamed, falling out of the chair, yanking the cord out of the wall. She lay on the floor crying. Her right hand was still gripping the handle of the mixer as a finger on the other hand was twisted through the blades of the beater. I stared, unable to move.

Having just arrived home, Mom and Dad heard me shouting from the kitchen all the way out to the car-park and rushed in the house. Mom got to the kitchen first. Her eyes widened as much as I felt mine were. "John!" She shouted. "Get in here!"

They rushed Joy to the hospital with the beater still attached to her finger. They had to cut through the beater blades to get her finger out. The finger wasn't broken, just sprained. When she got home, it was wrapped in a splint.

"Does it hurt?" I asked that night as we lay in bed.

"What do you think?" She snapped. "If you hadn't been so eager for the beater, this wouldn't have happened! Mom

MY SWAN SONG FOR JOY

had to call everyone and move my party to next week because of you." She rolled over and faced the wall.

I felt bad, but her words stung. I hadn't meant for her to get hurt. "Well, maybe if you had unplugged it, your finger wouldn't have gotten caught." Then very quietly I whispered, "It wasn't my fault." I rolled over and faced the other wall.

But I felt bad. Maybe she was right. Maybe it was my fault. I tossed and turned until I was staring at her on the other bed. She had gotten some pain meds, so she was already asleep. She was laying on her back with her arm dangling over the edge of the bed. I lay in the dark, staring at her splinted fingers.

"I'm really sorry, Joy," I whispered, as I drifted off to sleep. I wished that I could take away her pain and take her place, but I couldn't. So I prayed for her and thanked God that her finger hadn't been broken or fallen off.

23

The Problem with Favorites

Caracas, Venezuela

In Caracas, Joy and I shared a bedroom. Her side of the room was always tidy and clean. Mine wasn't unclean, but it wasn't orderly either. I had piles. Piles of clothes I hadn't put away, piles of stuffed animals, piles of random school supplies leaning against the desk, and the constantly growing stacks of books, notebooks, and drawing pads. Her bed was always made the right way with military precision while mine, even when it was made, never had that tightness. The only times it was ever made at all was because Joy threatened to tell on me if I didn't do it right, or if Mom saw and I got in trouble and had to remake it. I would hide my piles of things in closets and under furniture if I could get away with it. It drove my tidy Mom and fastidious older sister loony.

Truth be told, I'm the same as an adult. I confine most of my piles to my bedroom (usually), though there are almost always a few bags with things for events, piles of books, notebooks, drawing pads, and stashed socks throughout the house, much to Bek's chagrin.

One time, when Joy was particularly irritated about my stuff creeping onto her side of the room while I was doing nothing more than laying on my bed reading, she started throwing my stuffed animals at me.

"Why do you need all these different animals?" she shouted. "Just pick one!"

Dodging the monkey she'd aimed at my head, I stared at her. "Why do I have to pick one?"

She held my fluffy dog aloft but didn't throw it. A contemplative look slid over her face as her arm lowered.

"Because," she said, her words sliding out slow with her thoughts. "If you have one specific animal, or even two... I guess two's okay. It shows a bit of who you are."

I moved to the edge of my bed and dangled my feet. "What do you mean?"

She sat down on her bed facing me, tossed my dog toy to me, and folded her legs under her. She had this look, a look she often got when she explained things to me. She'd have one side of her mouth squeezed, that eye slightly closed, and her head tilted. It was a combination of suspicion that I might be trying to trick her, because she was always trying to trick me, and contained delight for the chance to display her knowledge. "Well, each animal shows things about a person and when others see what animal you like, they know a little about you that you don't have to explain. It's like symbolism in books. I don't know if you've gotten to that in your Literature classes yet."

We had, but I wanted her to keep talking, so I said, "Only a little."

She nodded. Sitting up a little straighter, she took on a teacherly air. "Let's take your monkey for example. Remember that kid we knew in Judebana who really liked Orangutans?"

I nodded, grinning. That kid was awesome! He wanted to be an orangutan when he grew up so he was always practicing climbing trees and swinging from branches and all sorts of weird orangutan habits. I didn't even remember his name since I just called him Orangutan Boy, though I pronounced it orang-a-tang to rhyme with fang. He said I could become an orangutan with him because I was so good at climbing trees and things. I told him I'd much rather be a chimpanzee since they're funnier. Then we'd chase each other making monkey noises and pretended to eat bugs out of each other's hair. Because of him, I'd started reading about all sorts of primates and learning about Jane Goodall who became one of my all time heroes.

"So his personality is like an orangutan, right? He likes to be in trees and he's happiest when he's alone doing his own thing and he makes stupid noises all the time."

"They're also really smart," I said, remembering how Orangutan Boy would tell me about how the orangutans were the most intelligent of all the primates and probably even smarter than humans but we're too stupid to realize it.

"Maybe," she said, "but the point is he reflects a lot of the orangutan through his personality. Do you get it?"

I shook my head. "I mean, I see what you're saying about him. I understand why that's his favorite animal but I don't understand why I can't have more than one or two."

She gave an exasperated grunt. "Cause if you do, they're not favorites! It's not how it works." She stood up and started pacing back and forth in our cramped room. She stopped and pointed at me. "Okay, okay, okay... So it's like me and swans. I like them because they're beautiful and they're really smart birds. They're name is even beautiful, swan in English and cisne in spanish. It sounds like how they are, soft and flowing." She looked dreamy and smiled, "Swan... Also, they swim really well like I do and they can fly, which I can't do but I would like to. They also sing, which I do too, though I sound better than any swan, and they are fiercely loyal to their swan family."

"They also walk funny and can be really, really mean." I tilted my head looking at her. "Well, you're like them in that way too."

Joy threw a pillow at me. I ducked, laughing.

"Whatever. I'm like a swan and a swan's like me. What animal are you most like? Once you figure that out, then you'll have your favorite."

I shook my head. "I don't think that's how favorites work. I can have a favorite of something that's just something I really like, but it doesn't have to be like me. Example... chocolate. It just tastes really good. Also, panthers are like my favorite cats. I love their black fur, that they can see at night, that they're really sneaky, that they move like water, and they have a fearsome growl. I'm noisy and can't see in the dark and my hair is brown and I trip over things all the time."

Joy gave a satisfied smirk. "That settles it, then. Panthers are your favorite animal."

I shook my head. "No! They're my favorite wild cat. I also love crows and hyenas, and all sorts of monkeys and jellyfish and octopuses... or is it octopi? Doesn't matter, I love them. Cephalopods in general are really cool. Also, it's a fun word. CE-PHA-LO-POD." I sighed. "Oh and hummingbirds! I love how fast they are and how they're almost always moving, even when they're still and how sitting on our porch has helped me find how to be still since if I move too much, they won't come get the nectar from the flowers and I will only be able to see them through the window. They're really cool when you sit still and they fly at your face. And I like bugs, especially fireflies. It's so cool how they can make light with their butts and I like dogs and cats and I think I like bunny rabbits, but I've never met one."

She laughed. "You've never met a hyena or a crow either."

I squinted. "You're right. But I really liked the pictures in a book we were reading at school. It was really cool reading about them. They're so weird! Also cockroaches are cool."

Joy made a grossed-out face.

"I know, hardly nobody likes them, but I do and a friend of mine does and it's fun to chase them, especially the really big ones." Venezuela had the biggest ones I had ever seen. I paused, studying her. "Don't you like other animals besides swans?"

She rolled her eyes. "Of course I do! They're just not all my favorite. Like colors. My favorite color is blue. I have no problem telling people that. But whenever anyone asks you what your favorite color is, you just get a weird look on your face and say things like, I like black and red and green and purple and blue... and you just list all the colors."

"I do not! Orange and yellow are not, and will never be, my favorites. I also only sometimes think green is my favorite. Usually it's clear, black, purple, red, blue and in that order... sometimes."

Joy glared at me. "Clear isn't a color."

"It can be!"

She squinted. "No, it can't."

"Whatever." I flopped on my bed.

"Anyhow, you can't even pick a favorite food. I know mine is spaghetti and meatballs."

"And sometimes pancakes."

She shook her head. "That's a different type of food. I was meaning dinner."

I crossed my arms. "I don't think everyone has to have favorites. I think some people, like me, don't. Or, our favorites change. Oooo, I like gazelles too! It's a fun word to say! Gazzzzzzzzelle..."

Joy snorted.

"So, why does it bother you that I don't have a favorite?"

Joy gave me a thoughtful look. "Well," she said slowly. "I guess, it makes it harder to figure out who you are."

I shrugged. "I don't know who I am. I mean, I'm Jeani, but I don't know what I'm gonna be when I'm a grownup. But I think that's okay. I know what you're going to be when you grow up."

"Oh?" She tilted her head. "What am I gonna be?"

"Bossy!" I laughed and grabbed my pillow to defend myself as she ran at me with her pillow. "Stop! Stop!" I squealed, my arms and my pillow over my head as she pummeled me with hers.

She fell on my bed beside me, giggling. Her elbow poked my arm as she turned her head to look at me. "You're hopeless."

I nodded, tucking up my knees and lying on my side facing her. "Hopeless," I agreed.

24

Dinner Interrupted

∞

Caracas, Venezuela

On the evening before Jackie's sixth birthday, the family had just sat down to dinner when the phone rang. Dad paused in saying Grace for the briefest of moments, then finished up and we started eating. Our family had a "no distractions at the table during meals" rule. There was one exception–emergencies. The phone rang a few times before the answering machine picked up.

Dad's baritone voice was loud and clear in the recording. "Thank you for calling the Vaughn household; we cannot get to the phone right now. Please leave a message at the beep. God bless you."

As it beeped, Joy whispered just loud enough for me to hear, "But nobody sneezed!" And we giggled.

Mom waved a hand to shush us as the machine began to record. "Johnny? Are you there? It's me, your sister Elizabeth and..."

Hearing 'Johnny', Dad had sprung from his seat and grabbed the phone. "Liz? What happened? Is everyone alright?" He paused, listening. Aunt Liz was Dad's older sister. All of his six siblings were older than him as he was the oops baby, being 10 years younger than his brother Clarence, the next one up. His sisters were all quite a bit older and motherly towards him since they had helped raise him. For any of them to call us in Venezuela meant big, and most likely bad, news.

His back was to us so we couldn't see his face, but his shoulders slumped. "Oh," his voice had gotten small and boyish. "Oh I see. Okay. You'll let us know when the funeral is?" He nodded at the phone. "Uh-huh." He threw the hand not holding the phone into the air as his tone became exasperated. "Of course we'll be there! How could we not? At least, I will." Another pause. "Yes ma'am, you're right, I'm sorry. I just..." He fell silent again, nodding and listening.

Except for Jessica, all of us were practically frozen, staring at Dad's back. We all knew something was wrong. It was rare to hear his voice get so small.

Pulling my gaze away, I looked around the table. I took in Joy with her empty fork near her mouth as she chewed in slow motion, Jackie looking like she was about to cry, and

Mom's bright green eyes wide behind her glasses. She had a forkful of green beans halfway to her mouth that was drifting slowly down to the plate, her mouth still hanging open. Then the baby laughed and clapped with hands covered in mashed potatoes, breaking the spell as potato bits flew across the table. Dad hung up the phone, and turned to us. His face was red. He opened his mouth like he was going to say something, then strode out of the room. Mom dropped her fork and ran after him. Joy and I looked at each other.

"Dad looked really upset," I said in astonishment. Joy nodded, as shocked as I was. Our Dad could be very stern and very silly, but he rarely showed true emotions. Being an engineer who had served in the Army, it just wasn't logical or practical. Plus, there was the whole "real men don't cry" ideology that he was brought up with.

"Bu-but they didn't even ask to be excused from the table!" Jackie started blubbering. "And who's having a funeral? A-and what about my party?" She was now wailing, tears streaming down her freckled face.

Joy and I looked at her, unsure of what to do. She'd had the good fortune to have her sixth birthday fall on a Saturday so a party was planned on her birthday. Just before Dad saying grace and the call coming in, she had been regaling us with the list of friends who were coming to her party and guessing what presents they would bring.

Joy, being the oldest, snapped into bossy sister mode. "Stop that. There's nothing to cry about. We don't know who died, so we're not going to speculate or be sad yet.

Also, they're adults, they don't have to ask to be excused. Now finish up your dinner."

"Bu-bu-but my party..." Jackie hiccuped, still crying.

"Stop crying. Your party will happen. There will be so much cake and ice cream and I even heard that there's going to be two surprise guests!" Joy announced. To emphasize her point, I made a goofy, questioning face, touching my finger to my mouth and tilting my head as if to silently ask, "Who could it be?" while making silly noises until Jackie was giggling.

Mom came back into the room looking sad. "Girls, I have some very upsetting news. Your grandmother died today. Your dad and I are figuring out what we should do. Once we know when the funeral is, your Dad at least will go. If we can figure out how to afford it, the entire family will join him."

Unable to stop herself, Jackie blurted out, "But what about my birthday?" She went full-on waterworks as Mom hurried over to hug her. "I-I'm sorry, Mommy! I'm not trying to be selfish! I-I just want to have a good party! Bu-but now Grandma died and I-I'm so so sad! And..."

"Shhhhh, sweetie!" Mom whispered, holding Jackie to her chest and rocking her. "I'm so sorry, but we're going to have to postpone your party."

Jackie cried louder and Jessica started crying too. Mom gave a meaningful glance at Joy who picked up Jessica. She bounced her on her hip, talking silly to her. I didn't know what to do, so I went back to eating. When Jackie glanced over at me, I made a face at her and she laughed.

Mom looked at me, but instead of telling me to stop like usual, she nodded gratefully. I watched her face and could see an idea forming. She leaned back from Jackie then put her face on Jackie's level so their noses were almost touching. "I just had a great idea!" She set Jackie down, then stood up and announced. "Let's have ice cream!" She walked into the kitchen and began gathering bowls and spoons. "I'm even going to extend all of your bedtimes to 10 pm! What do you think about that?"

Joy and I exchanged a look. We never got dessert without finishing all of our dinner and clearing the table and...

"Jeani," Mom said as she came in with the dishes. "Please clear the table." Joy smirked since she was still holding Jessica. "And Joy, start Jessica's bath." Before Jessica could get upset, she added, "Jessica, once you're bathed and in your nightgown, you can come back down for ice cream. Jackie, I want you to get all the ice cream toppings and put them on the table, okay?"

Jackie clapped and trotted into the kitchen. I cleared and wiped the table as quickly as I could. Jackie dumped all the ice cream toppings on the table, then arranged them as I set out the bowls and spoons. Joy came back in the room and got the huge tub of neapolitan ice cream out of the freezer. A few seconds later, Jessica comes tottering in wearing a pink nightgown. As we all sat around the table, Dad came downstairs.

"Where's your Mom?" We looked at each other and

shrugged. The phone rang. Dad went to get it from its cradle in the kitchen, but stopped halfway, remembering he'd left it up in the bedroom. He headed out into the family room to go upstairs.

Mom, who had been in the dining room using the other telephone, came into the kitchen holding a yellow memo pad that had a list of names on it and called up after him. "Liz is on the phone!" She saw us at the breakfast table with the ice cream and toppings. "Y'all go ahead and eat." Realizing we didn't have the ice cream scoop, she got it out of the drawer and handed it to Jackie.

"Me?" Asked Jackie. Mom nodded and we watched as Jackie dug into the ice cream with intense delight.

Mom motioned for Joy and I to follow her into the dimly lit dining room. "I don't think your dad and I will be joining you. Please clean up after you're done. Joy, you're in charge of making sure everyone gets to bed by 10 pm, okay?" Joy nodded. "No goofing around, okay?" We both nodded. Her serious face broke into a grin as she leaned in, whispering, "Save that for when you're clowns."

We grinned back.

Dad walked back into the kitchen calling, "Honey?"

"In here," Mom called. She turned to us. "Go get some ice cream, okay?"

"You don't have to tell me twice," I joked as we left the room. Joy punched my shoulder. "Ow! Why'd you do that?"

Joy rolled her eyes. "You're just so..." she shook her head and started serving herself some ice cream.

I rubbed my shoulder, wanting to know what I was just so. But Mom was always telling me to just drop it, so I did and got myself a heaping bowl of ice cream.

A few seconds later, Dad came over to us and motioned for Joy and I to follow him into the dining room. Joy followed obediently, abandoning her bowl of ice cream. I took my bowl with me. He had us sit at the table opposite of him and Mom.

"I just got news from your Aunt Liz that the funeral will be on Monday, February 27th, this coming Monday. Your Mom and I have talked about it and, while we would like for the whole family to go, we decided that the two of you are showing some great maturity and could decide for yourselves. It will be one of the quickest trips to the states we've ever taken. We'll leave tomorrow afternoon then turn around and come back in only a couple of days. We will have to start packing early in the morning if we decide..."

"I want to go," Joy announced. "Sorry I interrupted you, Daddy. But Grandma is the only grandparent we had left alive. I think we should all go."

I nodded. "I wanna go too."

Mom and Dad exchanged a smile, then Mom said, "Okay, it's settled. Now go eat your ice cream and head to bed. Tomorrow morning we'll be getting up super early and I don't want any grumbling grouses."

Jackie's birthday party was postponed until after the trip. Mom had already been calling all of Jackie's friends' parents that night. Jackie was sad, but when we got to the States, she got attention from our relatives about her birthday. Then, when she shared the sad story of having to cancel her party, everyone was so sympathetic. She even got a few gifts.

25

Grandma Vaughn's Funeral

Birmingham, Alabama

Dad's Mom died of Alzheimers at 81 years old. Her obituary:

"Mrs. Mary Elizabeth Vaughn, 81, of Birmingham, died Friday (February 24, 1984). She was a member of Avondale United Methodist Church and the Women's Christian Temperance Union. Funeral will be at 11 a.m. Monday (February 27, 1984) at Roebuck Chapel with burial in Forest Hill Cemetery.

Survivors include two daughters, Mrs. Elizabeth Davis,

Birmingham, and Mrs. Mary Louise Mardis, Tallahassee, Fla.; four sons, Charles L. Vaughn, Spring Hill, Fla., Marion W. Vaughn, Athens, Clarence N. Vaughn, Houston, Texas, and John E. Vaughn, Caracas, Venezuela; three brothers, Charles A. Rice Jr., Norfolk, Va., Raymond O. Rice, Miami, Fla., and Ernest Rice, Maxeys, Ga., and three sisters, Mrs. Kathleen R. Simmons, Forest Park, Ga., Mrs. Ludie R. Wright. Little Rock, Ark., and Mrs. Margaret R. Pierce, Lawrenceville, Ga. The family suggests any memorial be made to the church or the Alzheimer Association."

Joy was sitting next to me in the pew as we listened to the minister speak over our grandmother's body. She was lying in a dark wooden coffin in front of the pulpit. He had a very monotonous voice. The church only had a few stained glass, and a lower ceiling than most cathedrals. Still, his deep voice resonated and echoed. I was sleepy from the trip and his words kept blurring together. Even though Joy and I had slept on the plane, we had been up past midnight helping Mom and Dad pack. We agreed to pinch each other if we noticed the other nodding off. Dad was sitting next to the aisle, Mom was next to him with Jessica on her lap, Joy was next to her, then me, and Jackie. I was pretty sure Jackie wasn't going to fall asleep since she kept crying. I was sad too, but Jackie was a very sensitive soul. I gave her a hug and she cried harder. I glanced down the aisle at Mom, but she was crying too. Past her, I saw Dad silently weeping. I nudged Joy.

Her body jerked as she whispered, "I wasn't asleep."

Looking at her, I shook my head and pointed with my chin at Dad. "Dad's crying."

She turned and looked. It was the first time we had ever seen Dad cry. I found it so beautiful.

I don't remember much more from the trip since it was such a short one. There was a dinner where everyone got to tell stories about a grandmother I barely knew. I laughed at some of the funny ones – her not finding the glasses she was walking around with on her head, her sweeping her husband into a corner when he came home late (the humor of that tale lay in her being only about four feet tall and him being over six feet), the time she got her children confused – but I had none to contribute. I sat silent and sad as they talked about her mental decline, wondering if it would happen to my parents since my grandmother Seay had died of Alzheimer's too.

The night before we flew back to Caracas, Joy and I were lying on a pullout bed from an unfamiliar couch at a relative's house. I was trying to stay very still as I tend to thrash around in my sleep and I didn't want to wake Joy. But the house had strange noises and, even though I was tired, I just couldn't get to sleep. I was glad Joy was next to me.

"You awake?" Joy whispered.

Staring into the dark, I nodded with an uh-huh.

"I thought so," she snickered. "You were too still; it was

kinda freakin' me out." We both giggled, then she got serious. "What do you think it's like to die?"

"Well you go to heaven," I said without any thought.

"Well yeah," she sighed. "But what's heaven like?"

"There are streets of gold and little angels playing harps and God talks to you and everyone at the sametime 'cause he's God and... I don't know. Really yummy food?"

Joy laughed. "You're always thinking about food!"

"I am not!" I frowned. "I think about other things too like dogs and monkeys and this story I'm working on about Sam Nav the greatest detective who isn't the greatest detective but thinks she is and she's always getting in trouble like me. But there's nothing wrong with thinking about food. I like eating. You know, you die if you don't eat." I could feel Joy rolling her eyes, but I was pretty sure she was grinning, so I kept going. "Also, did you know that 100% of deaths are caused by not breathing?"

Joy laughed. "Stop it!" She commanded in a whisper, smacking my arm. "You're being disrespectful."

"How is knowing things ever disrespectful?"

From the other side of Joy, we heard Jackie make a sound. We both giggled. Jackie started speaking in Spanish. Joy turned towards her to hear better as I leaned over Joy's shoulder.

"No toca... muñeca..." were the only words we could understand.

"Don't touch doll?" I asked.

"Shhhhh!" Joy hissed. "You're gonna wake her up!"

"Shhhhh!" I hissed back. "YOU'RE gonna wake her up!"

"You're BOTH gonna wake me up!" Jackie grumbled. The light from the moon shone through the sliding glass doors on the other side of the room and splashed across her sleepy face.

"Sorry, Jackie," Joy and I said simultaneously as we rolled away.

"No!" Jackie laughed, sitting up. "Please wake me up! When else do I get to hang out with my big sisters? What're you talking about?"

I snorted. "You were talking in your sleep in Spanish. You said don't touch doll?"

"Oh," Her mouth held that oh shape as she thought about what I said.

"Yeah, you're a weirdo," Joy said.

"Do you remember what else you were dreaming?" I asked.

She shook her head. "What else were you talking about?"

"Heaven," I said.

"I like heaven," Jackie said, in case we had any doubt. "I hope to go there."

"Oh you will," Joy said. "I'm not too sure about Jeani, though."

"Hey!" I said, punching her in the shoulder.

"Ow!" Joy rubbed her arm. "Not with that attitude, you won't."

"Yes I will," I stated. "I accepted Jesus into my heart as my Lord and Savior, so no matter what I do, I have to go to heaven." I nodded into the dark. "Still, I wonder what Hell's like. I mean, I don't want to go there to stay, or anything. But it might be interesting to visit, just to see."

"You really shouldn't say that," Joy warned. "If you go to Hell, the Devil will keep you. So, don't say things like that."

"Yeah," said Jackie.

"I was just curious," I sighed.

"Curiosity is what got Adam and Eve in trouble, remember that," Joy said as she lay back down. "Now it's time to go to sleep."

"Yeah," said Jackie, also laying back on her pillow.

"But why?" I asked, still sitting up and too wide awake to go back to sleep. "Why would God, in all his infinite wisdom, make us curious but make curiosity a bad thing?"

Both Joy and Jackie were silent for a minute. Then Joy said, "Maybe you need to read your Bible more. I bet you can find your answer there. If you don't, I guess... ask? But don't ask me. Goodnight."

"Goo'night," Jackie, who was already falling asleep, mumbled.

I lay back down and turned on my side to face away from them. Out the window, a cloud drifted across the moon. I lay awake as the room went entirely dark. I decided that night I would do just what Joy said. I would read my entire Bible, cover to cover and take notes. Then, when I was done, I would ask the adults all the questions the Bible didn't answer.

"Thanks Joy," I whispered, knowing she wouldn't hear me since she was already sleep breathing. "G'night."

Jackie, fully asleep, mumbled something back to me and I stifled a giggle.

26

When We were Clowns

∽∞∽

Caracas, Venezuela

Even though my family lived in Venezuela for over five years, it never really became home. Our time there was regularly broken up with trips back to the states and most of our associations were with other expats, families of diplomats, and missionaries. But the trips back to the states were often hurried and brief.

In 1984, after attending our grandmother's funeral in Alabama, we did a quick turnaround and flew back to Caracas after only a few days. Once we were back, all six of us (or five since the baby didn't do much) focused on preparations for Jackie's birthday party that had been postponed due to the trip. Although we had cleaned the week before we left, the entire house was cleaned again, top to bottom. Even the little fenced in front yard with the mango tree and the run-down playhouse, was given a good tidying up. We decorated the house with tons of balloons and streamers and a banner that read, "Happy Birthday!" across the white brick fireplace we never used. I thought it was weird to have since it never got below 70° in Caracas. Outside, Dad put up some Christmas lights that thrilled Jackie to no end.

The day of the party, there were screaming six year olds everywhere. They all wore pretty dresses and suits since Jackie insisted on a fancy party. After the last kid had arrived, Joy and I disappeared into our room.

I removed my dress with such glee, Joy laughed. I put on Dad's old pants with suspenders, a crazy patterned shirt, and shoes he no longer used because the sole had worn through. Since the shoes were too big, I put on three pairs of socks and stuffed another pair into the toe of the shoes. It was going to be hot, but at least I wouldn't lose my shoes. Joy had gotten a flowered yellow dress that Mom no longer wore and combined it with an old plaid vest of Dad's that clashed. She had gotten some discarded high heeled shoes from one of the ladies at the church and wore two pairs of unmatched socks to keep them on. She had one of our oversized dress-up play purses. Then we snuck over to our parents' bathroom.

Mom had given us free range to use the make-up on the counter. Joy and I moved the make-up to the middle of the counter and climbed up. At eleven and thirteen, we were probably too big to be sitting on the counter, but we didn't care. Since we were in a hurry, we tried to put make-up on each other at the same time to save time, but we kept laughing and poking each other.

"I think we have to do it one at a time," I said.

"I think we have to do our own make-up," Joy stated. "Otherwise, we're going to take too long." Her giant crooked mouth made me giggle.

"I did your lips good!" I laughed.

"Well. You did my lips well," Joy corrected.

I stuck my tongue out at her, then we both got down to the business of putting on make-up. We had some practice from when we had been hired as clowns to earn money for the trip we took to the States alone, but we had always arrived at the parties with our make-up on. Joy had been the one to put make-up on both of us since she had a better understanding of make-up basics from the teen magazines her friends from back home in Texas sent her. So I smeared some blush while watching her carefully apply blue eyeshadow out of the corner of my eye. After a few seconds, I got a green eyeshadow and circled my left eye with it, then found an orange one and did the same to my right eye. She had very carefully used the eyeliner to outline her eyes even bigger than they were and draw on huge eyelashes. On my face, I drew a heart, a diamond, a club, and a spade.

"What're those supposed to be?" She asked, pointing to the club and the spade.

I pointed to the heart and the diamond. "They're from

cards, see?" I pointed to each in turn. "Heart, diamond, and that's a spade I think, and the other one. Is it a clover?" I could never remember what a club was called.

"Huh," she grinned. "Cute!"

She teased my hair and added lots and lots of hairspray so it stuck out from my head. I added blush to it so my mousy brown hair was kind of red. She braided her hair into two braids that hung over her shoulders. Seeing what I did, she added mascara to her brown hair to look like polka dots and added polka dots to her face. We hopped off of the counter, cleaned up the mess and Joy put the makeup in its carrying case to do some 'face painting' with the kids. Then we stood back to analyze our handiwork.

"Not bad," Joy said, putting her arm over my shoulder. "We make pretty good clowns."

I smiled, putting my arm over her shoulder. "We make great clowns!" I grabbed my yellow oversized sunglasses and put them on.

Joy and I snuck into the kitchen to get the rest of our supplies. I had stashed a whistle, candy, and a few decks of cards in one of the kitchen cabinets. I put the whistle around my neck, shoved the cards and candy into one of my pockets, then grabbed the stack of what I called my 'talking cards' off the counter and put them in the other pocket. I was a big fan of the Marx brothers and had decided my clown character didn't talk, like Harpo, who was my favorite, but I wanted to be able to still express myself. So I had made five cards that read NO, YES, MAYBE, YOU'RE BEAUTIFUL!, and the last just had a bunch of question marks all over it. We had stored water balloons in the vegetable drawer of the fridge earlier that morning. We got them out and carefully loaded them into Joy's large red handbag.

Mom was in the kitchen putting the finishing touches on Jackie's cake. She turned to us and smiled. "Y'all look great! You ready?"

Joy nodded. I held up my Yes card.

As we waited in the kitchen, she had all the kids assemble in the living room. Dad had moved the furniture to the walls so the kids could sit on the rug. He was the videographer of the party. Mom wasn't one for being up in front of a crowd, but had agreed to announce us. Joy and I could hear her from the kitchen.

"Ladies and Gentlemen, boys and girls, I am excited to announce that the two mystery guests have arrived!"

We heard the kids murmuring with excitement and Jackie's squeal was followed by a squeal from Jessica. Joy and I giggled.

"Please join me in a round of applause for Polkadot and Harper!"

Joy pranced out of the kitchen laughing and throwing candy at the kids. I did a cartwheel and a handstand, then jumped around blowing my whistle and gathering the things that had fallen out of my pockets.

"Hello new friends!" Joy said in her high, squeaky Polkadot voice, as she threw another handful of candy. The kids were all laughing and diving for the candy. "My name is Polkadot and this is my friend Harper! He doesn't speak, but he makes noises." I honked then blew my whistle. "He also likes to do tricks and is super tricky so watch out for him! If you won't get in trouble for getting dirty and maybe wet, go outside and play with Harper. If you want your face painted, stay inside with me!"

I blew my whistle several times, made honking noises, and ushered the kids through the sliding glass doors. They laughed and ran outside. Before I joined them, I ran over to Polkadot.

"Yes?" She asked, fluttering her eyelashes at me.

I held up the card that read, YOU'RE BEAUTIFUL, showing it to her, then the audience.

"Why thank you!" She gushed and turned to the kids saying, "Isn't Harper the sweetest?" I grabbed her purse and ran away laughing maniacally.

Polkadot stomped her foot and pretended to fume. "Oh, that Harper!"

Once outside, I blew my whistle and chased the kids, throwing water balloons from the purse at them. They squealed and ran. Most of my balloons hit the ground, only splashing them. One or two bounced instead of bursting. A boy grabbed one and threw it, hitting me in the face. As hot as it was, it should have been nice to cool off, but the impact hurt. I've never been much of a fan of balloons and the feel of it exploding against my cheek burned. Once the purse was empty, I ran back into the house to refill it.

But there was an ambush. Three of the kids tripped me and grabbed the purse. Fortunately, I landed on the rug. Unfortunately, I skidded across it on one knee. As they turned to take the purse to Joy, I ducked into the kitchen, a room they weren't allowed to go into.

From the other room, I could hear Joy talking in her high Polkadot voice. "Oh, thank you friends! That Harper is such a naughty clown. I'm glad you got my purse back."

Mom walked into the kitchen and found me sitting on the floor crying, but trying really hard not to. "Oh, did you hurt yourself?"

I held up the NO card.

"What happened?"

Dropping my Harper act, I told her about the water balloon and the tripping and showed her my rug burned knee. She got the first aid kit from the cabinet and bandaged it up. "You'll be fine." She grabbed a plastic bag from the stash in the laundry room that was right off the kitchen and held it out to me. "Here, you can use a grocery bag to carry the water balloons."

I nodded and thanked her. As I put balloons in the bag, I could hear Joy in the living room.

Polkadot was saying, "Oh, I don't know where Harper went. He might be hiding outside." A kid must've said something. "Well, that's true, but he is super sneaky. Did you check the playhouse or in the tree? He likes to climb that tree and eat the mangos! Go get him!"

I heard the kids run outside. Mom checked and saw only parents and the kids waiting to get their faces painted would possibly see me, then helped me sneak through the dining room. When I got outside, all of the kids were looking up into the limbs of the mango tree as one of the boys was trying to climb it. He wasn't having much success. I saw Jackie standing off to the side. When she saw me, I made a shushing motion. She grinned. I snuck up behind the group, crouching down so I was as short as them and looked up into the tree.

I knew the character I had created was supposed to be silent, but the gag wouldn't work as well with a card or a whistle or anything like that. So I said really loud in my deepest voice, "What are we looking at?"

Two of the kids jumped and one screamed. Jackie laughed and clapped her hands. I threw back my head and cackled, then chased them and threw my water balloons as I ran. The rest of the day was filled with more shenanigans, cake, and finally, to Jackie's delight, presents. The party, despite neither Mom nor Dad feeling very festive, was a great success.

That night, after Jackie and Jessica had gone to bed and Joy and I had removed all our clown-ness, Mom and Dad asked us to sit at the kitchen table with them. We were both exhausted and just wanted to go to bed, but we complied. They gave us each twenty bolivars for our performance even though we had been doing it as a present for Jackie. When we tried to refuse, Dad shook his head.

"You deserve it. You both kept those kids entertained when your mom and I were not at our best." He and Mom gave each of us a hug.

"We are very blessed to have the two of you," Mom said.

Joy, in her most Polkadot voice, replied, "we are the luckiest clowns to have such great parents!"

I made a honking noise, then laughed as I nodded rapidly in agreement.

27

Hansel and Gretel

∽

Caracas, Venezuela

In 1984, Escuela Campo Alegre announced that it would be putting on a production of Hansel and Gretel. Anyone who wanted to try out, from second to eighth grade, was allowed to do so. But since it was a musical, anyone who was in choir was expected to audition. Other kids who wanted to be in the show but didn't get cast, could be the cookie children that Hansel and Gretel freed from the witch at the end. They had one line at the end, "Thank you, Hansel and Gretel!"

The director divvied up the roles so that the main ones went to the Jr. High students, while the chorus went to the elementary students. Kindergarteners, first graders, and

High Schoolers didn't get to be in the show. The High School students had their own show and the kindergarteners and first graders were deemed too young.

Joy was in seventh grade at the time. I don't know how auditioning went for her, but in choir it was sprung on us. We had been learning the songs from the play without knowing that's what they were from. Then one day, as we were sitting in our homeroom class, our choir teacher came in and announced that if we had choir, we would be auditioning that day.

In my fifth grade homeroom, the entire class buzzed as we chattered about the auditions. Ms. Mafia, our teacher, stood at the front of the classroom clapping her hands, her sculpted black eyebrows pushing wrinkles up her usually smooth forehead into her coiffed blonde hair. She was young, in her twenties, and had made the mistake of confessing to the class that she had never taught above a third grade level. Any normal class might've taken pity on her. But ours was no normal class. She had started two weeks into the semester and her class was cobbled together from the two other classes that had been bursting at the seams. Other than my small group of friends and one or two other students, the rest of the class was populated with the kids who had already been sent to the principal's office at least once and most were already serving time in detention. She had been there a month and was still having trouble. A huge spitball hit the chalkboard just past her head, causing her to jump and the class to erupt with laughter.

"She's lost them already," Lara whispered, leaning across

the aisle so Saromi and I could hear her. We both sighed and nodded.

George, a kid from Germany who sat behind Lara and had a crush on her, was always trying to be part of our conversation. He said in his booming, heavily accented, voice, "is just sticky!"

Saromi giggled. One of the troublemaker boys punched George in his shoulder. He was trying not to laugh, but not doing a very good job of it. George rubbed his shoulder and glared at him.

"What's sticky?" The kid gasped out, "your pants?" He dissolved into laughter.

I jumped out of my chair and whipped around shouting, "hey! Leave him alone, you bully!"

"Oooooo!" Another boy intoned. "Does George have a girlfriend?"

I wrinkled my nose and crossed my arms. "No!"

In a soft voice I could barely hear, George whispering, "stop it. You make it worse."

I huffed, then sat down, still fuming as the boys made kissing sounds at us.

A loud screech caused everyone to cringe and cover their ears. I looked at the front of the room and saw that Ms Mafia was clawing the chalkboard with her long, perfectly manicured, bright red nails.

Without shouting, but in a loud clear voice, she said, "If you do not shut up and sit down, I will do that again." All noise stopped and everyone sat down.

Coming around to the front of her desk where she perched with her ankles crossed, dangling her high heeled shoes. She smiled. "Good to know I can get your attention. Now, this tomfoolery of throwing spitballs and bullying will stop today. If it does not, you will not get to be in the play."

One of the boys at the back chuckled. But instead of getting flustered like she had previously, she held her left hand out in front of her, inspecting and wiping each nail with her right thumb, then did the same with the right hand, as if she was getting them ready for their next chalkboard scratch. I watched her, my fingers ready to shove into my ears if she moved back towards the blackboard. But she just stood there for a few minutes.

She smiled again. "As you know, nobody is required to be in the play. So those who don't audition, will be in here with me. Now I was planning to give everyone who didn't audition an extra recess. But if you're going to be awful, we can sit in silence, no reading, no talking, until auditions are over." She sat there staring at us for about thirty seconds, then clapped her hands together. "Okay! Choir kids, line up at the door. Once they've all lined up, anyone else who wants to audition, line up behind them."

After I was in line, I looked back at the classroom and realized everyone had lined up. I smiled at Ms. Mafia. She winked at me.

Since we had been practicing in choir, when we got the sheet music, we saw that the songs were all ones we had been practicing. I got cast as a dew girl. There were sixteen of us. Our part was to dance around the sleeping Hansel and Gretel and sing the Dew Girl song while we sprinkled them with dew drops. When they woke up, they would be refreshed and reinvigorated.

I was so excited! The whole ride home on the bus, I was chattering with my friend Lara who got cast as a dew girl with me. We had been asked to find out if our parents could help with the production. I was explaining that my mom was really good at sewing and would probably be willing to help with costumes. Lara told me that her mom was traveling, but her dad would probably be able to help.

When the bus got to my stop, I hugged Lara and we promised we'd make plans to get together and rehearse our song. It wasn't until I was stepping down from the bus, that I realized Joy had run ahead of me and was already taking the steps two at a time up to the front door. I hadn't even seen her get off the bus. I waited for Jackie to join me. As we walked from the bus stop to the door, I told her all about my audition.

She ran along beside me asking questions, and making lots of oohs and aahs and saying, "I wish they let kindergarteners audition."

I agreed with her outloud, but was secretly relieved that they didn't since she was a much better singer than me. We reached the door, dumped our bags just inside the entry, and ran into the house.

"Mom!" I shouted as I approached the kitchen. "Guess what?"

Mom was standing in the middle of the kitchen with her arms around Joy. She smiled at me. "Your sister already told me."

I stared at Joy, dumbfounded. "She did?" I didn't even know that she knew. Shaking myself out of my stupor, I skipped over to them and wrapped my arms around both of them.

"Isn't it the greatest?"

Jackie, who had run in behind me, hugged mine and Joy's waist, happily shouting, "the greatest!"

Mom laughed. "I'm so delighted with how supportive you girls are being for your sister."

I nodded, beaming. "They're so great!"

"So great," Jackie repeated.

"Thank you," Joy said, untangling herself from the hug fest. "I should really get started learning my lines."

My arms fell to my side and I stared at her. "Your lines?"

Jackie, imitating my movement and tone, echoed, "your lines?"

Both Mom and Joy looked at us perplexed. Mom glanced at Joy who shrugged.

"Well, yes," Mom said. "I thought you were excited for Joy getting cast."

I clapped my hands. "Oh! I didn't know! I got cast too! How wonderful!"

My mini-me clapped and shouted, "wonderful!"

Joy smiled. "That's great! What role did you get?"

I smiled proudly. "I'm a Dew Girl."

"Lovely!" Mom beamed.

"And you?" I asked Joy.

She smiled and stated, "I got the role of Gretel."

My mouth fell open. My brain seemed to short circuit, repeating Gretel over and over. On one hand, I was a bit jealous. But on the other hand, I was super excited for her. On a third hand, I was just shocked that my super shy sister was going to be one of the lead actors. After a few stunned seconds, I shook my head and whooped.

Rushing over to her, I picked her up off the ground and swung her around. "My sister is Gretel!"

"Gretel!" Jackie squealed, clapping.

Mom laughed as I set Joy down.

"Can I help you rehearse?"

Joy, pretending to be dizzy from my spinning her, stopped and grabbed me by the shoulders. "You better! I'll help you too, deal?" She held her hand out to me.

I shook it hard and shouted, "deal!"

"Deal!" Jackie echoed, dancing with Jessica who had woken from her nap and wandered into the kitchen to see what all the shouting was about.

"Race you upstairs!" Joy shouted, pushing past me and sprinting for the stairs.

"Cheater!" I called, stumbling after her.

"No running!" Mom shouted, then sighed, "I don't even know why I bother."

I enjoyed the rehearsals, the singing, even the costume fittings where Mom would accidentally poke me with a straight pin when I got too wiggly. Joy seemed to be having even more fun than I was. Her popularity shot through the roof of the twelve story school building. I, of course, told anyone who would listen that Gretel was my sister. A few seventh and eighth grade boys came up to me and nervously asked if I thought Joy might want to date them. I would laugh and say, "we'll never know 'cause she's not allowed to date."

There were three performances. Two with Joy and her Hansel costar and a third with the understudies. Joy was so great each time. At the end of each performance, kids and parents would ask Joy to sign their programs. She got congratulated by a bunch of teachers, and even the principal. It was Joy's time to shine.

28

Flight Attendant

Caracas to Texas

Just before my family moved back to Texas permanently in 1985, Joy announced that she wanted to be a flight attendant. She knew she would be great at it! She loved traveling, visiting new places, and, even though she was shy, meeting new people. She was all about being in charge and bossing others around. Already fluent in Spanish, she picked up other languages easily. After only a few weeks with the Romanos family, she could understand basic words in Italian.

Joy was charming, people really liked her, and she was beautiful. She had long soft brown and, in the summertime, blonde hair that flowed like water. Her eyes, while brown like mine, were somehow prettier. Her skin might've been as pale as mine, but she sunbathed and tanned. She was slender and had a petite frame. But, at fifteen, she was the tallest she would ever get. She was only five feet tall.

Our Dad, in typical dad fashion, didn't take her plans too seriously and was blunt about it. "Well, you're going to have to grow several inches! Start doing those stretches! Stewardesses have to be able to reach to the back of the overhead compartments on a plane. You can barely reach the overhead compartment at all." Then, even though he was only about 6 inches taller than her and pretty short for a grown man, he patted her on the head.

Joy huffed and crossed her arms. "They're called flight attendants now."

Mom, in typical mom fashion, was a bit more sympathetic and encouraging. "John," she said in her stern, warning voice, "she may very well have a growth spurt yet. Joy, why don't you research being a flight attendant in the library and, the next time we fly, interview one?"

Even though she was somewhat discouraged by Dad, she took Mom's advice and researched. Before we moved, she even managed to convince one of her teachers to let her write a paper on becoming a flight attendant.

The next flight we were on, the one that flew us back to the United States for good, she came armed with a steno pad. She had written a bunch of questions on it, and was determined to interview not one, but all the flight attendants. I asked her if she wanted help. While I was naturally loud and outgoing, she was shy and quiet. (One of her nicknames in high school would be Joy Mouse.) But she just glared at me and said she didn't need my help. During the 8-hour plus flight, she ended up interviewing all three flight attendants and the one steward. They liked her so much, they gave her a tour of the cockpit and she got to sit with them, with our parents' permission, during the landing. Despite her shyness, she loved attention.

Once we got off the plane, she was mad at me. I didn't know why, but I could feel her anger coming off of her in waves. After about half an hour of riding in the car from the airport to our house in Jersey Village, I couldn't take her angry silence anymore.

"You got to go into the cockpit and meet the pilot and hang out with all the flight attendants. Why are you mad at me?"

She narrowed her eyes. "'Cause you're almost tall enough and will probably get taller while I'm probably the tallest I'll be."

Bewildered, I threw my hands up. "What are you talking about!"

She huffed, "You could become a flight attendant. I probably never will because I'm too short. They told me that."

I stared at her. "But I don't want to be a flight attendant. You have to know CPR and wear make-up and smile all the time. Also, if the plane crashes, everyone expects you to be in charge 'cause the pilots will be dead." I had been listening to her go on and on about what made a good flight attendant for weeks.

"Exactly!" She shouted.

Dad gave us a stern look through the rearview mirror. "You two keep it down back there. If we get into an accident, I will tan your hides!"

We both nodded. After a few minutes, she leaned over Jackie who was in the seat between us sleeping, and whispered. "That's what makes me mad. You have the advantage, but you won't take it. I bet you don't even know what you want to be when you grow up."

I shrugged, unable to understand her anger. But she was right. Other than knowing I would always write, I had no idea what career I wanted to have. It didn't really bother me. I felt certain I'd figure that out in high school. But she made me feel like I should already be thinking about it.

A few weeks later, she shifted her focus and decided that she would become a Spanish teacher. "I don't have to be tall to teach Spanish," she explained.

Joy was always the one with a plan. She said she could always adjust her plan around what life threw at her. I think life took that as a challenge.

29

Bedroom Window

Jersey Village, TX

I was staring up at the ceiling of my dark room wishing for sleep when the tapping began. I held my breath trying to find out where it was coming from. I realized it was the window and the sound was muffled by my ugly thick curtains. I slowly sat up as the tapping grew louder. After a few seconds of listening, I walked over to my bedroom door and opened it quietly. I could hear the television downstairs, so Mom and Dad were still up. I looked down the dark hallway to Joy's room. Her door was open and her room was dark. She still wasn't home. As I slowly closed the door behind me, the tapping changed and sounded a bit like... a song?

Careful not to kick any of the random piles on the floor as I made my way across my room to the window, I was pretty sure I heard humming. I threw back the curtains and saw Joy's face pressed against the glass, startling me. While I had expected it to be her, I hadn't expected her face that close. I stumbled back almost falling over a pile of books. She busted out laughing. Scrambling to my feet, and slid open the window. I thrust my head out.

"Joy! I thought you were a bird!" I don't know why I said that. I knew it was her.

Joy laughed harder. "A bird? That's new."

"What're you doing?"

Catching her breath, she stared at me and whispered. "Isn't it obvious? I'm sneaking in!"

I stood aside waiting for her to climb in the window. When she didn't climb in right away, I tilted my head and asked, "Well?"

She grinned. "Changed my mind. I want you to come out."

I stuck my head out the window. The air was crisp, with a cool breeze that sent a shiver through me. I got a faint whiff of smoke from her clothes mixing with the strong magnolia smell from the tree just a few feet beyond and below my window. I stared at her, still not fully awake, trying to process her words.

"Come on, Jeanine. Join me!"

I nodded and grinned. Dipping back into my room, I grabbed a sweater and my robe and pulled both over my nightgown. I climbed out awkwardly, pulling the window almost shut, leaving enough room to slip my fingers in and push it open.

"So the smell of smoke doesn't get in the house," I explained.

"I wasn't smoking," Joy said, then cringed. "My date was."

I shrugged and sat on the roof next to her. "Here," I said, holding a cookie out to her.

She snorted. "Where'd you get a cookie?"

I shrugged, producing another one out of my robe's pocket. "I brought them up to my room after dinner. I was going to leave one on your bed since you went out and probably didn't get dessert, and was going to eat mine after my bath. But I forgot about them 'til just now." I took a bite of my cookie. "They're chocolate chip cookies, your favorite."

"Ah," she said, taking a bite of her cookie. She picked some robe lint off of it and grinned at me. "Well, okay then. Thank you."

We stared out at the stars and the half moon. The night was so clear, we could see many of the constellations.

"Did you have a good date?" I asked.

She shrugged, not looking at me. "No. He was kind of a jerk."

I nodded. "You gonna see him again?"

"I just said he was a jerk!" she protested.

"I know," I quipped, "but I thought that was your type."

She laughed and punched me in the shoulder. "Like I need this!"

I was laughing too. "Just kidding."

The laughter faded and we fell silent. A dog two houses away started to howl. After a minute, other dogs in the neighborhood picked up the cry. Some cats were yowling on the other side of us.

"They're probably fucking," Joy said, trying to shock me with her swearing.

I nodded. "Yeah, probably."

"Remember that time we found those kittens?"

"Of course I do! I wish we could've kept them." I sighed, staring out at the stars. After a minute, I looked sideways at her. "Do you miss Venezuela?"

She shrugged. "I guess. But I like it better here. More stable."

I pressed my lips and sighed.

After a moment, she asked. "Don't you?"

Staring at my hands, I shook my head. "No. Nobody likes me." I chewed my nails.

"Why do you say that?" She asked.

I shrugged, then dropped my hand. "Well, not nobody. I mean, I have friends at church, sorta, and a few friends at school like Karen but... You know, I just miss Venezuela and my friends in Caracas. I liked it there."

"I did too, but it's good to be home."

"Maybe that's my problem. I don't feel like this is home."

She leaned back and stared at me. "Really?"

I nodded, not looking at her. "Really."

"So where is home for you?"

I shrugged.

"Do you feel like Caracas was home?"

I thought about that for a moment. "No. I mean, I liked Caracas, but it was always temporary. I knew we'd come back here. I thought this was home. I mean, it's where we've lived the longest, but it doesn't feel like home to me. It feels like this place I'm staying at. I don't know. I don't really have a home."

We fell silent. I didn't know what else to say or how to explain what I meant. School had never been easy for me, but I had never had a problem making friends until we moved back. Now, I was just too weird. I didn't fit in with any of the jr. high groups and I was always getting picked on. I had thoughts and urges I didn't understand, but Mom just said it was puberty. I hated puberty.

After a minute, I laid back on the roof, using my arms as a pillow and stared up at the sky. Joy did the same. I could tell she was frustrated, but I didn't know what to say about that either.

"Maybe I'm a nomad," I said suddenly.

She laughed. "Does that mean the road is your home? Are you like Jack Kerouac?"

I snorted. "He's a hack."

She gasped and pretended to clutch pearls. "How dare you say such a thing about my boyfriend!"

I laughed a bit too loud and Joy shushed me. We both held our breath, listening for Dad to shout up the stairs. When he didn't, we sighed.

I leaned a bit closer and whispered. "Do you really love Kerouac?"

"No," She giggled. "I just thought it'd be funny to react like that after you called him a hack."

I leaned back. "It was."

We sat like that for a few more minutes, staring at the stars. I started thinking about how things went when we were in Venezuela. How Joy had always been the shy one, but I never minded breaking the ice with new potential friends when we got to a new place. I was often too much or too weird for new people. They liked me, but–and there was always a but–they became her friends more than mine. But there, I had always been able to find other friends.

Something had switched when we moved back to Texas and making friends just became so hard.

"I love this," I said, pointing at the sky.

"Yeah? You come out here often?" She asked, turning her head slightly to look at me.

I nodded. "Whenever I feel overwhelmed."

She grinned. "Have you snuck out?"

I barked a laugh. "No. Where would I sneak out to? I barely have any friends. So, no shenanigans there."

Joy laughed. "Who says shenanigans?"

"Me." I grinned. "You know I like weird words."

"That's 'cause you're a weirdo." She bumped my shoulder with her shoulder. "Hey, why'd you get grounded?"

I sighed, drawing my knees up to hug them. "You remember that big binder of questions I was carrying around?"

She nodded. "Yeah, I remember you going around 'taking meetings' with the pastor and the youth pastor and the other deacons besides Dad and, didn't you even bother that group of missionaries that came to church?"

I nodded. "Yeah. I even went to other churches. They all just kept saying, 'have faith.' I can't follow something that makes me feel like I'm a horrible person. I hate how the Bible and the church treats women. Like our entire reason for living is to have babies. And, and I got through all the questions in my binder, but the answers were really unsatisfactory. So..." I paused and bit my lip. "Can I tell you a secret and you promise not to tell anybody, especially not Mom or Dad?"

"As long as you promise not to tell them about me sorta sneaking in like this, you've got yourself a deal."

I nodded and held out my hand. We shook.

"Okay. So yesterday, I burned all the pages in the binder in my Holly Hobbie trash can."

She snorted. "Well, it's metal so that's probably okay. Did Mom catch you doing it on the patio?"

I sighed and looked back at the stars. "Yeah, that would've been a really good place to do it. I, um, did it in my bedroom and... Did you know carpet can melt?"

She busted out laughing. I shushed her.

Below us, we could hear Mom and Dad in the breakfast room. Still shaking with silent laughter, she asked, "So, what did you tell them?"

"I said that a candle had fallen into the trashcan and burned some papers while I was taking a bath and it was my fault since I left the window open. Which, while mostly a lie, wasn't entirely untrue since I did drop a candle in there and my window was open to get the burning smell out and I did take a bath, only after."

She chuckled and looked at her watch. Then leaned close

to me. "Okay, I have an idea," she whispered. "But I'm gonna need your help." She cleared her throat. "So, I've got about 15 minutes until my curfew. If I change my clothes and put on perfume, they won't smell the smoke."

"You should also brush your teeth or rinse with mouthwash 'cause I can smell beer."

She gave me a thumbs up. "Good to know. Can you distract Mom and Dad so I can sneak down the stairs and pretend I'm coming through the front?"

I chewed my nails while I thought about it. "If I go downstairs, I can probably get one of them to go to the kitchen with me, but not both. That's a problem since the stairs go right into the family room. Why don't you climb down the way you came and just go through the front?"

"Well, now that they're in the breakfast room, they might hear me climbing down."

I nodded. "Okay, let's slide quietly into my room and you get changed, perfume, rinse out your mouth, all that. Then when you climb out the window again, I'll go downstairs to get a drink of water telling them loudly about a weird dream I had where a bird was tapping at my window and singing a Bon Jovi song, but when I went and opened the window, the bird must've flown away."

Joy put her hand over her mouth as she laughed. "You heard that?"

I grinned. "Yup. But I won't tell them I knew it was Bon

Jovi, just some radio song. I wouldn't want them to know I know any of the," I made air quotes, "Devil's music."

"Stop it!" She gasped. "They're gonna hear me laughing!" She was almost rolling on the roof trying not to laugh so hard. I quietly laughed with my hand over my mouth too. Once we calmed down, we slid into the house. Joy quickly got changed and, as she climbed back out onto the roof, I thundered down the stairs.

"Mom, Dad!" I shouted. "I just had the weirdest dream!"

As I told them all about my dream, I heard Joy coming through the front door. Our plan worked!

30

Playing Pool

∽

Athens, Georgia

The summer of 1986, my Dad's side of the family was in Georgia for a family reunion. We stayed at the Smith's house for part of the trip. Even though Linda and Leon were our parents' age, they were first cousins since Dad was Linda's uncle. But because it confused me, I called them Aunt Linda and Uncle Leon. With her tendency to address people properly, I don't think Joy ever did. Their two daughters, Lori and Lisa, were around Joy's and my age and were our second cousins. Our moms had similar sensibilities about naming their kids with the same letter since they each had married husbands whose names started with the same letter as their names. So, they were the L family and we were the J family.

In previous years when we visited, Lori, Lisa, Joy, and I

would make up dance routines in the basement where they had a jukebox. It was a real jukebox where you selected what song to play by pushing large lettered and numbered buttons and small records would be grabbed by a mechanical arm. You could watch through the glass as the arm spun the record in the air to put it on the spindle. I loved watching the lights come on as the record player gently set the needle in the record's groove, making music spin out to us. I remember lip syncing to and sometimes singing with songs like Sheena Easton's "My Baby Takes the Morning Train", Dolly Parton's "9 to 5", and Nancy Sinatra's "These Boots Were Made for Walkin'." When we'd perfected those performances, we would make our poor parents watch.

Jackie, when she was older but still so much younger than us, wanted to join. But we would tell her to go away. At least, Joy and I would. Well, really, I would at Joy's urging. I kind of relished the idea of being the one to shoo the little sister away instead of being the little sister who was shooed. Lori and Lisa, not having any younger sisters, didn't understand why we didn't want Jackie there. Then Jackie would cry and I would get in trouble for being mean to her and we'd have to include her in the dances. Once, when she said I was being particularly mean, I didn't get to join in and she did. I sulked in the corner while she performed my part. The sting was particularly sharp since she did it better than I ever did and was a superior singer.

I was actually relieved that summer to find out that the jukebox was gone. I don't think they got rid of it, but it no longer held center stage. As much as I had loved making up dances with my cousins and Joy, it caused too many fights with Jackie and I was trying to be better about getting along with everybody.

That morning around the breakfast table we were discussing what we would do that day. The kitchen had an open floor plan which included a breakfast area situated next to the entrance to the basement. There was a large sleek island the adults would cluster around and chat while they drank their coffee, except Mom who didn't like the taste of coffee, so she had a glass of orange juice while nibbling on doughnuts. All the kids had to take their doughnuts on plates to the table or we had the option to have cereal, which is what Joy chose since it was healthier. She was sixteen and watching her figure. I was fourteen and loved doughnuts.

Lori and Lisa told us about the pool table they now had in the basement. I was so excited! I had always wanted to play pool. Joy and I rolled our eyes at each other when both Jackie and Jessica, who were nine and six at the time, were told they could play too. But we said nothing.

"And Jeani," Mom said with a warning etched in each word, "be nice to your younger sisters."

"Me?!" I exclaimed. "What about Joy?"

Joy glared at me through the cascade of hair that was half hiding her face, and shook her head. "You know you're always the one telling them they can't play with us."

I was livid! Joy was always the one telling me to tell them to go away! But before I could say anything, Dad looked at me from where he was standing at the island. The expression on his face was all I needed to swallow my retort. I didn't want to end up grounded while on vacation.

We were told that we could play a few games of pool. After that, we would be expected to help out in the kitchen since that evening, other relatives would be joining us for a big dinner. There would be lots for the womenfolk, and that included all the girls, to prepare. The menfolk would be grilling outside and expecting us to do all the other food prep, cooking, baking, and even setting the table. (It was so unfair).

Our cousins' house was built into a mountain so the basement was only half underground. It was like the mountain was giving a one-armed hug to the house. The door on the opposite wall from the stairs, let out onto a patio. Their backyard butted up against a forest. As it got later in the evening, the sun would glare in the windows. When that happened, thick bamboo shades would be brought down and give the room a cavelike feel.

After breakfast, all six kids headed down to the basement, closing the door at the top of the stairs behind us. There was a bit of a mysterious feeling with the shades down. But as soon as Lori pulled the cord to lift them, the room was bathed in bright sunlight. There was a low hanging chandelier over the pool table, but it was off. I was a little disappointed to discover it was a smaller table and bumper pool, but was still excited to play. The table itself had dark wooden sides and a red felt covering under the bumpers. The pool cues were too long for Jessica to handle since she was only six. After she tried to lift one a few times, she looked like she might cry. But Lori and Lisa came up with an idea and said she could be the judge who decided who won. She liked that. We were going to split into sister teams, but Lisa pointed out that wouldn't be fair since Joy, Jackie, and I had never played before. So we split older against younger and, since there were three of us with Lisa, Jackie, and I, we got an extra turn too. Lori and Lisa patiently explained the rules of the game. Joy and Jackie listened intently and Jackie asked lots of questions. I tried to listen, but kept getting distracted with chalking my cue. Between my distraction and Jackie's questions, they had to go over the rules twice.

"Stop it, Jeani!" Joy snapped when she caught me making secret silly faces at Jackie during her turn.

"What?" I asked, putting the most innocent expression on my face.

Lori shook her head. "Jeani, we all saw you making faces." Lisa nodded.

"See?" Joy said, indicating to me with her cue. "She's always acting like a fool."

I sat down on one of the couches, holding the pool cue between my knees. "Sorry," I whispered. I didn't mean to be disruptive; I was just having fun.

After a few turns, I was done sulking, so I started being silly again. I tried very hard not to distract others when they went. But when it was my turn, I pretended I was a pool shark. Even Joy giggled at my over the top seriousness about lining up my shots and pretending to talk around a cigar like Groucho Marx.

I had recently read a book about the Marx brothers and watched several of their movies. Earlier in our trip I would randomly use my Groucho Marx voice to share quotes like, "Time flies like an arrow; fruit flies like a banana," when anyone asked the time. I also loved to say the quote, "Outside of a dog, a book is man's best friend. Inside of a dog, it's too dark to read." That one came up whenever someone said anything about books or dogs. My quotes were often met with the question, "What?" along with raised eyebrows. Every once in a while, there would be a snicker or two. I would explain that I had read some books on the Marx brothers and these were quotes by Groucho.

"But Harpo Marx is my favorite," I would continue even though nobody asked and I could tell most of our relatives were drifting away from what I was saying.

Aunt Linda indulged me and asked, "Is it because he plays the harp?"

"Yes!" I exclaimed. I was the harpist in my school's orchestra. "But that's not all. He doesn't have any lines to quote 'cause he talks with music. He could play six different instruments! I wish I was as musically talented as him. I can only play the piano okay, the harp pretty well, and the violin very poorly."

"But that's three. That's impressive too," she smiled.

I nodded, pleased with how encouraging she was.

Joy, from the other side of the table, laughed. "But we appreciate her quoting Groucho more than Harpo 'cause then she's not following me around making whistling sounds."

I nodded thoughtfully. "That's true. My harp's too big to carry, so I just whistle. But Harpo also communicate dwith whistling and horns. Mom said my whistling was giving her a headache so I'm only allowed to do it when we're outside. She said, if I wanted to emulate the Marx brothers, I needed to find something else." I sighed. "I guess I talk too much anyhow to be Harpo. I tried being as quiet as him but it's really hard. I also tried their physical comedy, but I kept hurting myself. So I learned Groucho quotes. Chico and Zeppo quotes didn't work for me and Gummo wasn't with them long enough. If I remember correctly from my reading, he only did the vaudeville act when it was onstage, not when it was filmed 'cause he went off to war. Did you know there were five Marx brothers?"

When no one answered, I became aware that I had lost even my most indulgent audience. I stopped talking and listened to whatever other topic was being discussed as I ate my lunch.

Once I took my last shot, and did really poorly, I laughed then said in my best Groucho Marx voice, "That was a great shot! Who're you going to believe, me or your own eyes?" I spun my pool cue as I wiggled my eyebrows as my sisters and cousins giggled. Then the cue crashed into the light over the table and time seemed to slooooooooooooow dooooooooown.

I heard a scream as pieces of glass rained on and around the table. Everyone else was far enough back, but one large shard came right towards me. I threw my arms up to shield my face. It hit my right arm hard enough to cause me to stumble backwards, slamming into Joy. But the glass hitting me didn't hurt. I slowly lowered my arms as Joy pushed me off her. Jackie, who was standing on the other side of the pool table, looked as white as a ghost. She seemed frozen with one hand over her wide open mouth and the other pointing at me. It looked like she was screaming, but at that moment, I could hear nothing. Lori and Lisa were also staring at me with wide eyes and dropped jaws. Jessica was in slow motion running towards the stairs, crying.

"Oh no!" I gasped. "I'm so, so sorry I broke the..." My words slowed to a stop and for what was probably a second but felt like an hour, I was frozen and couldn't breathe.

"Jeani!" Jackie shouted, shattering the silence and the slow movement of time. Suddenly everyone around me was moving super fast, I could hear screams and cries and everything was really loud. "You're bleeding!"

My head felt light as I looked down and saw a pool of blood at my feet. I was now the one in slow motion. My hand raised as if on its own to my shoulder and I looked down my forearm and saw that there was a clean sliced chunk of arm missing just above my right elbow. I stared at it as blood gushed out.

"Huh, look at that," I said.

"Why are you so calm?" Joy asked, coming to stand in front of me. "Nevermind. I'm gonna go get Mom and Dad." She took off after Jessica and passed her on the stairs. While everyone else's movements had sped up, I was still moving incredibly slow, like I was in a dream. My head turned as I followed her with my eyes, just catching up as she threw the door open and rushed beyond my sightline into the kitchen.

Jackie was suddenly standing in front of me, crying. I could hear Joy talking to Mom and Aunt Linda as I slowly brought my focus back to Jackie's tear-streaked face. She looked so funny, I started laughing.

She stumbled backwards, then turned and ran over to Lori who hugged her. Between sobs, she gasped out, "Why is she laughing? She's scaring me!"

Lisa, who had appeared at my side, spoke in her sweet gentle voice. She told me to lift my arm up so that the wound was over my head. "This will slow down the bleeding," she said, as she helped me raise my arm. "Right now, your heart is pumping blood at an extraordinary pace and lifting it above your head will slow that." I smiled at her as she gently guided me to the bathroom.

Behind me, I could hear Lori telling Jackie, "She's in shock right now."

I laughed, remembering that Leon, their dad, was a doctor. No wonder they knew just what to do. "I guess if I'm gonna get injured, getting injured in the house of a doctor is not so bad." My words sounded slurred. I laughed at them as Lisa walked me into the bathroom and helped me put my arm under the cold water.

"Oh, that looks really bad," I looked up to find Mom, Dad, and Linda at the door. I wasn't sure when they had gotten there or who had spoken. I laughed again.

Linda said, "I'll call Leon and see if he can stitch her up."

Joy was now in the bathroom with me. Lori and Lisa had gone to help clean up the glass while Mom and Dad were comforting Jessica and Jackie in the other room. I couldn't stop giggling.

"Quit that," Joy whispered. "You're freaking everyone out."

I looked at her, still giggling, and shook my head. "I can't! It's just so weird. It doesn't hurt. I can't feel anything and I'm just so... I don't know! It's weird. I feel really happy."

"It's the endorphins!" Lori called from the other room.

I stared at Joy, checked to make sure Mom and Dad weren't too close, then leaned in and asked, "Is this what it's like to be high?"

She laughed, then got a stern look on her face. "Why do you think I'd know?"

I tried to shrug, but only managed to lift my left shoulder. "I don't know... you're older and maybe you've done some things..."

She leaned forward and whispered in my ear, "If I had, I wouldn't tell you." Leaning back, she gave me a meaningful look.

I sighed. "If you told me in confidence, I'd never tell."

"Never tell what?" Dad's voice made both Joy and I jump. He was standing in the doorway.

"Nothing," Joy said. "She's babbling incoherently."

At the word babble, I started laughing again. "Babble! That's just such a fun word to say... babble, babble, babble..."

"You know," said Dad, "the word babble comes from the Bible and..."

"Yes Dad," Joy cut him off. "We know the story about the tower of Babel."

I laughed. "Bible babble, bible babble, bible babble... that's even more fun to say!"

Dad shook his head, a slight grin tugging at the corner of his mouth. "You seem to be feeling okay?" he asked.

"I can't feel anything!" I told him.

His grin disappeared. "That's a bit worrying, but I'm glad you're not in pain."

"Leon is at the hospital!" Linda shouted from upstairs. "If we get her there in the next half hour, he'll be able to stitch her up."

As Joy and Dad helped me wrap a towel around the wound so I wouldn't drip blood everywhere, I suddenly thought of something. "Did anybody find the part of my arm that got cut out? Do we need it to stitch it back on?"

"Ew!" Joy made a grossed out face. "I hope not!"

"No," Lisa calmly explained. "Dad'll just pull what's there together and stitch it. Your body will do the healing."

"Oh," I sighed. "Well that's good. I guess you can throw it away if you find it."

"Way ahead of you!" Lori announced, patting me on the head as I walked by her on my way out to the van.

Later that night, I was laying on the couch with my arm bandaged and propped over my head. We were at another relative's house, the gathering had been moved due to my injury, and all the younger cousins were in the living room watching a movie after dinner. Joy was sitting with her back against the couch. She turned her head to look up at me.

Whispering, she asked, "Tell me the truth. Did you really feel nothing?"

I shook my head. "No. It didn't hurt at all, not even when I was getting stitched." I adjusted my arm slightly. "It's starting to hurt now."

"Should I get you some medicine?"

I shook my head. "No, I don't want you to miss the movie. I'm probably gonna fall asleep soon." I yawned. "I'm so tired!"

Joy grinned. "Hey, good job on scaring Jackie. You had her terrified with all that laughing."

"I wasn't even trying. I wonder what that means, you know, laughing when you get hurt."

Joy snorted. "I think it means you're a weirdo." We both laughed until a few cousins turned and shushed us.

Then I said in a somewhat bleary Groucho impersonation, "I've had a perfectly wonderful evening. But this wasn't it."

31

Phantom of the Opera

◦∞◦

Jersey Village, TX

It was only a few days after my 15th birthday, and I was sitting in the family room of our house in Jersey Village, crying. Mom, Dad, Jackie, and Jessica were at church for Wednesday night service, but I had stayed home saying I had too much homework. After I finished most of my homework, I had tried watching Twin Peaks, my guilty pleasure show that came on Wednesday nights. But I was too upset and distracted. Joy was, as per usual, over at a friend's house studying or had a babysitting gig or maybe on a secret date. I could no longer keep track of her. I knew Mom and Dad would be home soon and I didn't want to answer any of the questions that would come if they saw me crying, so I went to bed. But it was way too early and I wasn't even sleepy. So I crawled out onto the roof and stared up at the sky. The sky was dark and the breeze calmed me. I laid back on the roof and breathed deep as I closed my eyes.

"Hey," Joy's voice startled me awake.

My body jerked as I tried to focus on her in the dark. Just her face was poking out of the house. She slid the window open wider and climbed out to sit next to me. I sat up and shivered, pulling my robe tighter around me. It never got really cold during the day, but at night it could get chilly.

We sat next to each other, staring up at the stars for a few minutes, then Joy laid back and I did too.

"Hey," she said, nudging my shoulder with hers. "What happened with Karen?"

I groaned and rolled over on my side away from her, covering my face. "Nothing." I whispered into my hands.

She pinched my back. "What was that?"

I moved my hands away from my face and whisper-shouted, "nothing!" Then covered my face again.

She pinched my back. I ignored her.

"Mom mentioned that she thought you were fighting?"

I stayed silent so she pinched another spot, then another, and another until I was twitching with her pinches.

"Stop it!" I hissed.

"No," she said, the pinches getting faster and harder. She suddenly switched to tickles catching me off guard. When I started to laugh out loud, she breathed into my ear, "all you have to do is tell me what happened and I'll stop."

I tried to wiggle away, but she had perfected holding me in place and tickling without mercy when we kids. I bit my bottom lip trying to pretend like the tickles didn't tickle, but it didn't work. Finally, I rolled over and pushed her saying, "okay, okay, I'll tell you!"

She stopped and leaned back. We both noticed that we had slid down the roof and were close to sliding off. Quick as we could, we scooted back up.

Catching my breath, I looked at her. She was sitting with one dainty ankle over the other as she leaned on her elbow. I sat up straight and wrapped my arms around my knees.

"Well?"

"Okay. So you know how we went to the Renaissance Faire with her and her parents for my birthday?"

"Yeah?"

I took a deep breath. "Well, mom and dad agreed that since we were getting home so late, I could spend the night at her house."

She tilted her head, "so? You've spent the night over there before."

"Do you want me to tell you?"

She snorted, then made the motion of zipping her lips and throwing the key off the roof.

"Okay. So you know how I told you Karen is like obsessed with the Phantom of the Opera?" She nodded. "She decided that after we got ready for bed, we should stay up and listen to the whole thing. So we did. I was sitting on her rug with my back against her bed as she went around the room lighting candles she bought at the Ren Faire and turning off all the lights. She put the tape on at full volume then came back and sat in my lap." Joy cocked an eyebrow. I shook my head. "I didn't mind. She smelled really good and, you know, I really like to cuddle. So we did that. But I was so tired, I fell asleep and, and she got mad at me for not staying awake."

I left out the part where Karen turned in my lap and whispered, 'you can be my Phantom and I'll be your Christine' then kissed me. I really liked kissing her. At first, it was just lips, then her tongue was in my mouth and mine was in hers. She let me touch her through her nightgown. The tape stopped, so she got up and switched to the next tape. When she came back, she sat on the bed behind me and played with my hair, kissing my head. I stroked her legs and kissed them and her feet. But I was really tired and fell asleep before the tape was over. When it stopped, she asked me what I thought and, she would tell me in school on Tuesday, I snored.

On Monday, I had tried to talk to her, but she ignored me and wasn't at lunch. When I got home that night, I called her house. But her mom said she wasn't taking calls.

On Tuesday, she was at lunch like usual, but sat on the other side of our friends group, away from me. I sent a note down to her, asking if she was mad at me. She sent it back and it read, "yes, you fell asleep and snored during Phantom, which you know is my favorite." After I read it, I looked over to where she was sitting, but she was already walking out of the lunch room and I wouldn't be able to catch her.

On Wednesday, I cornered her in the bathroom before classes. She made a face at me.

"What do you want?"

"I want to talk! I want to tell you, I'm sorry I fell asleep while we were listening to Phantom, I was just really tired from the Ren Fair. I really liked what I heard. And," I whispered the next bit, "I want to know what the kissing meant. I liked it."

I tried to take her hands, but she stepped back from me and hissed, "it seriously meant nothing. It didn't even happen." Then she pushed past me and stormed out of the bathroom.

I managed not to cry all through school or even when I got home, but was bawling once I knew I was at home alone.

Joy pointed to her mouth. I grinned, pulling an imaginary key out of my pocket and handed it to her. She dramatically unlocked her mouth. "That's so silly!"

I shrugged, "maybe, but she wouldn't speak to me the

whole time her dad drove me home, only grunting a goodbye when I got out. At school, she's been avoiding me and, well," I flopped back with my arms up over my head. "She was kinda my only real friend and it's the whole Estefani and Jaque and Laura thing all over again!"

She looked at me sideways. "This does seem to happen to you a lot. Why do you think..."

"I don't know!" I wailed.

But that wasn't true. With each of those friends, it was my fault. We decided to practice kissing or I tried to hold their hand or, like with Estefani, I told her I like, liked her. I knew I had wicked desires. There was something wrong with me. Why did I like girls like that? Why wasn't I ever attracted to the boys my friends said were cute? I was perverse. I sat up and took a deep breath, intent on confessing, but Joy shushed me and pointed to the garage where we could see headlights.

"They're home!" She whispered.

We crawled back into the house and Joy went to her room as I climbed into bed. I sighed, and stared at the ceiling, thinking about Karen. Maybe if I brought her a gift and apologized. But I wasn't sure why I had to apologize when she started it. I rolled over onto my side and stared at the wall crying in silence until I fell asleep.

32

Joy to the World

Jersey Village, TX

Joy and I were hanging out just the two of us—something that happened less and less since she became a full-grown teenager—in her bedroom. I was in tenth grade and Joy was in twelfth, soon to graduate high school and leave me. She had been grounded for staying out too late with her friends at a party. She told me about this game where everyone listed all the terrible things they would do when they grew up that would piss off their parents. She laughed about her friend who had hippy parents and said that all he had to do was grow up and become a corporate lawyer. When it was her turn, she went through what our parents would hate: satan worshiper, gay, drug addict, hooker, stripper. She said this started another game where everyone shared their stripper names. The way to make a stripper name was to use your last name and the street you lived on. She said she didn't need to use her last name 'cause her stripper name would be our street, Singapore Lane, and that her stripper friend would be Candy Cane.

I laughed from my spot on the floor. I was leaning against her dresser and she was lying on the bed, her feet dangling over the side as she idly tossed a wadded piece of paper into the air, trying to hit the canopy over her bed. In the background, a mixtape one of her friends had made was playing The Cure's "Just Like Heaven." After she finished telling me about the party, we both got quiet.

Just as she was just about to ask me to leave, I started babbling about why I no longer wanted to go to church or be a Christian and about all the research I'd been doing on other religions and spiritualities and my thoughts on all of it. She rolled over onto her stomach and stared at me. My frantic flow of words slowed until they stopped as I gave her a questioning look. She threw the paper at me. It hit my arm.

"Ow," I said, without much conviction.

She snorted a laugh. "Why do you do that?"

Her question confused me. I looked down at my hands to see if I was doing something weird with my fingers. Maybe it was my speedy babbling?

"Do what?"

She crinkled her nose and shook her head. "Make things harder for yourself. I mean, what does it hurt to go to church and make Mom and Dad happy?"

I snorted. "Says the one who's grounded."

"That's different," she said, waving a hand in the air as if my comment was smoke. "I stayed out too late. So I got grounded. So what? They're not actually mad at me. But if you stop going to church and don't believe in God and stop being a Christian, they'll not only be mad, but they'll be worried about you. Also, I'll never hear the end of it. Could you think about me?" She smirked, then got serious again. "The thing is, you don't have to believe, not really, and when you're an adult, you can believe whatever you want."

"But it's a lie," I said with the passion of the newly transformed.

"Then find something in it that you do believe. Like, for example, whenever we sing, 'Joy to the World,' I pretend they're singing about me and how awesome the world is because I'm in it." She sat up. "It doesn't have to be real. Just find something that you like. Maybe the idea of being nice. You're a nice person, usually. Or maybe being a sucker. You're good at that."

I shook my head, knowing she was teasing me, but I was so full of earnest conviction. "I just can't keep pretending like I love their God or believe the Bible when it doesn't make sense to me. I read it all! I asked a bazillion questions, and nobody could answer me. I told you about that, remember?"

Joy nodded.

"I hate all the stupid contradictions. I hate how much the

church makes me feel like there's something wrong with me. I mean..."

I paused and stared at her for a minute. I wanted to tell her everything, but I wasn't sure if it was the right thing to do since I wasn't even sure about it myself. But then I decided to trust her. Even when she was manipulating me, I always decided to trust her. I guess she was right, I was a sucker. So it wasn't too hard to do it when we were getting along so well. I crawled across the carpet and pushed her door closed. I sat leaning up against the door, facing her. "Can I tell you a secret and you promise not to tell anyone, especially not Mom or Dad or Jackie or Jessica?"

She stared at me without speaking as if she was thinking really hard about my request. I always liked that she did that. She never just brushed off a promise. If she promised something, it was for real.

"Okay," she said. "I promise not to tell anyone as long as not telling won't get me in trouble. If I think it's going to get me in trouble though, I'm telling."

I bit my bottom lip and thought about that. It wasn't the promise I wanted, but it was the promise she was willing to give. So I nodded. "You know how it's a sin according to the church to like a girl when you're a girl?"

She looked like she was about to say something sarcastic, but stopped herself and just nodded.

I took a deep breath. "I like someone. And the other day in her bedroom when we were listening to The Phantom of the Opera with the lights out and only a few candles burning, she sat in my lap and I held her and smelled her hair... her hair always smells like lavender, and..." I licked my lips and took another deep breath, feeling like I was going to cry. My voice got soft. "And she kissed me. I mean, I kissed her back, but she definitely started it. But now she won't talk to me. And I think she liked it, but I think it scared her. I don't know what to do. I really want to be her friend, but I'm scared she won't want to because that happened."

Joy tilted her head and I held my breath.

"Did you like kissing her?"

I nodded. "A lot. But not enough to lose her as a friend."

"Have you ever kissed a boy?"

"Well, there was that one boy, who kept following me everywhere on that last mission trip to Laredo, Mexico. Remember him?" She nodded. "He cornered me and kissed me. I liked that too. Not the cornering–that made me feel weird–but the kissing."

"Have you kissed anyone else?"

I nodded. "Two other girls when we were living in Venezuela. Oh, and um, that girl from my girl scout troop that I was really good friends with. You remember her?" Joy shook her head. "She had that blonde curly, rough hair and was always talking about how soft my hair was and petting me. It was so irritating. You know, the one you always said was too loud and bossy."

"Her? You kissed her? Why? She was a jerk."

I shook my head. "She wasn't that bad. But that's not the point... I didn't kiss her. She kissed me and it was messy and wet. It's part of why we stopped being friends and got into a fight and her mom kicked me out of the Girl Scouts."

At that, Joy laughed. "Wait... wasn't she the one who was such a lousy singer that she had to be one of the cookie kids for Hansel and Gretel even though she wanted to be a dewdrop girl like you?"

I nodded. "Yup! Her Mom was the one who barged into the dress rehearsal and threw a fit about her cookie costume needing to be on the stage because it was the best! But the night of the performance, she ended up in the audience just like all the other cookies." We both laughed.

Joy got a far away look in her eyes. "That was fun."

"Yeah," I sighed, thinking back to when we were in Hansel and Gretel in Venezuela.

"Hey," she said, poking me with her foot. I looked up at her sitting on the bed and saw that she was grinning with a sincerity she didn't normally show. "Listen, stupid. The church and our parents might see you as an abomination and say that you're going to Hell. But you're still just my annoying dumb sister." She shrugged. "You probably shouldn't tell Mom or Dad or the rest of the family, and don't worry, I won't either. For what it's worth, I don't think it means you're going to hell. No matter what spiritual pseudo-religious woo-woo you decide to believe or who you end up making out with, I don't think God cares as long as you're a good person. Now, get outta my room. I've got a date with V.C. Andrews's newest book."

I never got a chance to tell her how much that day meant to me. I hope she knew. Joy to the world indeed.

33

Stephen F. Austin State University

Jersey Village, TX

Before Joy chose Baylor University, she had been very practical by making lists, visiting schools, and getting scholarships as a junior. As a junior I, on the other hand, was struggling to keep a B- average, that was rapidly slipping into the realm of C, had no ambition beyond doing theater, working fast food to save up some money, and hanging out with my friends. If I had known then what I know now, I would have realized I was sliding into the first depression of my life. But all my parents saw was a rebellious teenager who had turned her back on God, the church, and them. They prayed for me nightly and loudly at the dinner table. When they could force me to go to church, they would. At church, I would be prayed over time and time again.

It wasn't until I got an invitation to go to Mass with my friend Michelle that I broke away from my parent's church for the last time. From then on out, I went to the church of Michelle. While we did go with her parents to Mass on occasion, mostly I would arrive at her house, go up to her room, and bow beside her bed.

"Oh great and wondrous one, I come to worship. In my devotion, I would like to share the offering of the sacred donut. My treat!"

We would laugh and go for donuts. It became our Sunday ritual.

About midway through Senior year, my parents were really getting worried. I still hadn't applied for any colleges, though I had collected informational packets on several, including Sarah Lawrence in New York where Michelle was most likely going. My mom, as kind as she could, explained that there was little chance of my getting into Sarah Lawrence and even less of a chance of us being able to afford an out-of-state private liberal college. She went on to talk about how Joy's 3.9 GPA and the scholarships she got were the only reason she could afford to go to Baylor, an in-state private college. I knew this, but instead of responding to her in a calm, and rational manner, I exploded. I accused her of never believing in me and only wanting me to get my Mrs. degree and pop out babies like she did. Then I stormed off to my room before she could ground me.

A few hours later, after the sun had gone down, Mom tapped gently on my bedroom door.

"What?" I practically snarled.

"Without opening the door, Mom's muffled voice said, "you have a phone call."

I sighed, got up off my bed, and stumbled over the mess on my floor. Without turning on the light or fully opening the door, I reached out and took the portable phone. Pressing it against my chest, I waited for Mom to leave.

After a few seconds of hearing her breathe, I said, "Thank you. And goodbye." I slammed the door and stubbed my toe as I made it back over to my bed.

"Hello?" I said, rubbing my toes. I was pretty sure it would be Xoch or one of my other high school friends.

"Hey sis." It was Joy.

At first, I was elated. Joy never called me from college. Sure, she'd talk to me for a few minutes when she called the whole family, but she didn't ever call just me. But then I realized I hadn't heard the phone ring.

"Did Mom call you?"

There was a pause. I sighed, gathered my cigarettes and my lighter and climbed out onto the roof. It was a warm and muggy night. All of the clouds were hanging low and oppressive. I lit my cigarette and coughed.

"Are you smoking?" Joy's voice held a note of incredulity that I found amusing.

"What if I am?"

I could almost hear her shaking her head over the phone lines. "Whatever. Listen, I'm worried about you, okay?"

I rolled my eyes, trying to blow a smoke ring. It was more of a smoke squiggle. "Yeah... you, Mom, and Dad have all said that. But I'm okay, okay?"

"Are you though?"

I pulled my robe tighter around me, even though it wasn't at all cold. "I mean, yes? I guess?"

"J9, what're you going to do when you graduate?"

She had called me J9 only a few times before. Over the summer, I'd told her that I really liked it. She'd said she would use it as my seriouser than serious name. I sat up, more alert than I had been in a few weeks.

"I mean, the plan is to go to college. What else am I gonna do?"

"I mean, you could not."

I tipped the ash from my cigarette onto the ashtray I had stashed out on the roof. "But then what would I do?"

"Exactly." She said the word as if I was a performing

monkey and I finally got that one trick that I could never quite get. Only I didn't understand what the trick was.

"Exactly what?"

She sighed. "Look. No one is saying you have to go to college. What we are saying is you have to have a plan and that plan can't be just to stay home and work at Whataburger, you know?"

"I don't work at Whataburger anymore, I work at Subs Etc."

"Really? That's what you're going to argue about? The point is you have to do more than fast food. You're too smart not to."

I looked at the phone skeptically. I didn't feel too smart and my grades certainly didn't shout smartness. I thought about saying as much, but didn't want to have an insincere discussion about how my smarts lie elsewhere and I should follow things I'm good at like English studies or theater. I sighed. "Maybe I'll go off to New York and work on Broadway."

Joy laughed. "You're gonna become an actor?"

"No," I said defensively, "there are plenty of other jobs in theater I could do."

"Okay, this is good! Let's figure out what you can do. Are you done with your cigarette?"

I nodded, crushing out the butt then quietly crawling back into the house.

"Well?" she asked.

"Ha! Yeah," I nodded at the phone. "I forgot you couldn't see me nod."

She laughed. I swished some mouthwash as I sprayed some lysol to cover the smell.

"Okay, I'm back in my room."

"Okay, check to see if Mom and Dad have gone to bed."

I crept down the carpeted hallway and stopped at the top of the stairs. I could hear Jessica's soft breathing coming from her room. There was no light or sound coming from downstairs. "I think so?" I whispered into the phone.

"Good," Joy's voice sounded really loud. I tiptoed down the stairs, hoping Jessica didn't hear.

"Mom said she was going to leave a pen and some paper on the table for you."

I turned on the breakfast room light and saw a yellow legal pad with a blue pen next to it. I clenched my jaw, feeling like I was being manipulated. I wanted to slam the phone down or scream into it, but I really liked that Joy wanted to help me. I swallowed and sat down.

"Okay," I said.

"Okay. At the top, I want you to write, My Life, and under that, make two columns. The left column will be what you want to do. The right column will be what you have to do to get there. Got it?"

"Got it."

"Okay, now in the left column, start listing the things you want to do, like write and theater and even bike to work every day. Then I want you to write in the second column what of these things you will need to go to college for or what you will need to do instead of going to college."

I wrote: be an author, an actor (maybe), work backstage as a techie, become a psychologist, a translator that speaks seven different languages, and figure out how to become a monkey... I giggled at that. "Do you want me to read them to you?" I started to say, but Joy cut me off.

"Look, I'd like to sit with you while you figure out your life, but I've really got to go to bed. I have to sing with the church choir tomorrow morning. Do you want to call me in the afternoon and we can go through your lists?"

My heart sank. I thought she was going to guide me through this. "Yeah, that's fine."

"Good. Love ya, sis!"

"Love you too," I replied. After we hung up, I put a few more things on the list, but decided I'd wait to fill it out more when we talked again.

When I called her back the next day, she was busy. I thought about talking with Mom about my list, but I had been so mean to her lately and I didn't know how to apologize properly. I called Joy a few more times, but didn't leave a message after the first time.

A few weeks later, Mom handed me a letter from Joy. She was always so good at writing letters. She told me how things were going with her, when she'd be home for summer break, and let me know that she was praying for me. But she didn't mention my list or that I had called.

I looked at my list. I didn't need to go to college to be an author, there were many authors who didn't. But going to college would probably help. Same with the theater stuff. I'd definitely need a degree to be a psychologist or a translator. I had crossed out becoming a monkey and added work with animals, though I didn't know what that would look like. I had read a bit about what it takes to become a veterinarian, and it was intense. Way more math than my dyslexic brain would be good with. But honestly, I just didn't know what to do.

So I made a different list. This one answered the question, which college would give me what I wanted. It had to be easy to get into, close enough that I could come home for the weekend, but far enough that I couldn't just live at home. It had to have good theater and writing programs. It also needed to be pretty. These were my reasons for choosing to go to Stephen F. Austin State University in Nacogdoches, Texas, one of the worst decisions I ever made. But those stories are for a different memoir as they're not about Joy.

34

What are the Chances?

Houston, Texas

The year I graduated high school, Joy was home for summer vacation from Baylor University and her studying to become a Spanish teacher. But instead of spending all her time hanging out at home, she decided to pick up a summer class at the University of Houston. Jef, one of her best friends from high school, was enrolled there. On July 2, 1991, Joy and Jef never made it to the University.

I wasn't with them, so I only know the story from retellings. So I'll let Joy tell this story.

"Now Joy," Dad says, handing me the keys to his Audi,

the sportiest car he's ever owned, "I expect you to drive responsibly and stay safe."

I resist the urge to roll my eyes. I can't even believe he thinks I need this lecture. I mean, Jeanine, sure, but I've always been the most cautious driver. Whatever, I'll be done with school soon.

"Of course," I say, taking the keys.

I pick up Jef and we're off.

It's a hot Houston day and the sun is shining bright. We have sunglasses on, the windows down, and the moonroof open. We look cool. Jef's raven dark and my honey brown hair blow in the breeze over our headrests. Well, her hair goes over, mine just blows against it 'cause I'm so much shorter than she is. We talk and catch up as Paula Abdul's "Rush Rush" comes on the radio. We both laugh and I turn it up. We start singing along, sort of enjoying, sort of making fun of it; quintessential Gen Xers that we are.

"Rush, rush / Hurry, hurry lover, come to me / Rush, rush / I wanna see, I wanna see ya get free with me / Rush, rush / I can feel it, I can feel you all through me / Rush, rush / Ooh, what you do to me..."

My left arm is partially out the window, swimming through the air, as we begin to exit the freeway. We're driving under an overpass when a loud thud-thunk-crack-crash shakes the car as the roof collapses and bows between us. I scream, yanking my arm back in, fighting the urge to jerk the steering wheel. I flash to my Dad going over and over the importance of staying calm in an accident. I gently maneuver us to the right, easing my foot down on the break. Deep breath in, I feel like my eyes are gonna pop out of my head, deep breath out, releasing all air as we slow to a stop on the shoulder. I can still hear Jef screaming. I sit for a moment, my entire body vibrating, my heart feeling like it's going to pound out of my chest. Lifting my right hand, I shakily push the hazard button.

"Jef," I call, "Are you alright?"

I hear her murmur something, but can't distinguish the words. But if she's talking, she's alive. Maybe hurt, but not unconscious. There is metal and fabric from the ceiling of the car in tatters between us. The windshield is smashed. There's blood, but I can't tell if it's coming through the glass or Jef's side of the car.

"I'm getting out!" I shout, just in case she's having trouble hearing me too. I pull the handle and push the door, having to push harder than normal, until it opens with a sickening crunch and scrape. It only goes so far, so I squeeze myself through the tight opening. Once out, I slide around the car, hugging close, to be out of the way of other cars flying past us. On the shoulder and slightly behind the car, I look back and feel my stomach contract. I swallow hard as I stare at the tangle of ropes and harness and the bleeding, shattered body of a construction worker lying on the roof of my caved-in car.

Jef, who is having trouble extracting herself from the car as well, finally gets out. She doubles over, leaning on her knees like she's gonna throw up. Taking a deep breath, she stands and slowly turns to look at the car. Her eyes widen as she clasps her hands over her mouth. Just as suddenly, she grabs her head, eyes squeezed tight, and leans forward again. I hurry over and touch her arm.

"You okay?" I ask, immediately, regretting the question. It's a stupid thing to say. Neither of us are okay.

She holds up one finger, nodding slightly, takes another deep breath, then stands up again. She's still wavering, her tan skin looking pale, but I don't think she's gonna puke.

"The roof hit my head so hard." She moans, squinting with eyebrows pinched.

I notice her sunglasses were knocked off, so I offer her mine that had by some miracle stayed on my face. She nods in appreciation and puts them on.

"Do you think he's dead?" I whisper, once again looking at the car where the man's arm had slid down and was hanging over the side. It almost looked like he was waving at us. I shudder and look away. There's just so much blood! Still not looking, I whisper, "sh-should I check him? Like take his pulse or something?"

Despite the heat of a Houston summer, Jef shivers. She starts to shake her head, takes a few deep breaths, and leans forward again. "I need to sit down."

I barely catch her words as the wind kicks up. Sirens are wailing in the distance. Taking her arm, I lead her away from the shoulder and help her sit on the cement wall. I glance over to the car. I still cannot bring myself to look at the man.

The police arrive, immediately followed by an ambulance.

A perimeter is set up, and someone is checking the man. Both Jef and I are checked over by medical personnel. I'm cleared. A police officer, who had been waiting, leads me a bit away from all the noise so he can ask me a lot of questions. I have to write what happened on the accident report. Even though I feel shaky, my writing is steady and in all caps so it's clear to read, "I WAS DRIVING S/B ON THE WEST LOOP. A MAN JUST FELL FROM THE OVERPASS AND LANDED ON MY CAR WINDSHIELD. I COULDN'T SEE AND MANAGED TO GET STOPPED ON THE SHOULDER OF THE ROAD." I sign it, Joy Vaughn. I wonder if I shouldn't have written out southbound, but it's too late now. After a few minutes of answering every question lobbed my way, many repeated several times, I ask, "What was he doing?"

One of the officers says, "From what we can tell, he was a construction worker working on the overpass you girls went under. The theory is that his harness broke."

All I can muster is a "Was?" I'm certain the word will be swallowed by the wind, but the officer hears me.

His face takes on a solemn demeanor as he nods. "Yeah, he didn't make it."

"Oh..."

I suddenly feel unsteady. Someone takes my arm and leads me over to the ambulance where Jef is. One of the EMTs is putting a brace on her neck.

I give Jef a questioning look.

MY SWAN SONG FOR JOY 279

She sighs. "My head. They're afraid I have a concussion."

"Do you wanna ride with us?" The EMT asks as he helps her into the ambulance.

I nod. "I mean, as long as there's room."

He nods. "You should probably get checked over again anyhow." They get Jef onto the gurney and show me where I can sit in the ambulance. "You can call your parents from the hospital."

Nurses, doctors, and even our parents keep asking, "What are the chances?" After I'm examined twice, they determine I'm fine. I escaped unscathed. Dad and Mom both say it was by the grace of God that I wasn't hurt and that both of us survived.

Standing beside Jef's hospital bed, we marvel at what happened. It's just so strange! I'm sad that she got hurt and feel a little guilty that I didn't.

"It's 'cause you're a shorty," Jef snorts, then touches her head. "Okay, laughing hurts."

"It's the weirdest thing that's ever happened to me." I shake my head. Then with a rueful grin, I add, "and I used to live in Venezuela!"

"Don't make me laugh," Jef says through gritted teeth.

I smile, wink at her, and say, "I can't help it. Making people laugh is what I do. It's even in my name!"

"I hate you," Jef smiles.

"I love you too," I say, laughing for us both.

I have the copy of the police report Joy held onto just so she'd have proof that it actually happened. That accident should have been the most bizarre in her life. But it was the first of three where someone ended up dead.

35

What the Water Wrought

San José, Costa Rica

Less than five years later, I wasn't there when Joy went to Costa Rica with her students. Even among the people who were with her in the raft, there is confusion about what happened. There is even video footage of that day. The rafting company had been filming a commercial. The footage, for obvious reasons, was never used for that purpose. It was, however, used by the insurance company and the police to investigate an accident that left one man dead and one woman, Joy, critically injured. My family and I have seen the footage. There is no way to tell if she was ever on the shore, if she dove back in, if she tried to save a dying man. But Joy was a good swimmer and that, more than anything, leads me to believe that it could be true.

I have thought on that day so very many times. I imagine what it was like to have been one of the students, the man who drowned, and Joy. It's always Joy's perspective that grips me. This is how I imagine that day through Joy's eyes.

This is my first time rafting and I'll be honest, I am terrified. But I'm a teacher, one of the chaperones, so I'm not about to let the students see my fear. I'm making lots of jokes; it's what I do whenever I'm in a stressful situation.

"Laughter is a great coping mechanism," a therapist told me after the accident where a man fell onto my car. "It is especially useful when you're dealing with things completely out of your control."

While this wasn't completely out of my control, it felt like it was. I had agreed that if we had time at the end of our trip, we would take the students whitewater rafting. So here we are. There are nine high-schoolers, the other teacher Julie, and myself.

"You sure this is a good idea?" I yell to Julie over the rushing water as we put our life preservers on.

She laughs, "Too late to back out now!"

I nod to the guide as he helps me into the raft. He assists each student to their seats and explains how the trip is going to go, what we need to do, and how to stay safe. I'm glad they already went over all of this before we got to the river because I can't hear a damn thing he's saying over the rapids.

Even before our rafts are in the water, the thunderous sound of the river is ear-splitting. It drowns out the bird and animal noises that surround us. It's overwhelming. But I try to focus on what a beautiful day it is. There are only a few clouds and the sun is high in the sky as we push off from the shore. I grip my oar tight as the raft seems to hit and jump, jerking forward, then to one side, then the other. I start laughing as I'm getting fully drenched by the spray. One of the students in my raft, or maybe in the one behind us, starts singing. I can't tell who it is or make out the words or the tune, but it makes me happy.

The rhythm of the river is carrying us along. We still have to shout to be heard, but we're able to pantomime to the trees and air above when we see the local fauna peeking out at us. So many glorious birds in an array of colors and mysterious creatures just behind the trees. Even though it's hot out, I find myself shivering with the chill of the river. My butt feels numb and my arms feel like noodles, but I'm enjoying myself. What a beautiful world we live in.

Our raft jolts, tossing everyone over the sides, and we splash in the water. Immersed, I sputter, but immediately start swimming for shore. All the practice of swimming in my youth pays off as I'm the first one to reach land. Or, at least, I think I am. There's so much chaos it's hard to see where anyone is! As I climb out and reorient myself to face the water, I scan the shore and see others climbing out too. I try to count, make sure all my students made it, but it's impossible as everyone keeps moving and I'm not sure if they're my kids or the tour guides or other tourists. I can hear voices mixed in with the roar of the river, but I still can't distinguish words. I start scanning the water and see someone drifting nearby. They're face down. Without thinking, I get back in and swim to the person. As I reach them, I realize it's someone I don't know. I reach out to him as the water rises in waves and cascades over the two of us, pulling us both under. I cannot breathe. I let go and paddle towards the surface when he grabs my life preserver. I look down into the face of the unknown man. There is blood coming from a wound on his head and spiraling in the water around his face. His eyes look sunken and his mouth is slightly open as if he cannot believe what's happening. I feel sorry for him, but he's pulling me down and I cannot pull him up. I try to detach his hand from the front of my vest as my brain screams for me to breathe. Finally free but the light is fading as I push myself up through the water. Is that up? I'm no longer sure. I try to hold myself still so I can reorient, but the force of the rapids keeps pushing me this way and that and the light is still fading and I cannot breathe.

Just breathe!

 Breathe...

  Breathe...

   Breathe...

There is no air, only darkness.

36

A Pregnant Pause

◦∞◦

Naperville, IL

A week or so after Joy had been brought back stateside, while she was lying in a coma, I discovered I was pregnant. My first impulse was to talk to Joy. I knew she would know what to do. For an instant, I forgot about her accident and only thought about my older sister who always had a plan. She would be disappointed in me; but that was okay, she was often disappointed in me. But then the images of her broken body lying there in a coma came crashing in on me. I started crying and shaking. Joy couldn't help me. I felt so selfish, focusing on myself while she was struggling to live. I felt so useless.

The air was warm, as I sat next to my ex on his roof, smoking. The sky was clouded so we couldn't see the sunset. The sky changed from a hazy gray to black. As the clouds cleared, a few stars showed their light despite the brightness of the street lamps. I was reflecting on the us that was no more. I had thought we were so good together. He had accepted me for me. He hadn't cared that I hadn't figured out what I wanted to do with my life, as he was still struggling to figure out his own. He supported my bisexuality and even confessed to his own bisexual interests. We experimented with different ideas and even had dalliances with another couple. We had been planning a life together.

But after Joy's accident, he pulled away. I could feel it, though he said nothing was happening. I heard rumors that he was cheating. I confronted; he denied; we reconciled. The day I discovered I was pregnant, I went to tell him. Before I could, he broke up with me, saying he wanted to stay friends. I went home and cried.

A week later, I went over to his place to talk, as friends. I was scared. Not of him, but of how my life was falling apart. I had already decided, but I was terrified of getting an abortion because it was surgery. I was frightened about what would happen if my parents found out. They, or rather Dad, had threatened to kick me out over sleeping at this man-child's house. What would Dad do if he found out that I had not only gotten pregnant, but had an abortion? My parents and my younger sisters had all marched in pro-life rallies. This was not a good time for me to be living at home. I tried to talk to some of our mutual friends, the only friends I had been hanging out with for the last several months, but they were still trying to figure out who to side with after our break-up. They had known him first, so... it was complicated. I couldn't talk with Joy about that, either. I felt so very alone.

As we sat out on his parents' roof, he wouldn't look at me. The dark curls around his dusky face hid his expression as I tried to explain what I needed. I had already decided when I was eleven that I wasn't going to have kids, and being pregnant didn't change that. He and I had even talked about it when we were together. He said he felt the same. He took long drags from his cigarette and said nothing, staring at the half moon. Most of the clouds had rolled away. His left knee poked out of a rip in his jeans and there was a scab that he absently picked at.

He's just a boy, my mind whispered as I stared at the scab, waiting for him to respond. He was only a couple years younger than me, twenty to my twenty-two, but he was a child. He won't be able to handle this, my mind said. I rejected that line of thought. After all, wasn't he the one who, even though I had never wanted to get married, had convinced me to accept his proposal only two months ago?

"Whatever you want to do," he said, "that's fine."

I bit my lip, then took a few puffs on my own cigarette. I wasn't going to get angry. I wasn't going to throw it in his face that I knew he had cheated on me. But I hated that he thought I was asking for his permission. I didn't fucking care if he was okay with it, I just wanted him to go with me.

"I know," I said, my words measured and calm, "I'm just asking if you will come with me when I go to the clinic."

He was silent for so long, I thought about repeating my question. Finally, he shook his head and said, "No." Flicking his cigarette over the edge of the roof, he climbed back through his window and left his bedroom.

I screamed. I screamed at the night sky until my throat was raw and one of his neighbors poked a head out of a window and asked if I was okay. I said no, but there was nothing they could do. I climbed back into his house and went after him. He had locked himself in the bathroom. I banged on the door.

"It's not like I fucking did this to myself! You were part of it. I'm not even asking for money, just that you go with me. Just that you be a fucking friend like you said you would. With all that's going on with Joy, I can't even wrap my mind around the fact that I'm pregnant. But I can't avoid it since it's my body! You're such a fucking coward. I can't believe you dumped me when I needed you most! And now you won't even be my friend? You're such a shitty person!"

I slammed my fist against the door one final time and fled. I don't remember where I drove to, but I found a place to park and a path to walk into the woods. It was full dark when I found a wooden picnic table. I sat with my feet up on the bench. I had picked up a stick and was hitting it against my belly.

"Why?" I whispered to my body.

We had used protection, double protection. Both condoms and the pill. But all six of the at-home pregnancy tests had come back positive. I dropped the stick and touched my belly, feeling heat and the welts that were already swelling. With my hands against my skin, I tried to imagine myself getting more and more pregnant, then having a kid and being a mom. But the image didn't fit. It wasn't me. I wasn't meant to have kids, and I was okay with that. Why did my body have to go and betray me?

I lay back on the picnic table and, as the sun rose, stared up at the clear pinkish sky with my fingernails clawing into my skin. I wanted to make myself bleed. I wanted to reach inside of myself and pull the fetus out. It was just a clump of cells that would grow like a cancer if I let them. I wanted to die.

I lay on that wooden table and was overwhelmed with the need to talk to Joy. Tears streamed from my eyes, down the sides of my face. But Joy couldn't help me. I closed my eyes against the ache in my heart. Where was she? Where was her soul? Did her spirit leave when she died, but not come back when she was revived? Was Joy's soul trapped inside her body with no way to connect?

Through the clouds overhead, the sky became lighter. I could hear voices off in the distance. I decided I didn't want to see anyone. I got up, got into my car, and drove.

We got the news that Joy was out of the coma a few days after that. She wouldn't be coming home right away, but as soon as she was able, she was moved to Marianjoy

Rehabilitation Center. I was still avoiding everything with classes and work, so I wasn't there when they moved her.

After another week or so, I found a friend to go with me to the clinic. I hadn't felt comfortable asking those who had been my closest friends since they were his friends too. But Leslie had become a friend through her boyfriend. She checked with her mom and not only drove me to the clinic to confirm that I was pregnant, but drove me to my appointment. She and her mom let me stay at their house for the next few days. I'd like to say that we stayed close, but Leslie was one of the people I shut out of my life when I was swallowed by depression. I'm not proud of how I treated her, especially after everything she and her mom did for me. But I am glad that years later, through social media, she and I have been able to reconnect and I got a chance to say thank you.

A few days after I came home, I still didn't feel well. Mom could tell something was wrong. One day, when I walked through the door after work at the theater, she asked me to sit with her in the family room. She was on the couch and patted the cushion next to her.

"How are you?" She asked.

I shrugged, fidgeting with my shirt. Out of the corner of my eye I could see her scrutinizing me. She was trying to figure out the best way to approach a difficult topic. This was something Mom was good at. She's the one who taught me, her tactless child, to be diplomatic in how I related to others.

"I know you've been having a rough time with the break-up. I'm sure us being gone so much with Joy has been hard on you too. But if there's anything you need to talk about, I'm here."

I nodded, feeling tears climbing up my throat and filling my eyes.

She leaned forward and looked at my face. "Oh honey!" She exclaimed, pulling me into a hug. It was too much. I was bawling. She cried too as she held me. "I know you're pregnant," she whispered.

I pulled back and looked at her. She handed me a tissue and took one for herself. After we wiped our eyes, I shook my head.

"I'm not pregnant," I whispered.

She lowered her eyes and sighed. "But you were." She stated this as if her worst fears had been realized.

I nodded. She hugged me.

"Can we not tell Dad?" I asked.

She shook her head. "I'm sorry, sweetie. But you know I don't keep anything from your father. What I can do is talk to him."

"He's going to kick me out."

She squeezed me tighter. "I'm pretty sure that won't happen. After all, I do have a say about what goes on in this house. Remember, it's my house too."

It was in the evening three days later when Dad called me into the living room. The living room was a room that always perplexed me. It was like the family room, only fancier. We'd had one in Texas and we had one again in Illinois. The houses in Venezuela were too small. It was where our parents would have important meetings with guests, where the Christmas tree was set up, and where we would spend Christmas morning opening presents. But it was also where we had to go when we were in trouble. It's where punishments were doled out and where lectures were given.

Dad had me sit on the piano bench, the only seat in the room that had no padding. He was wearing his blue work suit and looked down at me. He paced as he talked. This lecture was about me turning away from their God and opening myself to the Devil. It was an old lecture about my promiscuity. I was going down a dark path and had become a murderer. It wasn't until Dad called me a killer that I knew for sure he knew about the abortion. The lecture went on for over an hour. There were Bible verses thrown in. At the end of it, he said he loved me and I wasn't kicked out.

Yet he made it very clear that I was unsavory, a murderer, and merely tolerated. I decided then and there I would do everything I could to get out from under his roof. I would go to school, get my degree in Stage Management, and move away from his judgment.

37

The Day My Sister Became a Swan

∽

Winfield, Illinois

After Joy's whitewater rafting accident, there was something missing from Joy. I started to believe that Joy's soul had left her when she died. Maybe it floated away, then it couldn't find its way back to her when she was revived. I preferred that to the other thought I had–the idea that haunted me, that her soul was trapped and caged inside her broken body, her destroyed mind.

For a long time, I kept waiting for her to wake up. Not that she was in a coma anymore, but that she would wake up inside herself. One day she would lift her head, her hair flipping back in slow motion, like a shampoo commercial. She would have the biggest smile on her face and she would laugh. She would laugh and shout, "Haha! Fooled you! Like I'm going to have a major accident on April Fool's day. That would be ridiculous! You should have known it was a joke. Any book that had such a stupid plot twist would deserve to be thrown across the room."

Except, it did happen. She died, then she was alive. But she was different, so very, very different. Almost unrecognizable. One of my sisters mourned her as if she had died and stayed dead. She treated her relationship with our now brain-injured Joy as if she was a brand new person. It was a method that worked for her.

But I couldn't do that. There was too much history between us and I couldn't let go. Plus there were these small moments, instances where she would peek out and it would be Joy again. The Joy I knew from childhood, my best friend, my most ardent tormentor. She would be there behind her eyes, grinning at me.

The first time was the most startling. A rare moment of clarity a month after she came out of her coma. We were at Central DuPage, the Hospital she had been flown to. For a month or maybe a month and a half we were at the hospital. But it could have been Marianjoy Rehabilitation Center and it could have been a few months since she woke. The timeline was foggy when they were happening and just got more muddled as time passed. But those moments, the details, the conversations, are stark snapshots, vivid movies playing in my mind.

"You have to be the big sister now."

Joy's voice was graveled, having been little used for so long. Her stare at me was intense as her words settled in my shocked ears. We were in some sort of community room, maybe a cafeteria? The location wasn't as important as the fact that it was the first time we had spoken without family or friends around. I remember there were vending machines along a wall and we were sitting in a corner. There were other people at tables and moving throughout the room. It was bright and loud. But I could hear her soft voice. Joy was sitting in a wheelchair, unable to do much with her body. But her mind was, for that moment, her own. The delicate skin of her neck was raw from the bandages that had been removed, revealing a wound from the tracheal tube had been inserted. The rest of her skin, that was usually tanned, had become so pale, almost translucent. Her once lustrous long brown hair was oily and stringy and missing a patch from the back of her head where her skull had bounced against the board she had been strapped to on that journey from the side of the river to the road where an ambulance waited. It left a wound that would eventually heal, but never grow hair again. Her two front top teeth were loose and would eventually be removed and replaced. But her brown eyes had a rich and wise undertone I'd never noticed before. It would disappear within days after our talk as her injured brain got worse.

I sat stunned, unable to speak, her words reverberating in my mind. She was so different from the bossy older sister I knew growing up. Both of us, technically adults in our young twenties with only two years apart, were on completely different life paths. Hers had always been well mapped out and, even though it hadn't fully gone according to plan, she had her job teaching Spanish and was on her way to her next goal of marriage and kids before she was thirty. I, having dropped out of my first university, barely had a clue about what I wanted to do besides write, work in theater, and move out of my parents' basement.

Later, in my dreams, I would watch her changing, transforming, becoming something other. Sitting there in that wheelchair, she began to twist. Her lovely neck as it was still healing, arched and stretched. Feathers sprouted from the cuts and contusions all over her traumatized body, then grew from every pore. She squawked as wings bloomed along the mostly healed lacerations on her arms. Her legs, thin from lack of use, grew even smaller as her feet flattened and spread out, becoming awkward and unsteady. She stood, spread her arms, wings wide, her neck lifting her shrinking head higher as her mouth stretched to a beak. She brought her head down, beady eyes staring into mine. She had become a larger than life swan of dark portents.

"They need you." Her words were barely intelligible, clawing out of a throat that was still recovering from internal abrasions. "Please help them," she squawked so loud the place went dark and silent.

I blinked.

The swan disappeared, noises around us returned with the light. I was gazing at my broken sister.

"You're the oldest now," she said. "You have to take care of them."

I nodded. I owed fealty to my swan sister and I wanted to do everything I could to help my other sisters; to help my family. But I didn't know how. I was too busy wallowing in the mess of my own life. I was too busy avoiding; too busy in my mind trying to figure myself out, trying to find my place in the world.

I only saw my younger sisters when I would squint. They were so far away... not in physical distance, but in the space of mind and heart. My eyes had gotten cloudy, not seeing anything that was not me. My teenage sisters had changed too. That was not their fault. Our parents were exhausted, writing and rewriting what they thought our family should be. JacQueline was still growing out of calling herself Jackie and just starting to add the capital Q to her name. She was five years younger than me, an had, even before Joy's accident, become a dark room of migraine pain and silence. Jessica, verging on renaming herself to Kess, three years younger still, was a smile so tight she cracked at the edges. She spent so much time trying to make everyone around her happy, she forgot about herself. They were ever shrinking from my sight. But they hadn't gone anywhere. I was the one who was slipping away.

Joy had become a swan without wings. She could no longer move like us. Her words were squawks. Feathers landed on everything. Her attention was easily distracted. She could not form new memories. Her long term memories were difficult to access.

The care and feeding of the brain-injured swan, our Joy, fell to my mother. She rarely asked for help, though we knew she needed it. Our father did not understand her needs and I did not offer to interpret. It had been my mother's job to explain us to him for so long. But I could not fill that need for him, for her. My other sisters did what they could, but they were still so young.

When we were living in Venezuela, Joy had been my best friend; my only consistent friend as we moved from place to place. She was sometimes mean, constantly sarcastic, and often made me feel ungainly. But she was also my confidant, my champion, the most honest person I knew.

But this new Joy, this Swan Joy, she was not my Joy. I wanted my sister back.

38

Basement Flood

Naperville, IL

In July of 1996, there was a rainstorm that seemed to have no end. I had returned to living in my parents' basement between semesters at Illinois State University where I was in the Theater Program to get a degree in Stage Management and study script writing and directing. I had done some professional stage management work and was really good at it.

After Joy's accident and with the insurance no longer covering her stay at Marianjoy, Joy had moved back home as well. While her room before she had gone off to teach, had been in the basement with me, our parents set her up in the spare room on the second floor so Mom could more easily take care of her. I had landed a summer job in the costume department at the College of DuPage, where

I had gotten my Associate's degree and had worked on many shows. I was also contracted to stage manage and work on the crew for a few shows with the Buffalo Theater Ensemble and the college. It was good summer work, but it was really long hours.

In July, the biggest flash flood hit our area. I came home from the theater to total darkness. The electricity was out. I was so wet from the torrent of rain and exhausted from work, I barely noticed and went quietly down the little hall to the basement door, trying not to wake anyone upstairs. I opened the door to a pungent smell. Every once in a while, we would get a bit of water up from the sewers in the unfinished portion of the basement. I was so tired and just hoped it was very little. I would have to reset the sump. But then a shower... I really needed a shower. I flipped the light switch at the top of the stairs. Nothing. I tried the hall switch. Nothing.

I gritted my teeth and sighed. "Fuse box, sump pump, shower, then sleep."

I headed down the basement steps in complete darkness. Almost at the bottom, my foot landed in water. I was so startled, I stumbled, missing the handrail as I grabbed for it. The heavy bag I was carrying spilled forward, throwing me face first into freezing, brackish water. It was three feet of sewage water.

With my teeth chattering and wetter than I had been from the rain, I went upstairs and woke my parents and told them what I had discovered. Mom instructed me to take a hot shower while she found some clothes for me. I vaguely remember my sisters waking up, but I don't recall much else from that night.

That basement flood nearly broke Mom and me. She had so carefully boxed up and put down in the basement all of Joy's things from before her accident; before her transformation into a swan, in the hopes that one day Joy would be able to pick her life back up again. But the sewage water destroyed everything. It drowned Joy's stuff and my belongings. I would have been okay if I had only lost my clothes, furniture, and even little mementos. But it destroyed my writing. Almost everything I'd ever written by hand or printed was in the large lower drawer of my desk. The papers swelled with the water and I was unable to even open the drawer. That, along with the floppy disks I had saved my writing on were in another drawer that was under water. None of it was salvageable.

Mom and I methodically removed things from the basement. But when it became time to decide what to do with those things, we fell to pieces. We held each other, trying to squeeze the pieces back together, as we cried. My younger sisters tried to help, but weren't sure how. They watched us, feeling helpless. Joy was oblivious.

All around Dad, the engineer, were people he could not fix. He could not fix his oldest daughter who was now a broken swan. He could not save his second lost. He could not help his third daughter who had become a dark room. He could not understand his youngest whose smile would shatter into suicidal aspirations. But he could gather people to empty and clean the basement. He could fix the basement. So he did. We worked long hours to get the basement empty as the rancid water was slowly pumped out.

In the fall, as the work to restore the basement was still ongoing and my family was still in shreds, I returned to Illinois State University. I didn't want to think about home; I wanted to get away. But no matter how hard I tried, I could not escape my own mind. I was not well. I kept losing friends and I didn't understand why. I could not see that if I kept pushing them away, they would go and not return. It was me, not them.

Eventually, I dropped out. It was that or suicide.

The apartment I had been living in at school was toxic for me. People were coming in and out at all hours and my roommates were such consummate potheads that there was a constant cloud of smoke throughout the place. I tried pot a few times. While I liked the high, I didn't like how my joints reacted to it. They'd cramp up and I would be in pain for a few days after. It was a relief to move out, but I hated moving back home, again.

My father, who had renewed assisting my education financially once I got my AA degree at the College of DuPage, made it clear that if I dropped out, he would no longer help. I didn't blame him. He had two younger daughters who would soon start college, a damaged swan to care for, and a wife who needed him in ways he could not comprehend. He said I could come home, but if I decided to go back to school, I would be on my own. That was fine. I just needed a place to go to.

But then it began again...

I went back to the basement. It was fixed, but the same. Nightmares waited there. My dad, in a misguided but well meaning gesture, got me a waterbed. I had wanted one since high school. At first, I was excited. But the water reminded me of the flooding and of Joy's accident. Not wanting to seem ungrateful, I said nothing. Then, one night, I managed to puncture the bed in my sleep. I woke up thrashing in water, thinking I was drowning. My screams reached my parents. They came down to find me in a ball, rocking back and forth and drenched. My mom held me as I cried, still unable to verbalize.

The next day Dad said something about fixing the bed. I was adamant.

"No!" I practically shouted, then broke into tears. "I would rather have no bed. I can't sleep on water. I feel like I'm falling into sewage water and drowning every night. I'm so sorry!" I dissolved into tears. Mom wrapped her arms around my shoulders and held me to her as I sobbed. Dad looked on, a helpless look on his face.

I kept trying to help Mom with Joy, my swan sister. We gathered feathers, cleaned, and went to support meetings through the Brain Injury Association of Illinois. We did what we could, alway hoping that she would change back. But she never would. I had to change. I had to face that my sister was gone, my life was in shambles, and no one could save me. I had to save myself and find my own path.

In my dreams, my swan sister swam further and further away.

39

Caretaking

Naperville, IL

By 1997, Mom was Joy's full-time caretaker. She got support from the Brain Injury Association of Illinois through several programs they ran that Joy could attend. The family joined their support group when we could. I didn't attend a lot of meetings due to them being in the evening and I would be at rehearsals for this play or that, as a stage manager, assistant, backstage crew, or director.

One that stands out in my mind was where the brain injured individuals and their families / caretakers all met together. There was a heavily tattooed guy in a wheelchair who was very taken with Joy. He was about her age and, from what Mom told me later, had been fixating on Joy for quite a while. As a former member of a biker gang, he had been riding his motorcycle without a helmet and was in a crash that nearly killed him. He had recently made some great strides in expressing himself, but similar to Joy, had little filter for what he said. As we went around the circle sharing difficulties and celebrating accomplishments, before it was his turn, he blurted out, "I'm dating again."

His parents, who were sitting next to him, both looked surprised. "You are?" His mom asked.

He nodded, then said, "well, I would be, if I could go out on my own." He then stared at Joy. "You have to be my girlfriend. I've been thinking a lot about you and you're really pretty."

Joy was oblivious that he was talking to her, turned to me and said, "I have to pee."

Frustrated, he raised his voice and said, "Joy! I want to date you!"

Joy looked right at him and said, "of course you do. But I need to pee."

She stood up and I took her to the bathroom. When we returned, he and his parents had left. Mom told me later that his parents decided it was best for them to attend a support group at a different time.

Mom also worked with the Illinois Department of Human Services to get aid for Joy. The problem was, Joy fell into an odd category. She didn't need a nurse's care, but she needed someone who could handle her outbursts. Plus, there was the added issue of her age. A lot of the helpers were used to working with the elderly. Seeing someone so young was difficult to bear. One woman they sent over was Joy's age. They got along well. But, after a few weeks, she quit. Seeing Joy like that upset her and gave her nightmares.

One day, I came home from my job at the Olive Garden and found Mom sitting at the kitchen table staring out at nothing. She had a full glass of iced tea in front of her. Most of the ice had melted and tears were silently sliding down her cheeks.

She didn't look up as I came into the room and sat beside her. "We lost another one."

I didn't have to ask who she was talking about. This had been an ongoing conversation. It was one more helper that had been assigned to us from the state who couldn't handle working with Joy. There had been so many, I couldn't keep track of their names. Few lasted more than a week.

"And Joy?" I asked.

Mom looked up at the ceiling as Joy's bedroom was above us. "Taking a nap." She shook her head. "Even though she was here for almost a month, Joy never remembered her name. I don't even think Joy'll remember her at all. That's actually what got to her. Every day, she had to reintroduce herself to Joy. She felt like she was getting nowhere with her." Mom sighed and drank some of her tea. "She's right. Joy isn't making any progress. She's not getting any better."

I didn't have any words of comfort, so I hugged my mom. We both cried. I said I would try to help out. She nodded.

"I know you will." She patted my hand, then got up and went to do the laundry.

Almost a year later, she was in the same position when I got home from work.

"She was the last one, they have no one else to recommend. Joy is too violent or it's too hard to see her like that or, I don't know... they just have no one." She sighed. "At least with them not being able to find someone outside of the family, they said I could be paid as her caretaker. I'll also be able to get Jacqueline on the payroll when she's home for winter break."

At that point, I was working theater gigs at College of DuPage and with a few other theater groups and had just gotten a job at Borders in the cafe. I was making new friends and felt almost stable. I thought that I was maybe, just maybe, figuring my life out. I made a decision that I would help Mom in a more deliberate way. I would be better, I would do more.

"Mom, if you'll have me, I could also be one of her caretakers."

Mom smiled. "That would help so much, honey. Are you home tonight so we can sit down with our schedules?"

"Not tonight, but would tomorrow night work?"

She nodded, her eyes seeming to lighten with thought. "That'll also give me time to get the paperwork for you to fill out." She hugged me. "Thank you!"

After the paperwork was done, I spent two or three days a week helping with Joy. Even once I moved out and was living with Bek, I would come by during the day to give Mom a break. Since she knew me, Joy adapted well to me helping care for her. She even, for a little while, seemed to be doing better mentally. She was definitely doing better physically.

After her accident, the way Joy walked changed. Her movement was slow and halting. Mom had been taking her to physical therapy multiple times a week after she had been released from MarianJoy Rehabilitation Center. The more she got her footing, the more it became obvious that she was no longer my light-footed sister who moved like a swan over water. Her steps were clumsy and unsteady. Mom had tried to have the state appointed caretakers take Joy to physical therapy so she could do work around the house, or relax, while they were gone. But without Mom or someone she knew there, Joy got very upset and refused to get out of the car. She would scream and scratch and bite,.We lost at least one caretaker to her tantrums.

Once I started helping out with Joy a few times a week, I went with Mom and Joy to Physical Therapy. After a couple of times, Mom and I would alternate taking her when it worked with my Borders schedule.

The first time I went with them, it was a cloudy day. After

checking in, we headed into a room that smelled of sweat and disinfectant. It was not as overpowering as the hospital had been, but definitely strong. There were several beds and stairs and exercise mats and treads for walking with support and weights. Waiting in the area Mom led us over to was a young woman in scrubs with brown hair and pale skin. She had a wide smile and a friendly demeanor.

"Hi Joy! It's so good to see you again!"

I watched Joy look back at Mom. She didn't remember her, but didn't want to be rude.

"I guess so," Joy chuckled. Her slight embarrassment showed in the crooked way she held her mouth.

The physical therapist joined in with Joy's laughter. Mom and I smiled at each other. This was common; the new normal with Joy. When she didn't know someone who knew her or when someone was overly familiar, if she was in a good mood and not overwhelmed, she would laugh. If she was feeling overwhelmed or in a bad mood, she would be silent or, she would lash out with words and, sometimes, hands and fingernails. This happened very rarely but it did happen. She was in a good mood that day.

The overhead lights were those bright fluorescent ones that hurt my head since I had the beginnings of a migraine. I asked Mom if she had some ibuprofen, hoping that if I took it right away, it would settle my head down.

"I have some in the car," she replied, a worried look on her face. "Migraine?"

I nodded. She handed me the keys. I excused myself, got the pills from the car, and took them with some water from the water fountain.

When I got back to the room, Joy was walking and balancing herself between two arm rails. The mood had changed and the physical therapist was no longer smiling. Mom looked tense and Joy's lips were pinched tight.

I whispered to Mom, "Did something happen?" Her own lips tightened as she gave me a quick nod. I looked over at the physical therapist whose hand was wrapped in gauze. I pointed at it with my chin, "Joy?" Mom nodded.

I walked over to the end of the ramp where Joy was facing and started loudly cheering for her. "Look at you!" I didn't quite shout, not wanting to disturb anyone else's physical therapy plus my head was throbbing, but I spoke in a loud, enthusiastic voice. I smiled wide and gave an exaggerated golf clap. "You're almost to the end! Yay, Joy! You can make it!"

Her tight lips pulled into a smile and her movements became less stiff. Throughout our childhood I had found that my acting like a clown could break through her foulest mood. I squatted down and made faces at her until she laughed. Then stood up straight and applauded her again. "You can totally do this, Joy. It's a cake walk."

Her eyes lit up. "Do I get cake?"

I stopped myself from laughing and gave it some consideration. "If you finish everything here, maybe we can get cake. Whaddaya think, Mom?"

Mom shrugged. "Could be."

That was one thing we did with Joy. While we knew she wouldn't remember, we tried not to promise her things even if it meant it would encourage her. We didn't want to lie to her.

"Chocolate cake?" Joy asked.

Mom smiled. "We can discuss it but only if you finish everything. So not just this, but everything else, without argument."

Joy nodded and took a deep breath before continuing her walk. When she reached the end and was standing steady, I held my hand up.

"Highfive!"

"No," she said, then snorted a laugh. "I'm sorry!"

I laughed too and high-fived myself. "No worries." I winked, then turned to the physical therapist who looked more relaxed and less upset. "What now?" I turned back to Joy. "I mean, if you're okay with me doing it with you."

Joy nodded and the therapist looked surprised but grateful. I did everything Joy did, cheering her on and making silly remarks while referring back to her therapist for instructions.

When we paused for Joy to go to the bathroom, the physical therapist asked if she could chat with me. Mom said she'd take Joy. I was concerned that I was in the way.

"If you need me to step back or stop doing anything, just say so. I don't want to step on any toes."

She shook her head. "No! Just the opposite in fact. I think that because you and Joy are close in age, she sees you as competition and is pushing herself even further than she ever has. It would be great if you could come all the time."

I sighed. "I wish I could, but scheduling is hard. I have another job besides helping with Joy and work in theater too. But Mom and I are talking about my bringing her a few times a month. I'll come when I can."

She nodded, but looked discouraged.

"Tell you what," I said, having a sudden idea. "How about whenever she gives you pushback, you can tell her that Jeanine or Jeani, depending on what she's calling me that day... Oh! Or better... Ask her what her younger sister's name is and whatever name she says, she has two other sisters, say that you think that sister would do whatever she needs to do better than her. She's super competitive, especially with us, and that didn't change after the accident."

She nodded, grinning. "You know what, that just might work. Thank you." She shook my hand.

"Happy to help."

When Mom and Joy returned from the bathroom, we did a few more things. The physical therapist said things like, "I bet Jeanine could do that better than you," and Joy would get a real determined look on her face, then push herself even harder.

When we were done, Mom said something about needing to talk to the physical therapist. She tossed me the car keys so I could get Joy situated while they chatted. I took Joy to the bathroom one more time, then we headed out. As I helped her with her seatbelt, she settled back. "I'm tired."

I nodded. "I'm not surprised. You worked really hard today. Do you want to take a nap while we head home?"

She nodded, her eyes already shut. I slid the minivan door closed and climbed into the front passenger seat, making sure the doors were unlocked so Mom could get in. I was tired too and happy to sit for a bit.

On the drive home, Mom smiled at me. "Thank you for your help."

I smiled back. "Glad to do it. I just wish I had done more sooner." Mom stared out the windshield and I noticed she was crying. "You okay?" I asked.

She shook her head, still not looking at me. "I just wish your dad and I weren't so completely wrapped up in what's going on with Joy. I wish we were able to split our focus better between..."

"Mom, you're doing your best and we all know that."

She sniffled. "I really like what you did today. You challenged Joy in a way I can't and it was great. The physical therapist told me the suggestion you made and I think it'll be helpful. I like the idea of giving Joy challenges. She responded well while you were there. I just worry..." She paused.

"Oh yeah," I said. "What happened while I was out of the room?"

Mom shook her head, a discouraged look on her face. "Joy said she didn't want to walk. Instead of suggesting something else to do, the girl grabbed Joy's arm and tried to pull her out of the chair. Joy got frustrated and, I think, a little scared, so she scratched her and tried to bite her. When the therapist pulled back, Joy said, 'I'm sorry,' then growled at her. I was ready to ask for a different physical therapist. But, after she wrapped her hand, she sat across from Joy and apologized. She said she was wrong and should not have grabbed Joy. She then asked Joy if she would try and Joy did, though with a lot if huffing. That's about when you came in. I think you broke the tension and the rest was great." Mom gave a big sigh. "It's just hard not knowing how she's going to react from one moment to the next. I really appreciate everything you did today, but you don't need to feel bad about not being able to do more. We're all trying our best and..."

She lost her battle with the tears and, as she pulled into the driveway, she cried. I reached over and touched her arm, then started crying too. We sat like that, her holding my hand against her arm, as we silently sobbed.

From the seat behind us, Joy burped. "I'm hungry."

Mom and I laughed. We wiped our eyes and Mom fixed her makeup in the rearview mirror. I turned in my seat to face Joy.

"Well it's a good thing we're home! What do you want for lunch?"

She thought about it for a minute. "A sandwich? A peanut butter and banana sandwich on toast?"

I looked at Mom to verify that we had such a thing. She nodded.

"Sounds good!" I grinned, bouncing in my seat, "then we better get out of this van, don't you think?"

Joy looked at me like I had lost my mind. "Of course."

Each time I helped with Joy, I was helping myself. I got to spend time with Mom and our relationship grew in a way I hadn't thought it could. As a burgeoning teenage feminist, I said some very mean and dismissive things to her that I thought were unforgivable. But she forgave me, saying she always would. I will never regret that extra time with Mom and Joy. While it was never easy taking care of Joy, it was always easy caring for her.

40

The Swan at Graduation

Hannibal, Missouri

"Joy."

I look up and see my mom leaning into the van. She is smiling and motioning for me to get out. I think she has been speaking to me for a little while, but I don't remember what she's saying. Jessica... No, Kess now stands beside her. They're both dressed so pretty. The blue of their dresses is reflected in the sky behind them. I start to get out of the car, but realize I'm still buckled in. I try to undo the seatbelt, but it's stuck.

"Let me." Jeani climbs into the van from the other side and releases me.

She gets back out and I slowly get out too. Why am I moving so slow, I wonder. My joints ache and my body is stiff. Was I sick? I must've been sick. I walk with a slight wobble. Jeani gently catches me by my wing and walks with me.

What's wrong with me? I want to ask, but the sentence feels thick in my throat and I can't get it out. Jeani is talking. No, Jeanine... She goes by Jeanine now. Mom answers her and I think "Good, 'cause I have no idea what she said."

We walk into a large auditorium. I see Kess and Dad up ahead of us. We're following them to our seats.

"Where's Jackie?" I whisper to Jeani as we sit down. She leans forward and points to the front where we can see rows of navy blue graduation caps. I guess she's graduating. But the place is too big for a high school. How can she, my younger sister, be graduating college? I say nothing. I hate feeling confused. I hate not knowing...

"Joy, do you need to go to the bathroom?" I turn to look at Jeanine. Her brown eyes have an expression of concern. I nod.

It takes a bit to get out of the row. Now we're walking down a hall. I look at Jeani. "I have to go to the bathroom." My voice sounds froggy. Have I been sick?

She smiles and nods. She leads me to a door with a W sign on it. There is no one in the room. I head to a stall, letting go of her arm and stumble.

"Do you need some help?" She asks as she catches me.

I shake my head. She lets me go. I stumble once more but catch myself on the door and pull it closed behind me. I try to latch the lock, but my fingers are as useless as feathers. Why is everything so awkward and hard?

"Do you want me to hold the door for you?" Jeanine asks.

"Yes," I say.

When I come out of the stall, Jeani is waiting for me. I go to the sink to wash my hands. There are bits of paper towel all over the counter. I start to pick them all up.

"Joy, we don't have time for that. Why don't you go ahead and wash your hands? I'll get you a paper towel."

I turn on the water at one of the faucets and look at myself in the mirror. The face reflected back at me is not a face I know. She is older than I remember. I lean closer, staring into my own brown eyes. There is a smudge on my cheek. I rub it.

"Joy? We should get back."

I want to ask where we need to get back to, but Jeanine is handing me a paper towel to dry my hands. I take it, dry, then follow her out of the bathroom. My feet are once again wobbly, they feel too big for my shoes. Jeanine takes my wing and guides me. I want to push her off, but she's talking about how neat it is that we get to meet JacQueline's college friends. I can't help wondering how Jackie, I mean, JacQueline could be in college. I say something about that.

"I know!" Jeanine intones, "and graduating too. So weird, right?"

I agree.

After the ceremony, there are lots of people around. A crush of happy congratulations and excited graduates makes me agitated. I slap Dad's hand away from me and shrug off Kess's hug. If people don't leave me alone, I'm going to squawk!

I see Mom and Jeani talking. Jeanine comes over to me all smiles and holds out her hand. "Joy, do you wanna go for a walk? You can help me find Q."

I first want to push her away, but the idea of getting far from this crowd is very intriguing. I nod and grab her hand with my wing.

We're outside the building and I can breathe again. There are a few people here and there, but the majority are still in the auditorium. Jeanine and I find a winding sidewalk to walk on. She had been holding my hand, but once we're outside, I pull away. She lets me, but I can tell she is watching me.

It irritates me. I want to be alone, so I start walking faster. But my feet are ungainly and clumsy and I pitch forward. Jeanine catches my elbow and steadies me. I yank my wing away, squawk, and try to walk even faster. But my feet get tangled in each other and I start to go down. Jeanine dives forward to intercept me. I hear a sickening crack as her knee hits the concrete. But she twists and catches me, helping me ease to a seated position with no injury.

Beside me she gasps, clutching her leg as she slides onto the grass at the far side of the path. A man wearing a tweed jacket rushes over. He looks at me perplexed, then down at Jeanine who has her skirt hiked up as she's staring horrified at her knee. I stare too. It's getting bigger and bluer and looks like an egg. I look at her face. Her usual pinkish and freckled complexion is stark white.

"Oh goodness!" The man exclaims. "Are you okay? I mean, is there something I can do? Someone I can get?"

Jeanine takes a deep breath, then says in a shaky voice, "Can you get my Dad, John Vaughn? JacQueline Vaughn is my sister that's graduating. My family should be coming out of the auditorium."

The man nods and rushes off towards the building.

I watch him go. After a moment, I notice what a nice day it is. The sky only has a few wispy white clouds and, while the air is a little crisp, the sun is warm. I think it's spring. I'm glad I'm sitting down to really appreciate the weather. I hear a few birds in the trees on the other side of the path I'm sitting on.

But why am I sitting on a path and not on a park bench or something? I see one close by and start to get up to go over to it, but then I hear whimpering behind me. I turn to see Jeani sitting on the grass crying. As I'm just about to ask what's wrong when I hear someone shouting behind me.

"Jeanine!"

I turn. It's Mom. She and Dad and Jessica are running towards us. I wonder what's wrong. I see Jackie wearing a graduation gown and cap coming from a slightly different direction. Why am I sitting on the ground, I wonder. I start to get up, but can't get my feet under me. Jackie reaches us first and helps me up. Dad is beside Jeani, no Jeanine, and trying to get her to stand. Whenever she puts any weight on her right leg, she cries out and almost topples over. Dad and Mom get on either side of her.

"We're going to have to take her to the emergency room," Dad says gravely. "JacQueline, Kess, can you take care of Joy while we're gone?"

They both nod.

"What happened?" JacQueline asks.

Jeanine sobs out. "I'm so sorry, Q. It's your big day and..." She trails off. "Joy almost fell. I dove under her but ended up bashing my knee."

I stare at her. I almost fell? What's she talking about? I watch as Jeanine hops between Mom and Dad with her right leg bent and dangling. I wonder what happened?

"Joy, let's go inside." Jackie says, taking my wing. "Let's go get something to eat and you can meet my college friends."

"That sounds good!" Jessica says, taking my other wing. We walk towards the building.

After a minute or so of walking, I wonder where Jeani and our parents are. I figure we must be meeting them inside.

41

Bioluminescent

Clarendon Hills & Chicago, Illinois

In the summer of 2013, Mom and Dad came back to visit me in Illinois after they had retired to Huntsville, Alabama in 2007. Mom and I had been talking about them visiting me for a while, but things always came up. While I understood, it still hurt a little when they had no problem traveling to Texas to visit my sister JacQueline and her family. I mentally understood that it's more difficult to visit me because Bek and I have always had cats and Mom was severely allergic. Visiting me meant they would have to find other accommodations while they could stay with my sister and her family. There was also the advantage that visiting JacQueline meant seeing grandkids. Plus, there was always the issue of how best to take care of Joy. But emotionally, it stung. After all, they had friends in the area who had offered their houses.

So when they did come visit me and left Joy in JacQueline's care, it meant a lot. I took my folks to the Clarendon Hills Public Library where I had started working in April and they got to meet Lori Craft, the Library Director. At one point, Lori told my parents that I was a delight to have as an employee. My mom beamed.

Looking at me and smiling, Mom said, "I always like it when Jeanine works with books and people."

I had already been having the notion that being a Librarian was the path for me, but hearing her say that helped make it feel real.

We went to the Field Museum and saw the amazing exhibit they had that summer: CREATURES OF LIGHT: NATURE'S BIOLUMINESCENCE – New Field Museum Exhibition Explores Animals That Glow, Features Some Live Animals and Recently Discovered Species.

They were exhibiting the extraordinary organisms that produce their own light, something I'd read about in detail. They were going from North American backyard fireflies to glow worms from New Zealand, then all the way to the depths of the oceans for the creatures who have never known any other light but their own. They were even showcasing bioluminescent plants like mushrooms that grow on decaying wood.

As we walked through, the radiance coming from the different creatures caused my parent's faces to shine. They hadn't seemed too excited about coming, doing it more because it was something I planned for us to do together. But as we were reading the information and discussing the amazing attributes of these creatures and how their light affected the world around them, they started to really enjoy themselves.

The variety of the creatures was awe-inspiring. I knew about many of them, but I learned about many more. As we stood in front of one of the jellyfish tanks, I grinned. "I wish I could make my own light."

Mom and Dad exchanged a look then laughed. "You have always made your own light," Mom said. Dad grinned and nodded.

I smirked. "Do you remember when I learned that word, bioluminescence?"

Mom glanced at Dad who shook his head. "No," she said with a slight smile tugging at the corners of her lips. She took her glasses off and rubbed them with the bottom of her cream colored blouse. "But I'm sure you're going to tell us."

"So we were at the Seay's house in Huntsville and all us kids were out chasing fireflies. I said something about wishing I could glow. Joy said, 'oh, so you want to be bioluminescent?' I gave her an odd look, 'bio what?' 'Bioluminescent. It means to glow.' I rolled the word around in my mouth, you know, like I do with new words I really like." I stretched it out, emphasizing each syllable like I did when I learned new words as a kid, "bi-o-lum-i-ne-scent."

Mom nodded grinning as Dad snickered. He had teased me about doing that.

"Then I nodded and said, 'yeah, that's what I want to be.' Joy, Heather, and a couple of Heather's friends all huddled together, whispering. I heard one say really loud, 'she would never do that!' Heather and Joy, just as loud and in unison said, 'she would!' I stood there smiling thinking how great it was that my sister and my cousin were sticking up for me. I decided right then that whatever I had to do, I would do it. When they turned back to me, Heather was nodding sagely as Joy spoke. 'Okay, before we tell you what you have to do, you have to promise, cross your heart and hope to die, to not tell anyone, especially not Mom or Dad or Aunt Celia or Uncle Doug.' I promised and crossed my heart, then stared at them ready for my task, whatever it would be. 'You have to eat a firefly,' one of the other kids shouted. I stared. You know how much I love all critters. The very idea of eating a firefly made me queasy."

"Well, you did eat that half cricket when you were a baby," Mom said.

"She did? I didn't know about that!" Dad exclaimed.

Mom lightly swatted Dad's arm. "Yes you did, John. It was when we were in Memphis. I told you how I found the baby standing up in her crib with half of a soggy cricket in her hand and she was chewing on something. It doesn't take a genius to guess what was in her mouth. But she swallowed it before I got it out."

"Huh," Dad got a faraway look in his eyes. "I must've forgotten."

Mom shook her head then turned back to me. "So, did you?"

"Of course I did. I wanted to be bioluminescent. The group that had been around me when I was making up my mind had wondered off to play kick the can or something. They were talking about the rules in a circle, so I ran over and announced that I'd eaten a firefly. Someone said, 'that's a good start. Now you have to eat 49 more.' 'What?!' I shouted. 'Nobody said that!' They all nodded. 'Yeah,' someone else said, 'and it'll only make your butt glow.' Then they all burst out laughing. And that's how I learned the word bioluminescent and to not trust my sister and my cousin. Though I did have to relearn that several times before it stuck."

Mom and Dad were both laughing. Dad wiped his eyes. "I'm surprised you didn't come and tell us."

"Me too," Mom echoed.

"I had promised and both Joy and Heather convinced me I would get in trouble if I told anyone. So I didn't."

"Well, that's quite a story!" Dad said. "Come on, let me take my two girls to lunch."

I cringed a bit at the 'girls', but said nothing.

We ate at the Explorer Café, an area of the museum wasn't very crowded. We could still hear snippets of other people's conversations, but they were only echoes through the large open space and we couldn't easily distinguish words. Our conversation revolved around what we had seen and read. I commented about how weird it would be if human butts lit up like fireflies and we did weird mating dances. As I expected, Dad cocked an eyebrow and shook his head while Mom giggled.

"Joy would have given me the best, 'What are you talking about?' look," I laughed. Mom and Dad nodded, but but I saw them exchange a look as their smiles faded. Since we were finishing up, I asked, "What do y'all want to do next?"

Instead of answering, Mom took another bite and Dad stared down at the wrapper his sandwich had come in. The air became heavy. I looked between them, trying to figure out what was going on.

"What's up?" I asked, keeping my tone light.

Dad took a deep breath and looked up. "We need to talk to you about Joy."

I tensed.

"It's nothing dire," Mom quickly threw in. "We're just looking to the future."

Dad nodded. "As you know, your mom and I are getting older."

I resisted the urge to retort, and nodded.

He placed his hands palm down on the table, like he often did when things were serious. "And as you know, I've been having some heart problems."

I nodded again. He'd had a clogged artery and two stents put in and there had also been another problem that I didn't hear about until after it had occurred in 2012. I couldn't remember what all had happened, but it was something else with his heart. His tests afterwards had come back clear, but there was always concern since he was over 70.

"Your mom and I have been talking with JacQueline and her family about taking care of Joy. In fact, one of the reasons we decided not to bring Joy on this trip was so she could spend time with them and they could get a feel for how taking care of her full time would be."

I could feel the circulation to my fingers being cut off as I gripped my hands together in my lap under the table. But I kept my face calm and nodded, ignoring the questions exploding in my brain. The one that was the loudest was, "Are you dying?" followed by "Is this the only reason you're visiting?" But I stayed silent.

As if hearing my thoughts, Mom said, "Dad's not dying anymore than any of us are. But with Joy, we felt it was important to be prepared. So Jeff has started looking for a church for him to preach at in Alabama."

My brother-in-law, Jeff, was a minister. After seminary, (or maybe during? I'm not sure) he got a small parish in St. Jo, Texas. I always found it amusing that the town they lived in had my mom's name.

"The reason for this," Dad said, "is so they can be closer to help out your mom after I pass. We've already discussed it with both JacQueline and Jeff. They feel that this is where God is leading them to be."

They were now both looking at me expectantly.

"Okay," I said. I didn't know what else they wanted from me. I wasn't about to debate their faith or JacQueline and Jeff's faith in a God I'd walked away from many years ago. It wasn't worth even discussing religion with them on a philosophical level, much less on a practical level.

"You understand why we asked them, right?" Mom asked.

"Of course. We discussed this at Thanksgiving, remember?"

She nodded. "But your sisters were there. Even if you were upset, I don't think you would've said anything."

I smiled. Mom knew me so well! Even though I'm a confrontational person, she knew I would think about how my words affect others. She should know; she's the one who taught me. As a kid, I had no filter or sense of what was appropriate. I never got embarrassed by what someone else did, so I didn't understand why others would be embarrassed by what I did. Since my mom was so shy and easily embarrassed, she taught me to be considerate, diplomatic, and kind.

"So," she said, spreading her hands wide. "We wanted to give you the opportunity to discuss this with us." She brought her hands together and held them under her chin.

Glancing at Dad, I took a deep breath. "When y'all first told us that you were asking JacQueline to be Joy's guardian if something ever happened to either or both of you, it stung. It felt like I wasn't even considered. But it also made sense. I proved myself unreliable when Joy's accident happened. JacQueline and Jessica, even though they were kids, were there and helping the entire time. Q's also in a better place than either Kess or I to care for Joy. It may hurt my pride a bit since after Joy I'm the oldest and should be the one you can rely on, but I've not always proven to be reliable. JacQueline has. She may have some health issues, but she's always been there whenever you've needed her. Besides, my life is not constructed in a way that would be amenable to Joy's situation." I swallowed. "I love Joy; I love all of you. But I'm also realistic enough to know that, even though if it came down to it I'd take care of Joy, I am not the first choice. And that's fine."

They both exhaled and relaxed. We all got up and hugged.

But they were wrong. It wasn't Dad who died, it was Mom. That visit was the last time I saw her. But her kindness, her advice, her light still shines on. She was the essence of bioluminescence.

42

A Mother's Broken Heart

Huntsville, Alabama

In December, after my parents visited me in Illinois, Mom collapsed in the garage. She was rushed to the hospital and my youngest sister Kess called me. I had been having an allergic reaction to something, had taken Benadryl and gone to bed. I was out cold and didn't hear my phone ring the half dozen times she called. Finally she called Bek, my bestie and lifemate, who was able to wake me up.

"They've taken your mom to the hospital for surgery," Bek told me, her face twisted with worry. "But it's her heart so they're not sure she's going to make it."

I thought for sure I must be dreaming. Benadryl always knocks me out and gave me weird dreams, but Bek assured me I was not. There was no way I would be able to navigate an airport in the state I was in. I started talking about driving to Alabama. Without hesitation, Bek said she'd drive me. I'm so glad she did since on the drive there, we got the call that Mom died during surgery. She had a ruptured aortic aneurysm. She died of a broken heart. We pulled over and I wailed.

When we got there, I wondered if Joy understood what was going on. I wondered how Joy was processing these events. As I remember the events of that day, I peer through my swan sister's eyes.

It's cold as I get out of the car. The breeze tickles my feathers; ruffles my hair. We're in a parking lot that's mostly empty. I think it's morning? It's hard to tell since the sky is clotted with clouds. There is a slight sprinkle, a cold drop here and there shocking my skin. We hurry to the building. Well, they hurry, I move slow, my swan legs not so good on asphalt. As we enter the church, I catch my reflection in the glass door and notice that I'm dressed nice. It must be a holiday or something. Why black? It's not my color, but it is a nice dress. Maybe we're just having Sunday service.

Then I see Jeanine. Her face is tight, like she's trying not to cry. She looks tired. I'm confused; she doesn't go to church. Her friend Bek is standing beside her. I like Bek. I remember Bek, but I didn't know her from before. She has lots of tattoos, like Jeanine, and she's tall, not like Jeanine.

"Joy? Do you want to stand with me?"

I turn. It's Kess. My baby sister. Not that she's a baby anymore. She's taller than I am. She smiles and holds her hand out to me. I take it. We wind through the press of people into the auditorium. There is music playing and the screen behind the podium is showing pictures of Mommie. There is one from when she was a little girl, one from when she was in high school, another from her wedding, and on and on they go. I feel a tremble in my hands, a fluttering in my chest as I am stopped before I get too far down the aisle. The person who stopped me has a familiar face, but I can't remember her name. She starts talking to me about Mom.

"Excuse me," Jeanine says, stepping past the woman to me.

Behind me, Kess asks, "Do you need to go to the bathroom?" I turn and nod, realizing I do, forgetting the squawks of frustration that had been building inside me. Kess, Jeanine, and Bek make a barricade around me as we head to the bathroom.

I'm standing in a line with the family. Except Mom... Where's Mom? I look around, but don't see her. JacQueline is next to me. I turn to ask her where Mom is, but she's talking with someone. Another line of people stands in front of the line of my family. They walk to us, hug us, and tell us how sorry they are. Sorry for what? I want to ask, but I don't. It's hard to understand what everyone is saying because there's music playing and other people talking, so I just go along with the hugs and keep nodding until someone says something about Mom dying.

"Mommie died?" I whisper to Kess who's standing on my other side.

She nods. I can see she's crying. I want to cry too and hug her. But someone pulls me into a hug and someone else is hugging Kess and they're talking. I lose the thread of what they're saying, what anyone's saying, and I just nod and keep my face looking interested. But I really don't know what's going on.

I'm hungry... I think.

There's music playing. I turn and look onto the stage where there's a movie screen and pictures are being shown. But they stop and the music fades.

We all sit down. The service begins. The pastor looks familiar, but I'm not sure who he is. He mentions Mom, my mom, he says Jo. Why is he talking about Mom? I look around for Mom. But she's not sitting with us. Where would she be sitting?

I have to pee.

The service is almost over. But I really have to pee. JacQueline notices I'm squirming in my seat and asks me if I have to pee. I nod, but we're sitting in the front of the auditorium.

"Can you wait a few minutes?" JacQueline asks.

I nod so we wait until everything is just wrapping up. As

things end, I see Kess come over to JacQueline. They talk for a bit, then I go to the restroom with Kess.

After we get out, we're standing in the lobby of the church and everyone is moving around and talking. There's a corkboard with pictures of Mom on it. There are other people too, but Mom is in every picture.

Where's Mom? I think. But I don't ask because people are talking. There are so many conversations and I just want to leave.

"We're going to go eat now," JacQueline says, taking my hand. Dad is beside her. We walk through the church. There's a hall behind the sanctuary. It feels familiar. I follow my family into a large room. It's a gym, but set up with tables and chairs for eating. Along one side are other tables heaped with food.

"I'm hungry," I say.

Dad laughs. "Well, then we came to the right place!"

Others laugh too. But it is a nervous laughter. I don't know why.

We get to the front of the line. The food smells so good. But after I fill up my plate and sit at the table to eat, I notice Dad is talking with someone and crying. Dad never cries. Suddenly hands are on my shoulder and someone is hugging and shaking me from behind. I manage to get a forkful of spaghetti into my mouth and chew while they're talking in my ear. I can't really understand what they're saying, it's just so noisy in the gym with everyone's voices echoing, but I nod pretending to know what they're saying.

But I don't understand. Or maybe, I can't remember. Each time they tell me, it's a surprise and it hurts. But it only lasts until I get distracted by... anything. I don't have the memory for it. My swan brain cannot retain. Even me telling you this here, is just J9 trying to understand my mind.

Mom died on December 22, 2013 of an aortic aneurysm. Her heart ripped and tore and she fell in the garage and died on the surgery table while Bek and I were on our way to Huntsville. She died of a broken heart. She was an organ donor, so I never got to see her body before they dismantled her for parts. A part of me wishes I had the confirmation of her death through seeing her body. Another part, a bigger part, is glad that the last time I saw her was when she and Dad visited.

43

The Loss of Memory

~

Huntsville, Alabama

I wake.

I look around me. I am in a familiar room. But, is it familiar? No. The things in it are familiar. They are mine... I think. I see a wood carving with Joy painted on it. My name, it is mine. It was a gift from... I don't remember who. I see my swans. So many swans. I love swans. I've collected them since... I can't remember. I see furniture. It is familiar, but it is not mine. I think it's Jeani's. Am I in Jeani's room? Why would I be in her room? Am I going to be late for school? I look at the clock by my bed. The red light says 5:30 am and it is dark outside. I don't need to be up this early. I know there is a reason I woke up, but I can't remember what it is. I close my eyes. As I drift back to sleep, I shift uncomfortably in the bed. It is wet and cold. I dream I am sleeping on a pond, floating on the water and I am a swan. Everything is peaceful.

"Joy."

I wake.

The room around me is familiar, but not, at the same time. A woman stands by my bed. She too is familiar, but not. Mom? No. Jackie? I think that's right, but she's too old to be Jackie. Three children come into the room. I know them... At least I think I do. They are... who are they? The little boy gives me a hug, tucking himself under my wing. I know him. I love him. Caleb. My little buddy. The two girls, a blonde and a redhead, I know them. I love them too. How do I know them? Katie and, and Sydney! These names belong to them. Are they cousins? No. They are Jackie's. How are they Jackie's? Jackie is so much younger than me. Do I have children too? Why can't I remember them? Am I married? I was always meant to marry. I want to ask, but I don't have the words.

Someone is talking.

I look at the woman. I almost say Mom, but she's not Mom. I look around the room. I am sitting at a kitchen table in a breakfast area just outside the kitchen. The woman who is speaking is in the kitchen. There is a bar with barstools between us. On top of the bar, clothes are folded. I look in front of me. There is a coloring book. I like coloring. Colored pencils sit in a box beside the book. I take one out. Someone has been coloring on this page. I don't want to color where they have been coloring. I turn the page to save their work. There's a dog on this page. I like dogs. I wonder where Midnight is. I turn to ask mom, but it's not mom it's... Jackie?

My mouth is open, like I was going to ask something, but I forgot what it was. I look back at the book in front of me. I look at the pencil in my hand. It is the wrong color. I select a different colored pencil. I color.

"Joy?"

I look up. A woman... (Mom? No, not Mom) stands in the kitchen.

"Why don't you clear the table?"

Her voice is familiar. Jackie? No. This person is too old to be Jackie. But I know her. I nod and close my book. I pick it up and stack the colored pencils on top of it. I stand and pick up the coloring book and pencils.

"Joy?"

I look over. It is Mom, my mother. She is smiling. She looks older than I remember. Her once brown hair is mostly gray and her face is pale with more wrinkles than I remember. But her green eyes are still shining behind her glasses. She is so beautiful.

"Why don't you put that on the counter behind you?"

I turn. There is a stack of coloring books and a pile of colored pencils. I add mine to the stack. I wonder where they all came from. Are they mine? I look at my hands.

"Joy?"

I turn to Mom. Not Mom. Hair and eyes brown and a rosy face. Jackie? No, JacQueline. She is no longer a little girl. She is holding a damp dishcloth out to me.

"Where's Mom?" I ask.

She looks pained. She takes a deep breath. "Mom died."

I start to cry. "Mom died? But…" I want to say, but she was just here. Only, I'm no longer sure. Was she here? Was that now? Did that happen at another time and I was just remembering?

Jackie nods and comes over to me. She sets the dishcloth on the table. She is also crying. She hugs me.

"Do you want to pray for her?"

I nod, then shake my head. "No, you pray."

She nods. We sit at the table.

"Dear Lord. Thank you for loving our Mommie so much. We miss her. But we know that she is in a better place with you. Amen."

Jackie squeezes my hand then goes back to the kitchen.

I look over at her. She is crying. I don't know why. I notice the dishcloth on the table. I take it and wipe the table.

When I am near the window, I see a bird. It's a hummingbird. I go to the window. There is a hummingbird feeder with hummingbirds all around it. I remember the hummingbirds out on the tiny patio we had when we were living in Caracas, Venezuela. They loved the flowers that grew there. Jeani liked to sit out there with them. Sometimes I joined her.

Should I go outside? It's a sunny day, but I'm pretty sure we're not in Caracas. There is grass and a little wall, a tiny hill. It looks familiar but I don't know where I am.

"Joy?"

I turn my head and look over my shoulder. I see Jackie standing in the kitchen. She is holding out her hand. Her face looks sad but I don't know why. Maybe she has one of her migraines? I look down at my hand and see a dishcloth. I wipe the table and bring it to Jackie. No, not Jackie, JacQueline. She hands me five plates. I try to think of who they're for. Me, her, Jessica, Jeani, and Mommie I guess. Daddy must be out of town again. I set the plates on the table, then think, or is it, me, her, and her three kids? I wonder where her husband is. What's his name? Jeff? Maybe he's out of town or working late at the church. I go back over to the kitchen and get the silverware and napkins to finish setting the table. When I'm done, I sit in my spot.

After dinner, I go to the bathroom, then come back to find a coloring book and colored pencils at my spot. Jackie (not Jackie, JacQueline) brings over a medicine cup full of pills.

"I can't believe I forgot to give you these with dinner again," she laughs. I toss them back like a shot.

I remember a different shot of the alcoholic variety that I had when I was in college. It wasn't at college; I was visiting home and out with a few high school buddies. Drinking at Baylor, where I went to college, was more than frowned upon since it was a dry campus. If found out, you could get expelled. But back home, it was fine! I was dressed up and my friends and I were at a bar lookin' good. There were a few other friends, but they had stepped away. I think someone had volunteered to be designated driver or maybe I did and I was just having the one shot before dancing? That was okay. My friend was happily telling me about something as the music drowned her voice out. I don't remember what it was, or maybe I never really heard it, but I remember smiling and nodding and swaying to the music.

"Joy."

A woman stands beside me with a glass of milk. There are pills in my mouth. I take the glass and drink them down.

I set the glass next to my coloring book. I open the book. Someone has already started a lot of these pictures. I turn to a page where nothing has been colored. It's a swan. I love swans. I wish I could be a swan. They're my favorite animal. I select my yellow colored pencil and begin with coloring the top of the bird's beak. I color the bottom in orange. I do the dots inside the diamonds on the frame of the page in red along with some of the berry looking bits in the swan's feathers. I start to color the diamonds pink, but the tip of the pencil breaks. I notice that the swan has an eyebrow. I pick up a blue marker, blue is my favorite color, and color the eyebrow then the rectangular frame. The marker is fading so I set it down and pick up the blue colored pencil to finish the diamonds. The feathers are white, like a swan, so I think I'll leave it. But then I decide to put my name in blue in the swan's feathers, Joy C. V. I start to color another feather...

"Joy."

44

Pancakes

Naperville, Illinois & Huntsville, Alabama

In the year 2000, after I had moved out of my family's home for the last time, but while they were still living in Illinois, I would come back and help with Joy's care. Sometimes, I'd arrive early enough to get Joy out of bed then have breakfast with her and Mom. Both of my younger sisters were adults, but JacQueline was away at college and Kess was helping out when she could. Both Kess and I were working at the Borders in Wheaton, but we had different schedules.

On days that we had pancakes, Joy would almost always watch me, then give me a weird look.

"What?" I'd ask, picking up my pancake with my fingers and taking a bite.

"You're supposed to use a fork," she'd say, waving her syrupy fork, a bit of the syrup landing on my hand.

I'd wipe the tiny droplets off, then ask, "Do you use a fork with toast?"

She'd wrinkle her nose at me. "No! That's stupid."

"Well," I'd say, taking another bite of my pancake, making a big show of chewing and swallowing. "If you don't pour syrup on it, a pancake is more like toast and you can eat it with your fingers. Right, Mom?"

Mom would shake her head. "No. Don't get me involved. I can't understand how you can enjoy pancakes without anything on them. When you were little, you would drown your pancakes in syrup."

I'd shrug. "Tastes change, I guess. I just like them without anything. Pure, as it were. Though I sometimes put peanut butter on my pancakes."

"Ew!" Joy said. Then, "I'm sorry," her voice shaking with giggles.

"Don't be!" I'd grin. "You don't know what you're missin'."

"And I don't want to know, either!" Then Joy would give a full toothy chuckle. Those two front teeth, the ones that made her smile so toothy, weren't her real teeth. Her natural two front teeth had been knocked around during the rafting accident and, after a few years, had to be replaced.

Mom and I laughed too. Then we went back to eating our

pancakes. But a couple of minutes later, Joy looked at me quizzically.

"What?" I asked, knowing full well why she was giving me that look.

"You're supposed to use a fork."

I smiled and waved my half-eaten pancake at her, saying in a silly voice, "Not if they're naked!"

Then she snorted with laughter.

"Pancakes."

It was one of the last things Joy said. She smiled at the thought of pancakes in the morning... a morning she would never see. A morning that would be so dark for us who loved her, so bereft of light, that it might as well have been night. I hope she slept through everything that happened. I hope she died dreaming of pancakes.

"Joy," My youngest sister Kess says, "please hold still."

"Where am I?" I ask her as she combs my long brown hair. It's wet; I must've just taken a shower. Or had I been swimming? I'm sitting on a bed in an unfamiliar room. It's very dark out the window I'm facing and I'm in a nightgown, so I know it must be bedtime. I wonder why Kess was putting me to bed instead of Mom. But before I ask, she's talking.

"Joy, you're at my house, remember? Jeff, JacQueline, and the kids are visiting Jeff's family in Missouri for Thanksgiving, so you get to stay with me. Pretty cool, huh?"

I nod. "Will we have Thanksgiving with Mom and Dad?"

Kess pauses combing my hair. Her entire body goes still as she looks off to the side. Her green eyes are shining. They're so much like Mom's eyes that I, for a moment, think she is Mom. Wasn't Kess just a teenager? She is the only one of us kids who got Mom's beautiful eyes.

"Ummmm, we'll have Thanksgiving with Dad and Margaret. You remember Margaret, right?"

"Margaret Boreman?" I ask. "She was one of my best friends in high school."

Kess grins, but her grin feels sad. "Not that Margaret. The Margaret Dad married. Remember?"

I nod, not understanding, then hear a huffing sound coming from the other room. "What's that?"

Kess laughs. Her lovely cherubic face spreads wide with a smile.

I smile back. "I like that."

"What?" She asks, startled.

I point to her face. "When you smile."

Her smile widens. "I smile because of you."

I nod, "Of course! That's why my name is Joy."

She laughs again and I join her as a dog's nose pushes the door open. I crane my swan neck forward, staring.

"Is that Midnight?" I lean even further, thrilled to see our parents' black lab.

Kess goes quiet again, her green eyes somber. "No. Midnight died a while ago."

I nod, then shake my head as a slow moving beagle ambles into the room. "No, that's your dog." I reach out, leaning over the side of the bed to pet her. She smells like the outdoors and dog food. "What's her name?"

Kess tilts her head, the seriousness still in her eyes, but with a bit of mirth whispering at the edges. "I think you know it."

Patting the beagle's black and tan marked head, I concentrate really hard. She sniffs me, then sniffs the bedsheet. "B-B-B-B-Bessie?"

The delight has come back into Kess's voice. "Close. Now add a T."

"Bestie?"

She laughs. "Now move that T around…"

"Betsy!" I gasp.

"That's right!" She hugs me and hugs Betsy too. Betsy gives a little huff, then wanders back out of the room.

"Now, to the important stuff," Kess says, as she helps me lie down and tucks me in. "What do you want for breakfast?"

"Pancakes," I say with no hesitation. I love pancakes.

"I thought you might say that," Kess teases. "I already picked all the ingredients up at the store." She kisses me on my forehead then stands and turns off the light. "I love you, you know."

"I know," I say. I yawn, closing my eyes and falling asleep.

In my dream, I am a swan flying high in the sky above everything. It's night, not the usual time for swans to fly, but I am not a usual swan. I stay aloft, high above my body and the cares of the world. I do not hear or see the wall breaking, the truck crashing, the crushing of my body, or the man inside the truck, cursing. But I sense something is broken. I feel cut off from my body. I fly lower and see Kess bolting upright in her bed. From dead asleep to wide awake in less than a second. She thinks there's been an earthquake. She's not too far wrong, as the foundation of her life splits apart... again. I watch her as she shouts my name, helpless to tell her, "I'm here!"

I watch as she rushes across the house through rubble that has become smoke. Drywall ground to powder blurs her vision, getting in her eyes, hair, nose, and mouth. I watch her choke and cough as she grabs her phone, calls 911, calls Dad, calls JacQueline, calls Jeanine, calls her friends. I watch as neighbors gather around the now partially demolished house trying to understand. Kess, her face smudged and streaked with tears and dust, stumbles over to the truck inside her house. The truck that had broken through a wall, destroying the safety of her home, shattered all sense of peace.

She screams, "GET OFF MY SISTER!" as she bangs the door.

The man cowers in the cab of his truck.

The truck hit the wall so hard that water is spewing into the air from busted pipes. Sirens blaring in the distance are getting closer and louder. Neighbors and police are making their way through the rubble into the house and to my sister. They are pulling her off the truck as she cries and wails. Her sounds are the keening of a banshee that pierces the very fabric of serenity.

My view of the scene is starting to fade as Dad and more emergency vehicles arrive. Sounds are falling away when I know they should be getting louder. I feel I'm being pulled further and further from the scene before me.

"No!" I shout, flapping my wings as hard as I can, trying to get back. But it's useless. The stars in the sky are going out one by one and I am falling upwards into their darkness. There will be no pancakes ever again.

45

The Swan and the Ram

Dreaming in Illinois

After understanding the specifics of Joy's demise, I began having recurring dreams; nightmares. In one, Joy was standing in the middle of a street in Guadalajara with cars speeding all around her. I was not able to get to her. I called to her in English and Spanish, but she couldn't understand what I was saying and all the cars were honking. The drivers all looked like the picture of Joy's killer. Just before she got hit, I woke up.

In another, I was driving like mad to find her, to stop her being killed, but I was always late. I was always just around the corner from her but could never see where she was, then I would get lost.

The worst dream, the one that became the litany of my sleeping mind, was the one where I was there in Alabama but helpless; the one Joy was a swan.

In that nightmare, I was standing outside Kess's house. I knew that this was the night it would happen and I had come to stop it. I thought, at first, that I was a time traveler, here to save my sister. I tried to call Joy's name, but found I had no voice. I leaned against the outside wall of the house, screaming without sound.

Joy, my oldest sister, my Swan sister, slept beyond that wall. I knew what was about to happen. But just like Cassandra, I spoke my prophecies to an uncaring world. No one could hear me as I was but a shade, a future shadow. Their future, my past, all wrapped in a gauze of dream cloth.

Behind me, I heard the beast snorting, hooves scraping the ground. I could not turn. Behind the beast, a man yelled at his mother. He was angry, his mind muddled, his perception altered. (Even in my dreams, I was not privy to the reason for his rage. I just knew the fire of it.) His mother felt the violence brewing in her son. She locked the key to her truck in a safe and left the heat of his fury. He took an ax to that safe. No one would stop him. He would unlock his rage. Nothing would get in his way. The beast was fueled by fury.

He strode out of his mother's house, keys in hand, to her truck. It was a truck but not just a truck, it was a weapon in the wrong hands. A Dodge Ram, a ram. That Dodge Ram truck transformed into a ram that was a beast of violent and explosive encounters. The man climbed into the ram; onto the ram. He was no longer a man, he altered his form, shifting into the thing he inhabited, as a storm of rage inhabited him. He became The Ram. A seething storm of anger, drugs, and alcohol fueling him, powered the beast he had become. Red fury blocked his view, his perception of the world beyond his aspect. Hooves striking sparks as he pounded the ground, sideswiping a car, breaking fences, crashing through bushes. He was aflame.

The sky was overcast, but not raining.

It's not raining...

Why was there no rain? For what was about to happen, there should be, should have been a torrent; a downpour. If there was rain, my Swan Sister might have swum away. The world should mourn. There should be no sun ever again.

I stood between The Ram and my youngest sister's house. Wishing, just that once, just that dream, for the power to stop him; for the power to sacrifice myself for her, even if only in a dream. But I was a ghost, a mere whisper of thought.

In the real world, in the world where this impossibly improbable thing actually happened, I was hundreds of miles away in an airport. But the dream was more than a dream. It was a fact. It has already happened and my dream-self is but smoke as the Ram passes through me.

The silent air was cut by an angry bellow as a horrid crash of metal blasted through the wall of my youngest sister's house with such force it shook the very foundation. The wall collapsed and the Ram was still running. My oldest sister, my Swan Sister, was in the bed against the far wall, sleeping. (I hope she slept. I hope she heard, saw, felt nothing.) The Ram blazed through the room, destroying everything in its path, crushing her brittle skeleton beneath his fury. As the air was filled with drywall dust, feathers, splintered wood, broken bones, and water from mangled pipes, the house engulfed the Ram, holding him where he stopped.

I am glad the Ram was trapped.

Over and over in these dreams, I watched my youngest sister, Kess, come running. She was terrified and angry. Her green eyes were filled with such pain. She blinked away tears that wouldn't stop flowing. She screamed and banged on the door of the truck. It was not a beast, not an animal, not a ram. It was a Dodge Ram truck that sat upon our oldest sister; our broken swan. There was a person behind the wheel. A man who held such anger in his heart he cared not who he hurt. He, a stranger, rammed into my sister's home, crushing the most fragile of us all. This person killed our Swan Sister.

I wish he were dead.

If he had died too, this would be over. I would still be angry, mournful, confused, but at least, it would be over. I would not be wrapped in vengeful thoughts. Other times, I'm glad he's still alive and caged. I wish for him not to know sleep. I hope he is tortured by his own mind. I want him to have no peace. I want to know that, if he does sleep, his sleep is as dreadful as mine. I want to know that he suffers every day as we suffer, awaiting his trial.

46

Journey Adjourned

Chicago to Guadalajara

I was at the O'Hare International airport on the night of November 24, 2018 and it was almost midnight. Overhead, the speakers crackle to life and announce my flight at the exact same time that my phone buzzes. I answered while gathering my bags off of the chairs I'd been sitting on. Passengers on all sides were doing the same. A child began to cry.

"There's been an accident…" There was no preamble, just the voice of my youngest sister, Kess.

I cradled my phone close and learned that the accident happened at Kess's house. I learned that Joy was part of the accident. I felt my insides become liquid.

"What happened?"

"There was a truck and, and…"

Her voice faltered, wavering between loud enough to hear and so faint I was straining. After she repeated herself, I understood that a truck crashed into her house where Joy was sleeping. Kess was asleep in her room on the other side of the house. But the voices all around me were getting louder. Around Kess, voices are vying for her attention while her dog barked. I didn't know what to do. Kess apologized and told me she had to get off the phone… I did too.

"As soon as I land, I'll call." I said. "I love you!"

"I love you too," she said, then she was gone.

I held the phone next to my ear a bit longer, listening to nothing. The line I was standing in started to move, jerking me out of my daze, and all the sounds came rushing back at me. I called Bek and asked her what she thought I should do. She said I had to make the decision, but reminded me that I was in an airport in Chicago and my sisters were in Alabama. Even though it hurt, I decided to board the plane.

My feet felt like they were made of solidifying molasses as I boarded the plane to Mexico. The logical part of me said I should go, but after that call from Kess, I worried about Joy. What did Kess mean when she said there was an accident? I felt the world is once again wobbly as the worry nibbled at my mind. What if something horrible had happened? I feel panicked. Should I get off the plane and stay?

No.

    Breathe...

        Everything will be fine.

I focused on the trip and even got into a conversation with one of my fellow travelers. She didn't speak much English and was delighted when I spoke to her in Spanish. She shared that she was returning home to see her family, a daughter and grandkids. I explained that I'm studying to become a Librarian and would be taking part in the Feria Internacional del Libro, the International Book Fair, with my grad school class. I told her how excited I was to merge my passion for library work with my love of Spanish and other cultures and how cool it was that I was going to be purchasing books in a variety of languages. She told me about her childhood in Mexico. I shared about growing up in Venezuela. I even talked about Joy being a Spanish teacher.

But even as I had this conversation, I felt like I was sitting outside myself. I kept being reminded of that first day of April when Dad greeted me at the door.

That too was an accident.

        I've been here before...

hing is everfine.

Hours later, we landed in the crepuscular light of predawn. The airport in Jalisco, Mexico was a tram ride away from where the plane lands. The sun was just starting to peek over the horizon as I climbed down the aircraft ladder. As soon as my feet touched the tarmac, I checked my phone and saw that there were several voice and text messages. Instead of reading or listening to them, I called Kess.

She told me Joy was dead.

"Dead?"

I repeated, standing stock still as the line of passengers swirled around me. The air was so thick, I couldn't breathe. Rolling suitcases knocked my ankles and someone grumbled when their shoulder bag hit my back. But I didn't care; I barely felt anything.

I was no longer moving...

                thinking...

                              breathing...

This wasn't the first time I'd heard those words, nor was it the first time they'd been true. But it was the last time my sister Joy, my swan sister, died.

Inside the airport, it was very crowded. A cacophony of greetings and squeals and rapid fire talking in both English and Spanish and other languages I couldn't pick out. The sun glared through the glass building, causing me to squint. The air smelled of sweat, fast food, cologne, and perfume so sweet I felt nauseated. I wanted to crumble to the floor and wail, but I took a few deep breaths with my eyes closed, until I could walk without heaving or crying. I stepped into the fray and looked around for someone with a sign. I finally found Sergio, a friend of my teacher Ann Barnhart, who was couriering students from the airport to the hotel.

He had a wide smile and greeted me with, "¡Bienvenidos a Guadalajara!"

I greeted him in Spanish then, unable to stop myself, launched into telling him about Joy.

He shook his head. "No mucho Inglés."

"Lo siento," I apologized, immediately switching to

Spanish, the words tumbling out faster than I could think them. "Quando el avión llegó aquí, llamo a mi hermanita que está en Alabama porque me llamó justo antes de subir al avión que hubo un accidente. Cuando llamé, ella me dijo que nuestra hermana mayor estaba muerta."

Tears were streaming down my face as I looked into such kind brown eyes. He gently guided me out of the pressing crowd and asked me to explain it again. I took a deep breath and told him that Joy was dead. I explained the whole situation, Joy's brain injury, how our family cared for her, how she was at Kess's house because JacQueline's family had gone to visit the in laws, how she just so happened to be sleeping in a bed that was not her own when a truck came crashing through the wall of the house and crushed her in her sleep.

We were both crying at that point and this stranger I had just met, gave me the hug I needed. I knew I didn't need to explain all of that, but I couldn't stop myself. I felt like a faucet that once turned on, wouldn't turn off until the sink had flooded.

He asked me what I wanted to do.

"I – I want to..." my voice choked up and I took a deep breath. "Go home. Necessito ir a mi casa, hogar... necessito mi familia."

He nodded and guided me to a bench then called Ann. I heard him relay everything I had just told him then brought the phone over to me.

"I am so sorry!" I sobbed into the phone.

"No. You have nothing to be sorry about! Sergio is going to try to get you another flight back to Alabama..."

"Chicago," I said with a shaking voice.

"Chicago?"

"Yeah, my family lives in Alabama, but my partner and I live just outside of Chicago and I need to see her before I go to Alabama."

"Got it. Chicago. But if he can't, he will bring you to the hotel, okay?"

"Okay, thank you!"

"Of course. Please hand me back to Sergio."

I held the phone out to him and he took it. He stepped a little bit away so I couldn't hear him this time, but he seemed to be mostly listening.

My heart was pounding, I closed my eyes and went back to deep breathing. Joy is dead. The words kept playing over and over in my mind. But in between those words were other thoughts of how I wasn't going to get to do all the things I had come here to do. Self pity slid into my sorrow, giving it a bitter taste in the back of my throat.

We weren't able to find a flight, so Sergio drove me to the hotel. It was a beautiful sunny day and we rode with the windows down. He asked me how I knew Spanish, so I told him that my family lived in Venezuela when I was little. He nodded and said I spoke beautifully. I thanked him. Then we rode in silence for a few minutes.

At a stop sign, he said, "No es lo mismo, pero mi padre murió en un accidente de caro cuando era joven. Fue muy inesperado y mi familia se ayudó mutuamente inmediatamente después de que sucedió."

I listened as he explained his father's car accident and how it brought his family closer together right after it happened. He talked about how the shock was overwhelming and he felt powerless, like the world had turned its back on his family as life went on around him.

"Lo siento," I said when he fell silent.

He nodded, then said, "la razón por que estoy hablando de esto es porque recuerdo que justo después de enterarme, no podía pensar con claridad y lo único que tenía sentido era estar con la familia."

He paused as he made a quick, almost 180 degree right turn that put us on an uphill road. His driving was fast but sure, even with all the traffic. It reminded me of the taxi drivers in Caracas.

He glanced over at me. "Una cosa más. Recuerda siempre que tu duelo tomará el tiempo que necesita y debes respetarlo."

I nodded, not fully understanding. Years later, that advice of respecting my grief and allowing it to take the time it needs, would come back to me and help me. At that moment though, my appreciation was for his understanding that I needed to be with my family.

We arrived at the hotel and he insisted on carrying my

luggage. Ann, who I'd only ever known online through our virtual class, greeted me with a hug like this wasn't our first in person meeting. I melted into her, crying on her shoulder. She introduced me to Lisa, the other professor chaperoning the trip, and she hugged me too. I told them that I was supposed to be meeting with a book distributor who I had an agreement with for shipping the books I bought back to the Oak Park Public Library. I was actually surprised that I even remembered that.

Ann helped me find my contact who was so very kind and understanding as I explained the situation. She then whisked me back over to Lisa who helped me find a flight. She had me go with an airline she had points with and insisted on using her points for part of the cost. This kindness put me in tears again. Ann came back from speaking with Sergio. By the time we had my flight figured out, he had left to pick up some other students.

"Oh no," I said to Ann as she sat on one of the plush lobby couches, "I didn't get to say thank you properly."

She and Lisa exchanged a smile. "No worries, he'll be the one driving you later back to the airport, so you can thank him then. In the meantime, I know you've been traveling since last night. Are you hungry?"

I nodded.

"Let's go over and get some breakfast in ya. I highly recommend not eating your favorite food or even something you've always wanted to try since, with the state you're in, it will become associated with the death of your sister." She waved her long fingers in the air and shook her head. "That's just my experience. You might process things differently."

"No, I appreciate the advice. I don't even know if I'm really hungry or just thinking I should eat since I haven't since yesterday afternoon. I might not even keep it down."

Lisa, who was now standing next to Ann, said, "don't worry about that."

We headed over to the dining area. I remember introductions and shaking hands with a few other people, but I have no idea who they were. The food smelled delicious and spicy, but I took Ann's advice and ate something relatively bland that I wouldn't miss if I stopped eating it due to a negative association. I have no memory of what it was. Ann then suggested I should wait in my room until it was time to go back to the airport.

"I doubt you'll be able to sleep, but it might be good to just rest and meditate for a bit, you know."

I nodded, grateful for the opportunity to get away from the lobby that was becoming more and more crowded. I started towards the elevator with the key Ann had handed me, then stopped and turned back to her.

"The room! I – I got..."

"Don't worry about it," Ann said. "Rest and get back home. That's all you need to think about right now."

When I got up to the room, another wave of sorrow washed over me. It was a nice hotel and the room was lovely. I would've been sharing it with a classmate I had only met online. But now, I wasn't even going to get to meet them. I flopped on my temporary bed and screamed into a pillow.

It took me more than a day to get back from Mexico. I tried to go to Chicago first, thinking I'd leave from there with Bek. But it was winter in Chicago and there was a snowstorm and my flight got grounded in Dallas. There was no news about when Chicago would open up again; just the ominous warning that the storm was building. I joined the long line of frustrated people who were getting new flights since theirs were canceled and half of the system was down because so many calls were being made. When I finally made it to the front of the line, a few airline reps helped me find a flight to Huntsville with just one connecting flight in Atlanta. But I had to make it to the gate on the other side of the terminal. I asked them about the connecting flight's ticket, but the printer was down so they said I should get the ticket at the booth when I landed. I called Bek and updated her on what was happening as I practically sprinted the length of the terminal. I just made it before they closed the gate. But there was some confusion and they did not have the ticket for my connecting flight. Because of grief, sorrow, or lack of sleep, or all of the above, I forgot to get the flight number. When I arrived, there was no one at the desk to print the ticket. When I got to the ticket counter, they had no record of me. I ended up having to purchase another ticket. But I eventually made my way across the country to Huntsville.

I arrived exhausted. Dad picked me up at the airport. He

explained in more detail what had happened to Joy. Having heard it from Kess on the phone and then from him, it should have felt more real, but it didn't. It was just too bizarre. We rode in silence the rest of the way to the house he shared with his new wife, Margaret. (Dad had remarried less than a year after Mom died.) He set me up in one of the rooms. After calling Bek again and confirming she was on her way, I went to sleep.

When I woke, my youngest sister Kess was in the house. JacQueline arrived with her family and other family members arrived as we went to the airport to pick up Bek. Then we were at the morgue. Everything was moving so fast. A man asked if we wanted to see Joy's body. I remembered how unreal Mom's unexpected death had been and still was for me and wondered if seeing her body would have helped, so I said yes. Bek came with me.

The air was stale and dry as I entered the white room where, the smell of formaldehyde and the buzz of the overhead florescent lights assaulted me, pinging the migraine that was already growing. But I opened my eyes wide against the brightness, taking it all in. Around me, it felt like the room was holding its breath. I stepped towards the only piece of furniture in the room, a metal table. The cloth covering her body was lowered so I could see Joy's face. My breath hitched as I was reminded of how she looked when I saw her in a coma after her whitewater rafting accident half of a lifetime ago, slack and peaceful to an obscene degree. But there were no wires going from her to a bunch of machines. No beeps to indicate her pulse, her life. She was not breathing. I almost announced that she was not breathing, but managed to stop myself. Joy was dead. I knew this. After a few minutes of staring at her, I reached out and touched her cheek. Her sallow skin felt like paper. I realized I had also stopped breathing as my lungs started to burn. I still waited to step out of the room before I took a breath.

Bek placed a hand on my arm, steadying me. I looked at her and nodded that I was fine. We walked away from the room that held Joy's body.

When we arrived in the other room, the family was picking out Joy's urn; such an odd ritual. We agreed on a blue one since that was her favorite color. Then we went to a large office where the whole family, including Margaret and one of her daughters Allison (her other daughter, Lora, wasn't able to be there), discussed what should be in the obituary. I didn't want them there with my family, but I said nothing. I knew I was being selfish. They may not have known Joy as long, but they loved her too. I spoke up when the mortician was listing family for the obituary and insisted that Bek should be included.

"We've been together almost twenty years," I said, looking at Dad. Even though our relationship is unconventional as she's straight and I'm queer and we're polyamorous, she's my partner, my lifemate. She was there with me, and I wanted that acknowledged.

Tight-lipped, Dad agreed.

Even small victories are worth the effort.

From the Berryhill Funeral Home & Crematory:

"Joy Clarece Vaughn, age 48, of Owens Cross Roads passed away Sunday, November 25th.

She is survived by her father, John (Margaret) Vaughn; sisters, Jeanine Vaughn (Rebecca Huston), JacQueline Vaughn Roe (Jeff), Jessica Vaughn, Allison Tofflemire (Steve), Lora Bennett, and nieces Katie Roe, Sydney Roe, and nephew Caleb Roe.

She was preceded in death by her mother, Josephine Seay Vaughn.

She was born in Miami, Florida in 1970. She graduated from Baylor University in 1993 with an Education Degree in Spanish. She was injured in a white water rafting accident to the point of nearly drowning on April 1st, 1995. Her injury occurred in Costa Rica where she was chaperoning a trip of 11th grade students studying Spanish. She lived in many places. She lived in Venezuela for five years where she fell in love with the Spanish culture. She studied extensively and taught at Batavia High School in Batavia, IL. She was a member of Southside Baptist Church where she was a member of the special needs class.

Visitation will be Friday, November 30th from 10:00 – 11:00 a.m. at Southside Baptist Church, followed by a Celebration of Life at 11:00 a.m. officiated by Pastor Michael Walker and Pastor Jeff Roe.

In lieu of flowers the family would like donations to the Alabama Head Injury Foundation."

They let us look it over and the mortician asked if it was all correct. Dad said yes, and the conversation moved to the funeral plans.

But they had it wrong; they had to. If she died when the police said she died, the obituary would have read November 24th. Her killer rammed through the wall of Kess's house and crushed Joy before midnight. They said she felt nothing; she died instantaneously. They didn't get her body out from under the truck until after midnight, but by then, she was already dead, right? Right?

I wanted to correct them on the date, but my mouth was dry and the words had bunched in my throat. I swallowed several times, but when I felt I could speak, I didn't. I was afraid if I did, they would tell me that I was wrong. They would say that she was alive under that truck and she had suffered. Or maybe she was alive but unconscious? I didn't know. All I knew was I didn't want for her last moments alive to have been in misery. If I could never know for sure, I didn't want to even know the possibility. I felt sick thinking about it. I rushed out of the room saying I had to use the bathroom.

I closed myself in a stall and cried. This was so wrong. All of it was wrong. I wanted my mommy, I wanted my Joy, but the Joy from before; my first best friend; the Joy who was never my swan sister. Why did I have to lose her so many times?

Through my tears, I whispered, "I miss you, Joy."

There was a light tap on my stall as the toes of two black boots could be seen under the door. "Hey, just wanted to make sure you hadn't abandoned me in Alabama with your family."

I snorted at Bek's words. "I would never."

Taking a deep breath, I stood and stepped out into Bek's arms. Life was once again plunged into darkness, but at least I wasn't alone.

47

House Spirit

Huntsville, Alabama

In early March of 2019, my youngest sister Kess found out that she had breast cancer. She called her right breast, the one with the cancer, Marcia and the other one Jan, referencing the "Marcia, Marcia, Marcia!" scene from The Brady Bunch. Humor, when you can find it, has always helped in times of crisis. She had to go through chemo. In August, after her cancer was in remission, I went to visit her. I wanted to go sooner, but I was struggling with the whole idea of flying, something I'd been doing since before I was born. But with the help of a great therapist, I worked through my anxiety. A lot was tied up in finding out about Joy's death while I was in an airport. But I could finally handle flying.

By the time I got to Alabama, the house Joy died in had

been repaired and Kess had moved back in. Since I was there for her, that's where I stayed. The house didn't belong to Kess, she was renting from our cousin Colin, one of the Seay kids who visited us in Venezuela. Our families have always been close. In fact, Mom's friendship with my Aunt Celia is a big part of why she and Dad decided to retire near Huntsville.

Colin and his family were living in Qatar when Joy's accident happened. He had to fly back to oversee the construction and deal with the legalities of it all. He wasn't there when I visited in August, but he had been there in December for Joy's memorial and I got to see him then. I felt he was having similar conflicteed feelings. Mine were a tangle of grief about Joy and a deep sense of disappointment over missing the International Book Fair with a weird sense of guilt connected to even thinking about the trip I had missed. I surmised that his were tied to his house being destroyed, having to deal with a crime scene and construction, while also coping with his cousin Joy dying in his house. But he did and he got the house fixed all while living in a different country.

Kess had set me up in the room near where Joy had died, but not the same room. A bathroom was between the two rooms. That first night there, despite being exhausted from my travels, I couldn't sleep. I had been planning to do a ritual and meditation at some point in my trip and decided that was the night. Even though Kess's room was on the other side of the house with the living room, dining room, and kitchen between us, I made sure her door was closed and she was sleeping. I had initially thought to do this with Kess, but there are some rituals that need to be done alone. Kess was the only one in the family who was okay with my witchcraft and paganism. I told her that I was going to spend some time in the room doing witchy things and she was fine with it.

I quietly stepped into the room, turned out the light, and slid the door shut. I sat in the middle of the floor. Closing my eyes, I stretched with my mind, my heart, my soul. I breathed slowly, meditating on finding my sister, finding Joy. I explored every inch of the room then pushed out beyond the room into the bathroom, into the room where I had been sleeping, the living room, the dining room, the porch, the kitchen, the laundry room, Kess's bedroom, even her bathroom. I could feel my sleeping sister and even a faint glow of her dog Betsy who had died right after Joy. Throughout the house, there were memories of Joy that breathed in the corners, but not her. Pulling back into myself, I smiled and opened my eyes. The one thing I would not have been able to bear was the thought of Joy, who had been trapped in her body for almost twenty-four years, was now trapped in a house. But the house was not haunted. She was free of it.

Staring into the darkness, I continued my meditative breathing and thought about the house. All around me were new walls, new window, new ceiling, new carpeting, new paint, new... just about everything. Not quite at the Ship of Theseus level as the structure, the foundation of the room and the house had survived and been witness to the events of that night. The house had felt the force of the truck crashing through its walls, destroying the room, crushing my sister. I was sitting in a house that failed to keep Joy safe.

I could hear the wind through the window. Around me, the house settled and sighed. I took the small pack I had brought into the room and took out the items. The bag was actually a scarf I had tied with string and would serve as a makeshift altar. On the altar I placed a small incense holder, a candle, a small bowl, and a bell. I also had a piece of paper on which I had written a letter to the spirit of the house. After opening the window, I lit the candle and the incense. I sat in the flickering light of the candle and read my letter.

"Dear Spirit of this House,

I believe that, like everything in the world, houses have spirits and it is to you I speak. I do not know you, but you are the spirit of a house that failed to do what a house is built for. You failed to keep your occupants safe. You were made to protect those inside your walls from the outside. But you didn't. You allowed a truck to come through your walls, uninvited, and kill my sister. Please know, I have no anger towards you. The force was too great; you could not withstand. But I charge you, the spirit of this house, to double your protection of my other sister, my youngest sister Kess who has been through so much, lost so much, yet has come back to live inside your walls despite what she knows. She was there when you failed and yet she again has put her trust in you, in your walls, in your roof, in your foundation to keep her safe when she sleeps and is at her most vulnerable. Please keep her safe."

Setting down the letter, I blew out the candle and, once there was no light in the room, I stood and spoke to the darkness. "Spirit of this house, I do not have much to give you, but I offer you these words I have written, this light, the scent of this incense, and the music from this bell."

I burned the letter and set it in the bowl. As it burned down, I rang the tiny bell in a gentle rhythm over it and hummed until it was ash. I walked through the room ringing the bell in all the corners. Once the incense had burned all the way down, I blew out the candle a final time, closed the window, and went to bed.

Goodnight, Joy. I miss you, my first best friend, my swan sister.

48

Joy's Ashes

∽

Gulf Shores, Alabama

Because of Kess's cancer , because of the tragic circumstances that destroyed her house and killed our sister, because her dog died, because she survived it all, my youngest sister was gifted a beach trip – all expenses paid. It was a gift from a group at the news station where she was working.

She decided to make it a sister trip, a trip for us to say a deeper and less frantic farewell to Joy in March of 2020. Joy, like Kess, had loved the beach more than any place in the world, making it a perfect goodbye. The gift was for Gulf Shores, Alabama. While not the place Joy would have picked, she would've said any beach is better than no beach. So that's where we took Joy's ashes.

Even though I had traveled by plane to check on Kess

and family in August, I was still anxious when it came to airports. I checked my phone probably a million times while waiting to board my flight. But all was well. After I arrived in Huntsville, we traveled by car to the beach. JacQueline had the biggest car, so we were able to travel together. We took turns driving for the six hour drive.

JacQueline regaled us with tales of our niblings, Katie, Sydney, and Caleb, her husband Jeff and how her writing was going. Kess talked about her Editor job at the news station, dog Louisa, her roommate Sierra, and Sierra's dog Princess. I told them about how Bek was doing, about work at the Oak Park Public Library and all the shenanigans of our resident cats and the foster kittens. I also shared how hard it was returning to grad school after taking a year off after Joy died but how glad I was that I did. This opened the conversation up to the struggles each of us had been facing. JacQueline and her family had been struggling with their purpose in Alabama since caring for Joy was the reason they had uprooted, moving from a small town in Texas where Jeff had a parish.

"But my whole reason for being here is gone." She was in the passenger's seat, wearing big sunglasses that covered most of her face. Even so I could see her giving Kess, who was driving, a sidelong glance and peaking at me through the rearview mirror. "I know this isn't what y'all believe, but there is a reason why God brought us here. I'm just really struggling to understand it."

I sighed, "I wish I could believe there was a reason for what happened to Joy."

Kess, my agnostic sister, nodded. "Me too."

With her mom-green eyes not leaving the road while she drove, she gave a quiet confession about how hard it had been for her to be living in the house where Joy died. Both JacQueline and I nodded along, tears puddling in our eyes. How could it not be?

Then she added, "I wish I could talk to Mom."

"Me too," JacQueline breathed, wiping at the tears that had escaped.

I nodded, not trusting my voice as tears fell. The car was silent as we all thought about how Joy's death brought up so much pain connected to our mother dying five years earlier. I felt I'd never really mourned Mom when she died since we were immediately focused on Joy's care.

The weather was beautiful and breezy as we drove into the small vacation town. JacQueline pointed out a building with a giant purple octopus on it, breaking the somber air. We all laughed, speculating about the kind of building it was. Despite it being right around spring break, there were few cars due to the Pandemic gaining traction, even in Alabama. We saw hardly any other tourists.

We found our no-contact beach condo and unloaded the car. The condo was lovely and had a decent sized kitchen. We each got our own room with a bathroom attached. We even had a balcony where we could see the beach. We each established our places: JacQueline loved sitting on the balcony and writing, Kess loved laying out on the beach, and I loved the water. For the short time we were there, I swam almost every chance I got. The water was chilly, but totally worth getting to swim. JacQueline and

Kess joined me a few times, but weren't quite as eager to swim as I was. Each evening, we would sit in the living room sharing memories of our lives with Joy.

On the last day, the flock of us carried our swan sister's ashes onto the beach right at sunset. There were a few stars dotting the darkening sky and the wisps of clouds added a bit of mysticism to the swirls of orange and pink in the west and blues in the east. The air was cool, but not cold. The waves were soft and gentle in their rhythm. We stood in the shallow water, the waves lapping at our ankles and toes. We took turns saying words and prayers. As the water kissed my feet and the sand tickled my toes, my sisters and I smiled at each other with shining eyes as tears slid silent and unchecked down our cheeks.

"May your afterlife be filled with peace and be everything you want and need it to be," I said, finishing up my wish for Joy. I tossed the small handful of ashes. The breeze off the gulf shifted slightly and blew it right back at me.

"I've got Joy in my eyes!" I laughed, rubbing them.

"And your hair!" JacQueline shouted over the wind, brushing my hair as the waves started spraying us.

"Maybe we should go back inside?" Kess asked, "I mean, since we're done and salt water isn't the best for washing eyes."

"Good point," I giggled, rubbing my eyes andstumbling after them as the wind whipped all around us.

I kept imagining Joy standing there with her hand on her hips looking amused and disappointed at me in a way only she could. "Only you," she would say, shaking her head and grinning.

After we got cleaned up and changed our wet clothes, we went out for Italian. Originally, we intended to share an order of spaghetti and meatballs (minus the meatball for this vegetarian) since it was Joy's favorite meal, a fact that had stayed constant, even after her brain injury. But neither Kess nor I really wanted spaghetti and JacQueline said, "I'd rather not get something I can easily make at home."

We laughed and decided Joy would be okay with us getting what we wanted. We each got a different pasta dish and discussed the different reactions Joy would have given to our choices. We could each hear her in our minds saying different things.

"If that's what you want, I suppose..."

or

"That's just pasta, little sister..."

or

"Spaghetti would be better, but..."

or

something sarcastic. She was a Gen Xer after all. Then she would have made faces at each of our plates. We shared memories of Joy and toasted her. It was a good night.

That last morning, I got up early and strolled down to the beach by myself. I had my journal and a towel. The sun was already rising when I got there, blanketing the beach in a golden hue. The seagulls were diamonds in the sunlight and the waves were a cacophony of elaborate furls as they danced to the music of their own making. Sitting on my towel watching the few early risers walk and jog by, I journaled a bit, then leaned back and closed my eyes. I listened to the sounds around me...to the deep rhythm of the waves, to the faster beating of hammer on wood as another hotel or condo was being built, to the birds calling each other, to the people chatting in the distance, and to the wind whispering in my ears.

All around the world, the pandemic of COVID-19 was gaining momentum. During this trip I had learned that my library had closed and the latest update was that we would be closed through the end of March. Chicago and most of Illinois were in almost complete shutdown and Alabama had just gotten their first confirmed cases.

I wondered how my swan sister was doing in the ocean or if her ashes had combined with the sand. I wondered how her soul was faring in the afterlife. I thought on what it might be like, knowing I will never know until I embark on that journey. But I wouldn't be joining her any time soon. Life felt tenuous, but was still worth living. I wasn't done yet.

In the periphery of my mind, I was concerned about getting back home to Illinois and what the shutdown would mean for me and how my grad school class on

Community Engagement would work and if my family and friends were safe and what was going to happen with my job and...

        and...

                and...

                        I blinked.

I stopped thinking about all the what ifs. There, on that beach in Gulf Shore, Alabama as the waves came and went, the sand was solid. All around me the air smelled hopeful. I was, for that moment, at peace.

EPILOGUE
The Trial

The trial that took place on September 13, 2021 was declared a mistrial due to improperly filed paperwork. It was rescheduled for Monday, February 7th, 2022. By that time, I was a certified librarian had been at my job long enough to take a whole week off. I was vaccinated, would wear a mask and keep my distance. It would be a trial by judge, no jury.

The day of the trial, the judge was sitting above everyone and behind a plexiglass barrier. He was a large man with cherubic cheeks and brown skin. To his left was the stenographer. Along the right wall was the defense, and the prosecution was along the left wall. A brown-haired, fair skinned woman sat directly in front of the judge's bench facing us. Her podium was lower and there was no plexiglass between her and the rest of the room. She did all the swearing in.

Kess sat in a chair facing the bench and relayed the facts of what happened. She told how she woke to the house shaking, the dog barking, and clouds of dust in the air. She stumbled through the house calling 911 and calling out to Joy, who she had put to bed mere hours earlier. She described the debris, the broken walls, and the red Dodge Ram truck inside her house. She, with a calmer voice than I would have been able to maintain, explained how she climbed through the detritus of her house shouting for her sister and yelling at the man sitting inside the Ram.

I listened and watched the judge's kind face struggle to hold its composure. My gaze shifted to the sallow face of my sister's killer and stared. He looked back at me then quickly looked away. I kept staring. I was right in his line of sight. He looked down at the table before him. I kept staring and thinking, "You killed my sister. Never sleep, never sleep, never sleep."

Kess finished her testimony. I wanted to applaud, to stand and give her an ovation for telling it so well. I was in awe of her composure. Just listening to her, tears were streaming into my mask. I had to lift it and wipe the tears from the creases of my nose so I wouldn't drown in the salt of my sorrow and rage.

The defense attorney...

Can I just take a moment to describe the defense attorney? This pasty-faced man literally hooked his thumbs under the lapel of his jacket, then strutted around like Foghorn Leghorn from Looney Tunes. His Alabama accent was thick and he spoke fast. The man who killed my sister could not afford an attorney, so he had been appointed one. I later learned that this lawyer was the third one to be appointed as two others had turned him down.

The judge asked if he wanted to cross-examine Kess. He

declined. As Dad later put it, "Jessica's testimony of what happened that night was so good that the defense attorney didn't even try to downplay it or challenge it. She did an awesome job." He was so proud of her.

The police officer who had been at the scene was called to the stand. The prosecution was represented by Shawna, a sensible pale blonde lawyer wearing a crushed velvet skirt with a black turtleneck. She showed him pictures of tire marks. Since the court had been rearranged for COVID-19, putting the witness's chair facing the judge and in front of the plexiglass in front of the audience, I was able to see the pictures. They had used bright orange paint to highlight the truck's tracks showing the path off the road where it side-swiped another car, drove through a fence and bushes, then into the backyard of Kess's house, ending at a truck-sized hole in the wall of the house.

Next, Detective Abernathy, a fair-skinned clean-cut young officer in a suit, took the stand. He was one of the officers at the hospital and, later, became the lead on the case. When he was cross-examined by the defense, there was a discussion that, as the phlebotomist was drawing the defendant's blood, the Detective hadn't had eyes on the entire process. But he stated that he and a few other officers were in the room the whole time. The defense then asked about the blood being stored, since it was a holiday weekend and Detective Abernathy couldn't send it to the lab until Monday. The detective stated that it was kept in a locked box in his locked cruiser the entire time. Oh! But was that box refrigerated? It was not.

After the detective's testimony, there was a break. Dad wasn't going to be able to stay for the second half of the trial so he took us out for lunch. We found a brewery called Breezr that served vegan food in downtown Huntsville. Getting my teetotaling meat-eating dad to buy vegan food at a brewery tickled me. It was really good too!

Before we got back into the courtroom, I saw the man who killed Joy in the hall talking with his mother. I caught his eye just as he was ushered into the courtroom. There was no guilt or remorse, just an irritation at having to go through all of this. I took a deep breath and made my way into the courtroom. I sat beside Kess, across the room from him. He looked at me, at us, then quickly looked away.

The expert witness arrived. He was the scientist who headed the lab and signed off on the toxicology report. He was a serious, tired-looking man with a bald head, a tightly-trimmed goatee, and a somewhat ruddy complexion. After the swearing-in, the defense attorney threw question after question at him.

He explained that his lab, along with blood reports from court, analyzed evidence for autopsies. The toxicology report they received for this case indicated that the amount of alcohol in the defendant's blood, at the time the blood was taken, exceeded that of several cases involving overdoses. Basically, he was surprised to find that my sister's killer was alive.

The defense attorney then switched the questions to how blood should be handled.

"How does your office handle blood when it's received?"

"Very carefully," the expert said, taking a sip of water.

"What I mean to say is, do you immediately refrigerate the sample?"

"Yes."

The attorney got excited about that. "Then, wouldn't you agree, that the police cruiser, where the blood was left over a holiday weekend, should have had a refrigeration unit in it?"

"Not necessarily. It's not required; my lab is just overly cautious."

"Well then, could the sample have altered chemically during that time it was in the police cruiser without refrigeration?"

"No. The only thing that could have happened is it could possibly have become less potent."

He then launched into the science of the chemical compounds in the blood and how it can be affected by time. The lawyer deflated. Switching tactics, he asked about the time between the accident happening and the blood being drawn. Was it possible that the defendant was not drunk while driving?

The expert hesitated, seeming to need a moment to compose himself. After taking a deep breath, he launched into the science of how much alcohol he would need to have drunk in order for the numbers to be where they were when the blood was drawn.

"But it's possible?" The lawyer asked.

"It's possible, but keep in mind that my calculations do not factor in any degeneration that may have happened to the blood over the holiday weekend."

Then it was the prosecution's turn.

"Just to get a better picture," she said in her amiable way as she strolled over to the witness, "for him to have the level of alcohol in his blood at the time it was drawn yet be completely sober during the crash, he would have had to down a whole bottle of Jack Daniels right before getting in the car. Is that about accurate?"

"Something like that, yes."

"So not the two shots of vodka he said he took?"

"Not unless it was followed by a whole lot more."

"No further questions."

The judge asked the defense if he had any other witnesses. He did. He called Tony Wu, the killer himself. But first, a short break. Kess and I decided to stay in the courtroom. Shawna came over and explained that she would do very little cross-examination if any.

"I'm surprised he's taking the stand," Kess said. "He didn't at the first trial."

Shawna snorted. "They know they're losing so they're grasping at straws. Unless there's something obvious, I'm going to let him do it all himself. His attorney knows it's a risk to have him testify."

As we were called to reconvene, there was a bit of commotion on the other side of the courtroom. Tony had gotten hand sanitizer in his eyes. He was waving his hands and blinking his eyes as a few different people handed him tissues and a water bottle. When things settled down and he sat, he kept rubbing his eyes that were now red.

Tony was sworn in and told us about his childhood. He worked in his dad's Chinese restaurant for long hours and little pay and he had anxiety and he was on medication and he was introduced to drugs and he became addicted. He decided to get sober, but his friends and brother were toxic for his sobriety, so he moved to Taiwan, where he had family on his father's side. When he came back to Alabama only months before the accident to take care of his mom, his brother immediately tried to get him to do drugs. A week before the accident, he got into a fight with his brother who, he said, poisoned him with molly. He discussed how he had antidepressant and anti-anxiety drugs from here and from Taiwan. Then, on the day of the accident, a horrible fight broke out with his whole family. He said his mom always took his brother's side, so he decided to end it all. He took pill after pill and washed it down with vodka. He said he didn't even remember getting into the truck.

He turned and looked right at Kess and I. "I am so sorry! I wish it had been me and not your sister! I didn't mean any of it. I am so, so sorry!" His face was contorted like a kid playing at being really sad.

We stared at him. He was sorry... He was sorry he got caught. If he had been truly sorry, he would have pled guilty from the beginning. But he dragged this on forever.

"You will not address the family of the victim!" The judge boomed. "You will only address the court!"

Tony's head dropped. I looked at the judge who was staring at Tony with fire. He took a breath then, for the briefest moment, looked at Kess and I with kind eyes. I nodded my thanks. I knew at that moment what the verdict would be.

The closing statement from the defense was weak. It focused on how it wasn't proven that Joy died from being crushed by a truck. Despite Joy having no pre-existing medical condition that would cause a heart attack, he pointed out that the prosecution had not brought in the EMTs who rode with Joy to the hospital, therefore it could not be concluded how Joy died.

The prosecution was incredibly eloquent, but it boiled down to her explaining just how stupid that was.

It took less than four minutes for the judge to make his ruling. Tony Wu was found guilty of manslaughter. His sentencing would be at the end of March. Since he was a flight risk, all of his travel documents (drivers license, passport, etc.) were taken from him. A bail was set, but he had no way to pay it.

On March 30th, 2022 Tony Wu was sentenced to 20 years imprisonment, the maximum for manslaughter.

I thought I'd be more elated, but I'm just relieved. In some ways, it's over and we got a modicum of justice for Joy. In other ways, it will never be over. Joy is still dead... she will, until I die, be my dead sister.

I miss you, Joy.

Printed in the USA
CPSIA information can be obtained
at www.ICGtesting.com
LVHW091200081124
795950LV00006B/548